MIND GAMES

Exposing Today's Psychics, Frauds, and False Spiritual Phenomena

André Kole
& Jerry MacGregor

Mind Games
Exposing Today's Psychics, Frauds, and False Spiritual Phenomena
Copyright ©2002 by André Kole and Jerry MacGregor
All rights reserved

Cover Design by Brent Shetler
Interior design by Pine Hill Graphics

Packaged by ACW Press
5501 N. 7th Ave., #502
Phoenix, Arizona 85013
www.acwpress.com
The views expressed or implied in this work do not necessarily reflect those of ACW Press. Ultimate design, content, and editorial accuracy of this work is the responsibility of the authors.

ISBN 1-892525-76-3

Printed in the United States of America.

To Tim Kole and Jenny Lynn,
my son and daughter-in-law,
who are carrying on the Kole magical legacy
in an excellent and grand style.
—André Kole

This book is for Molly,
one of my favorite performers.
—Papa

CONTENTS

A WORLD OF ILLUSION

I love magicians because they are such honest people. They tell you they are going to fool you and then they proceed to do it. But no matter what happens at the show—when you get home you will still have your watch, your wallet, and your appendix. And that is more than I can say for some of my non-magician acquaintances.

—Elbert Hubbard

A magician is one who uses natural means to accomplish a supernatural effect. There is nothing supernatural about what he does; he only creates the *illusion* of the supernatural. Every week thousands of people enjoy André Kole's *World of Illusion*, the spectacular magic show which has been touring the world for more than 30 years. In that two-hour stage show he supposedly walks on water, contacts the spirit world, "reads" with his fingertips while blindfolded, and levitates high above the stage. In seeing André's performance, some people are convinced he has special powers or is working in league with the devil to accomplish such alleged miracles. We assure you he is not.

André Kole is a world-class magician whose magical creations are much in demand by other performers. Magical luminaries such as David Copperfield, Siegfried and Roy, Harry Blackstone Jr., Doug Henning, and Melinda have consulted with André on creating illusions.

7

A religious skeptic until the age of 25, André's careful study of Christ's life and miracles convinced him to give his life to the Lord. He concluded as did Nicodemus of old, "No one could perform the miraculous signs...if God were not with him." The most famous magicians require several trucks and tons of equipment to perform their "miracles." But Jesus cannot be accused of such trickery. As the Son of God, He had power to do what mere man cannot do. Therefore, every time André has a performance he is careful to explain that what the audience is seeing is only an illusion. It is because of his expertise in the field of magic, along with his ability to spot a secret gimmick, that has led to the creation of this book. People the world over are being taken in by a lie: that they can tap into some sort of super mental power, which can cause them to know the future, move objects, or even discern the thoughts of others. Tens of thousands of people are calling psychic hotlines, seeking assistance from spirit guides, and checking their horoscopes in the paper. Even Christians are being influenced by this sort of deception, listening to success-gurus talk about "visualization" and worrying over alleged demonic powers.

During André's travels in 78 countries, he has searched out claims of the supernatural made by witch doctors, psychic surgeons, mind readers, and all sorts of others purporting to possess amazing mental powers. He has failed to find anyone able to demonstrate legitimate psychic power. Though he has pledged a $25,000 reward to anyone who can successfully demonstrate genuine psychic ability, no one has ever claimed the prize. Yet he still hears of individuals who claim to levitate, predict the future, and speak with the spirits of the deceased.

Dr. Jerry MacGregor is a writer whose "Mind Games" lecture reveals to Christians how psychics perform their alleged miracles. In his demonstration, he predicts the future, tells complete strangers what they are thinking, and reveals the influence of occultic thinking in modern society. Yet he has no special powers—it's all a trick, using the same methods applied by those who bill themselves as genuine psychics. Even though Jerry is careful to point out that there is nothing supernatural about his performance, he is regularly accused of using some special "power" to accomplish his feats of mental magic. This sort of confusion has led Jerry to join André in investigating psychic phenomena.

This confusion over the issue of psychic phenomena stems from three facts: First, as a society we have incorrectly interpreted Scripture through experience, rather than interpreting experience through Scripture. Second, the influence of New Age thinking has become so prevalent that things like "mind power" are going unquestioned, to the detriment of proper theology. Third, there are few Christians researching alleged psychic activity who are skilled in the art of deception.

Most people are not aware of what those trained in the art of magic can accomplish. Illusions performed by twentieth-century magicians would baffle ancient practitioners. Changing a stick to a snake, as Pharaoh's magicians did in Exodus 7:11,12, is child's play when compared to a modern magician causing elephants to appear and disappear. André Kole has collaborated with David Copperfield to accomplish such amazing feats as levitating over the Grand Canyon, walking through the Great Wall of China, and causing the Statue of Liberty to disappear. But as incredible as these illusions sound, there is nothing supernatural involved. He could explain the mechanics of these spectacular illusions to anyone in a matter of minutes.

The so-called psychics of today are much like the ancient practitioners of magic, trying to convince others that they possess supernatural powers. Ancient temple priests, medicine men, and soothsayers played on the superstitions of their followers. In 135 B.C. a Syrian named Eunios stopped a rebellion of Sicilian slaves with his awe-provoking demonstration of fire-breathing. Although he claimed a goddess made him immune to fire, the chronicler Florus revealed that Eunios secretly stored the fiery substance inside nutshells hidden in his mouth. Lest you think those primitive and uneducated people fools, remember that in our own day many people believe that others have "channeled" a 3500-year-old warrior, been abducted by aliens, and had angels deliver golden plates written in a language that could only be translated while looking into a seer stone!

With this book we hope to clarify the various mind games that are being foisted upon an unsuspecting public. We are also following in the footsteps of sixteenth-century Christian scholar Reginald Scot, author of *The Discoverie of Witchcraft*. Scot abhorred the barbarous persecution targeted toward helpless women falsely accused of witchcraft, and was shocked at the belief that works accomplished by the power of the Most High God should be referred to as the power of Satan. Scot also worried that the churchmen of his time were fostering a belief in the power of witchcraft, and felt that "this absurd error is growne into the place which should be able to expel all such ridiculous follie and impietie"— the same concern we echo today in regard to the belief in psychic and occultic power. "In like manner," wrote Scot, "he that attributeth to a witch such divine power as dulie and onlie apperaineth unto GOD (which all witchmongers do) is in heart a blasphemer, an idolater, and full of gross impietie."[1] His conclusion was that belief in the so-called supernatural powers of those considered witches stemmed from incorrect theology, coincidence, and deliberate fraud. The latter encouraged Scot to expose some tricks performed by the magicians of his day, thus gaining for Reginald Scot a place in history as the first book explaining magic secrets ever written in English.

As Scot did 400 years ago, we hope to do again. He wanted to educate those who were being misled. More than that, he wanted to warn the church against attributing supernatural power to people, and to stop any sort of belief that Satan can perform miracles. Just as God used Elijah to challenge the false prophets of Baal in order to prove Satan could not impart miraculous powers, we want to challenge the false prophets of our day. It is our goal that many Christians will reconsider their thinking in light of truth. And as always: If anyone involved in the psychic world can display supernatural mental power, André Kole will pay that person $25,000. Since so many people believe in that fallacy, we await the day when someone offers incontrovertible evidence of psychic power. In the meantime, we are confident that the money will never have to be paid.

André Kole & Jerry MacGregor

CHAPTER ONE

They Told My All About Myself!

Betty was nearly jumping up and down in excitement. "You won't believe this," she exclaimed, "but this guy really read my mind. He knew exactly what was happening in my life. *He told me all about myself!*" Then, seeing skepticism on the face of her listener, she added, "And I didn't reveal anything!"

When asked for details, Betty explained that she had called one of those psychic hotlines after watching an infomercial on late-night television. "All he asked for was my name and birthdate. Then he started talking to me, revealing some of my deepest thoughts. It was as though he could see right into my soul. At first I thought he was just reading something about my astrological sign, but then he began telling me things no one could know.

"For example, he told me that I have a tendency to be critical of myself, and that I've got a great need for others to like and admire me.

He talked about my secret doubts over making good choices, my worries about revealing too much of myself, and my unrealistic expectations for my life." Lowering her voice, Betty added, "He even knew about my concerns over some sexual issues—*no one* could know about that; I've never talked about it with anybody. It was almost scary. That man read my mind—there's nothing you can say to convince me otherwise!"

In a typical church multipurpose room in Arizona, 75 high school and college youths gathered for a special program. The guest speaker planned to illustrate psychic power that he claimed could "be developed by anyone who trusted God completely with his life."

The demonstration began with two students placing a blindfold over the speaker's eyes, and putting tape around the blindfold to ensure that no light entered. Then students produced various objects from their pockets and purses—a comb, a pocketknife, a wallet, even a pair of scissors. While holding his fingers about 12 inches from the object, the speaker correctly identified each item. He claimed the gift of "second sight" allowed him to view each object in his mind's eye.

Next the students were instructed to write questions on a piece of paper and pass them to the speaker. *While still blindfolded,* he held each paper in his hand and answered the questions. In some cases he revealed intimate details about the person who wrote it, though he had never met anyone in the room. At the end of his demonstration, the speaker declared that by blindfolding himself he had developed his other senses more keenly. He reemphasized that "God gives each one of us special gifts, and we need to discover and use those gifts to help others."

More than 10,000 people had gathered for a Navajo tribal fair in eastern New Mexico. During the festivities, a half-dozen tribal leaders in full ceremonial dress spread a blanket on the ground. A medicine man threw a dozen eagle feathers into the middle of the blanket, and the leaders sat in a half-circle around it, chanting and beating small drums.

After a few moments the feathers began to move. Gradually they stood erect on their quills. The Indians, seemingly in a trance, continued to chant and beat their drums while the feathers moved in intricate formations, as a precise military drill team. Those who watched it were convinced they had seen hard evidence of *psychokinesis*—the ability to move objects solely through the power of the mind.

The small room was crowded and warm. On three sides a fine screen allowed a slight breeze to drift among the observers. Pressed against one screen were the faces of several Filipino natives, each hoping for a glance at the miracle about to take place. On a narrow table lay a young woman draped with a white sheet. She looked up at an overweight, middle-aged man in a colorful native shirt. Surrounding this "doctor" were several assistants and two magazine reporters from the United States.

The surgeon quietly assured the young woman that she would feel little pain, and if she believed in God's power, she would walk out of that room healed. He opened a Bible to Psalm 23 and read, "Yea, though I walk through the valley of the shadow of death, I will fear no evil, for thou art with me." Closing his eyes for a moment, he prayed silently. Then a nurse lifted the sheet and lowered the front of the woman's pants, exposing her abdomen. The doctor took a cotton ball, dipped it into a bowl of water, and began to swab a small area of the patient's skin. As he did this, a small amount of blood appeared. Suddenly he plunged his hand deep into the woman's abdomen, appearing to go almost through her body. A moment later his hand reappeared, holding what appeared to be a piece of diseased tissue. "This is your appendix," the doctor said triumphantly. "You should feel a lot better now."

He dropped the diseased organ and cotton ball in a bucket below the table, rapidly swabbed the area with a clean piece of cotton, and covered the woman again with the sheet. The observers could see no evidence of any incision. The marvel of "psychic surgery" had again been demonstrated. As he helped her to her feet, the doctor encouraged the woman to read the Bible every day and continue to trust God. The whole operation had taken about five minutes.

With a loud yell the witch doctor, wearing only a grass skirt and numerous strings of beads, called the natives to the center of the village square. He shouted that the gods had cursed the village because of one man's guilt. Unless the culprit was punished, there would be a plague and many people would die. Dramatically he grabbed his rifle and called the offender forward. The crowd withdrew toward their grass-thatched huts and watched in silence as the witch doctor raised his gun and shot once. Blood spurted out of the man's chest, and he fell dead.

The dead man's body was placed inside a crude coffin. Several men dug a grave outside the village, while the witch doctor uttered incantations to break the evil spell. Then the box was buried.

Three days later the witch doctor made another dramatic announcement: The gods were satisfied with the retribution for the unnamed crime, so the dead man could return to the village. All the villagers quickly ran to the gravesite, and several young men dug down to the box while the witch doctor chanted. The coffin was raised up and set beside the grave. With a dramatic yell, the leader ordered the villagers to open the box. The young man who had been shot and buried for three days slowly began to move. With a dazed look, he sat up and was helped to his feet.

"All readings done by angels," the sign read. The woman performing the readings was seated at a table in a shopping mall, part of a "psychic fair" the mall was hosting. Amidst people selling crystals and books on astrology, the psychic reader was charging $20 to anyone who wanted his or her fortune told.

Gloria, a bit of a skeptic, paid the fee, mixed some tarot cards, and watched as the psychic reader dealt the cards facedown into the shape of a cross. Then, as she turned over each card, she would reveal something about Gloria's personal life. The psychic reader was able to divine that Gloria's major goal in life is security, that she had recently faced a major change at her job, and even that her husband was struggling with a serious health problem. The reading became more involved with each card, ending with a dramatic yet hopeful declaration that Gloria's life had great potential if she would take some appropriate steps to handle the stress in her life.

Gloria walked away amazed, but as a Christian she was also wondering if the psychic reader had received her information from demons.

These stories are just a sampling of numerous true and unusual phenomena that André and Jerry have encountered throughout the world. Each incident had religious significance, and the feats performed supposedly were evidence of genuine spiritual power. But *none of the situations were supernatural.* None were genuine miracles. Most casual observers would assume they were, since there is no logical explanation for what occurred. They would doubtless argue, "I saw it with my own eyes!" The things they saw are apparently not humanly possible according to the laws of nature, so most observers conclude that the incidents can only be explained in light of the supernatural. But if those same people could increase their frame of reference, they would discover that there are other, purely natural explanations.

Since the late 1950s André Kole has performed illusions in more than 70 countries of the world, baffling millions of people. Audiences have seen him "levitate" several feet above the stage, discern the thoughts of total strangers, read books with his fingertips while blindfolded, and cause the "spirits" to throw pans and place a bucket on the head of a spectator. Yet all those feats, though perhaps *appearing* supernatural, are accomplished by natural means. The audience has been tricked. As André likes to say, "Any eight-year-old can do what I do on stage—with 15 years of practice."

While artistically presenting illusion as reality, he has also studied numerous religions and so-called spiritual feats, attempting to discover if any paranormal phenomena are authentic. André has looked for evidence of genuine ESP, psychokinesis, prophecy, psychic healing, and levitation…and has found none. In talking with people around the world, he has discovered that most believe in God and the devil. Most also believe that certain people are capable of displaying supernatural powers—what some people would call psychic phenomena. But what he has concluded from his 35 years of research is that *every verifiable instance was composed of clever tricks*—magical effects being presented as supernatural phenomena.

MAGIC, NOT MIRACLES

Take for example the supposed resurrection from the dead performed by the witch doctor, which André observed in Africa. In his investigation, André discovered what really happened: The doctor had prearranged the event with his victim, who had placed a balloon full of pig's blood under his shirt. The witch doctor fired a blank from his rifle, and the villager grabbed his chest, punctured the balloon, then fell over as though dead. Once inside the coffin, the man slipped out through a trap door in the back of the box, which then was buried empty. When the coffin was dug up, the victim, who had remained hidden for three days, climbed back into it through the same trap door. Then he simply carried out his performance of being raised from the dead.

What appeared to be a dramatic miracle was just an illusion. But the native villagers were impressed, and were reminded again to follow the leadership of their witch doctor. Such tricks are handed down secretly from one generation to the next, and witch doctors in Africa actually have asked André to teach them some more up-to-date tricks, so they can increase their influence over their followers.

But villagers in Africa are not the only people being fooled today. Millions of supposedly well-educated Americans are being deceived by charlatans who pretend to have supernatural knowledge or skills. Some of them claim their power comes from God and draw many to their unorthodox theology. For example, the man pretending to see things while blindfolded was performing an old magician's trick, though he claimed it was a special God-given ability. Tied in a certain way, the blindfold allowed him to see the objects being held before him. The "psychic surgeon" in the Philippines was also a fraud, performing slight-of-hand tricks with glycerin and chicken livers, then claiming to be withdrawing the patient's appendix.

Others claim that their power is from Satan. The Native American shaman who apparently levitated eagle feathers may have claimed to be using supernatural power, but he actually relied on small threads and puffs of air by which he could manipulate objects. The woman doing readings at the psychic fair didn't gain her information by angels or by demons, but by common sense and "cold reading," which we will discuss in detail a bit later. She made some general statements that are true of almost everyone, then watched for nonverbal cues she could use to follow up. The information about a sick husband started as a lucky guess about "someone close to you struggling with an illness," and continued as she watched the response in her client. Dr. Jerry MacGregor, a Christian who lectures on fake psychics, gets exactly the same type of results at his shows, revealing that anyone can *appear* to have psychic ability if he or she will merely memorize a script and learn to read people's responses.

Many psychic believers have promoted the possibility that individuals have latent power that can be developed, if they will learn the techniques which are available to anyone...for a stiff price. The man answering the psychic hotline not only wants to keep his client on the line (and therefore earn more money), but also wants to cross-sell tapes and books that purport to "build" psychic powers.

It's easy for Christians to assume they can't possibly be deceived by such frauds—*but that is a dangerous assumption.* We should be equipped to talk intelligently with those who are looking into the occult for purpose and answers in life. Christians should have a healthy respect for the power that the kingdom of darkness holds over people, but we should not attribute more to Satan than he deserves. The devil would like us to believe that his earthly servants possess more power than they actually do. In fact, as we will see, he only presents a poor imitation of God. Christians should take courage: God has the real power! He doesn't need cheap imitations to impress us.

THE CHRISTIAN AND PSYCHIC POWER

There is a subtle deception that has crept into some churches. A few men and women, posing as servants of God, have misled believers by displaying supposedly supernatural gifts, when in reality they are using cheap tricks and deception. One televangelist, Peter Popoff, claimed to be able to discern the names, addresses, and concerns of those attending his crusades—until researcher James Randi proved he was secretly getting information fed to him by his wife, who was reading the information off cards the participants had completed earlier, then sending it to him by means of a tiny radio receiver.

Another man, a conference speaker, claims that God has given him the gift of prophecy, and he demonstrates it by "predicting" words that members of the congregation will suggest. But his ruse is an old magicians' trick, in which he knows the words ahead of time, taking all the mystery out of his performance. By doing these sorts of scams, such performers make a mockery of Christianity before the world and draw attention away from the real work of God. As believers, we must be able to distinguish between the *acts of God* and the *chicanery of men* who are using God as a means to promote their own selfish ambitions. They may be relatively few, but they are like a cancer in the body of Christ, drawing people away from the truth. Christ warned us to be careful:

> *See to it that no one misleads you. For many will come*
> *in My name, saying, "I am the Christ," and will mislead*
> *many.... Then if any one says to you, "Behold, here is the*
> *Christ," or "There He is," do not believe him. For false*
> *Christs and false prophets will arise and will show great*
> *signs and wonders, so as to mislead, if possible, even*
> *the elect (Matthew 24:5,24 NASB).*

In this book we will examine some of the most common phenomena that mislead people. Based on our research and personal observations, we will answer some of the most asked questions, such as "Does ESP exist?" "Is there any truth to astrology?" "Are there really UFOs?" and "Can someone really bend spoons using only his mind?"

But first, it is important to ask *why so many people are being deceived.* Why do people attend seances, even though it is impossible to communicate with the dead? Why do they listen to "seers" like Jeane Dixon, the late psychic whose percentage of correct predictions is no higher than chance? Why do so many people spend money they can't afford in order to talk on a psychic hotline, or to visit psychic healers in the Philippines or Brazil? Why do people attend exotic fire-walking seminars? And why do people who are crippled and confined to wheelchairs continue to flock to alleged faith healers who create the illusion of healing yet have no measurable track record for genuine organic healing?

We believe that Christians must first understand *how* people are deceived, so that they can discern accurately between what is true and what is false. If there is a God, and if He sometimes intervenes with genuine spiritual power, then it is important to know how to identify that power and separate it from deception and fraudulent power. To that end, there are at least six basic reasons why people are misled.

A TABLOID MENTALITY

First, *the media blows many stories out of proportion.* Not everything you read in the paper is true. Tabloid publications such as the *National*

Enquirer and *Globe* regularly print articles under sensational headlines. We have all found ourselves standing in line and seeing "UFO's: At Last the Proof" or "The Gift of Prophecy: Psychic Demonstrates 89% Accuracy." But even respected periodicals can print misleading stories. Not long ago, the generally conservative *Reader's Digest* published an article titled "New Evidence on Psychic Phenomena," purporting to reveal proof of psychic powers (later proven to be a hoax). Such respected magazines as *Science Digest* have featured articles entitled "Physicists Explain ESP," and the *Instructor*, a magazine for teachers, ran the story "Your Kids Are Psychic!" with a subtitle "But they may never know it—without your help." Television programs like *Unsolved Mysteries* and The Learning Channel's *The Quest* have promoted the popular notion that there have been hundreds, if not thousands, of verified psychic phenomena.

After seeing these stories, a casual reader would assume that ESP is an established scientific fact, even though that is not the case. Some articles reveal scientists' uncertainties, but the tone of the headlines and the first few paragraphs lead readers to believe that many people have genuine psychic abilities. Television documentaries can be even more deceiving because they seldom provide enough time to explain all the divergent facts and opinions. Kendrick Frazier, editor of *The Skeptical Inquirer*, keeps a watchful eye on claims by various publications. In a story titled "Articles on the Paranormal: Where Are the Editors?" he explains:

> *The problem is not of factual inaccuracy. Usually the facts are correct. The problem is with the selection process that determines which facts are included and which facts are omitted. Often the facts omitted are those that might weaken a seemingly good story. Hard, skeptical questions are not asked. The overall result is to drastically warp the article's perspective to give a dramatic, but not altogether accurate, view of the subject.*[1]

For example, Frazier cites an article in *California Living,* a Sunday supplement magazine in newspapers such as the *San Francisco Examiner* and the *Los Angeles Herald Examiner.* The article, "The Psychic Body Finders," reports of cases where psychics supposedly helped police solve crimes. Frazier points out the story's shortcomings:

> *The hard questions weren't asked: How often do these "psychic bodyfinders" fail? How many guesses do they make before they get one right? And how specific are they? Why do we hear only of the "successes"? And the article makes no mention of the only controlled study I know of that examines the claims of so-called psychic crime-fighters, the one in which the Los Angeles police department found them to be of no use at all in criminal investigations.*[2]

Even major news bureaus are guilty of maintaining a tabloid mentality when it comes to alleged psychic phenomena. In our own discussions with Associated Press editors, we were told that paranormal "news" is almost always reported in the "human-interest" section of the newspaper. That means the stories will not receive the same thorough scrutiny they would get if they came to the "national news" desk. Human-interest stories are intended to entertain more than to inform, so they don't receive the same thorough treatment a hard news story does. Besides, most people *want to believe* in psychic miracles, so the stories are not written critically, but complimentarily.

For example, when one national television program was doing a report on an "unsolved" psychic incident, they invited skeptic and psychologist Ray Hyman to discuss the case. Dr. Hyman proceeded to explain exactly what the alleged psychic had done, and how he had made it appear to be a miracle. Yet, while the program trumpeted the psychic and his purported abilities, Dr. Hyman's explanation was left on the cutting room floor. Why? Because the producers decided if he were to explain what happened, it would no longer be "unsolved"! They feared no one would be interested in watching someone prove a psychic to be fraudulent, so they cut all explanations from the program. It is precisely this sort of mentality that perpetuates the myth of psychic power.[3]

FUZZY FACTS

This leads directly into the second reason people are misled: *Determination of the facts is often difficult.* One of the problems in evaluating reports of unusual mental phenomena is that only certain facts are selected. Unfavorable facts are usually omitted. Many reports are exaggerated, and in some cases reports are actually fabricated. Most of the psychic mysteries we have investigated have grown even more impressive over the course of time. The specific facts of the incident in question are hard to come by, even when talking to the participants.

For example, André enjoys listening to people try to describe some of his illusions. Once when he was in Madras, India, he appeared to cause his daughter to float within the framework of a large pyramid. The next day a waitress excitedly told him what some of her customers had said about the show. According to them, André had not only levitated his daughter but had also caused her to float out over the audience, turn in a large circle, and do some impossible gymnastic feats.

André's good friend David Copperfield made a small Lear jet disappear from an airport on one of his television specials, but André has heard people say that David made a 747 jet disappear *while it was flying through the air.* Such exaggerations are common and usually unintentional. People easily blow the facts out of proportion, and they often don't remember all the details correctly, so it is wise to be skeptical about eyewitness reports that deal with any supposed supernatural event.

Any criminal investigator will tell you that eyewitnesses have a track record of being unreliable. Psychologists tell us that the images recalled by a terrified woman who has witnessed a brutal crime may not be accurate. Her fear causes her mind to play tricks. André's coauthor, Jerry MacGregor, experienced that firsthand: Jerry was once held up at gunpoint by a thug in a ski mask, but he was able to provide the police with the detail that the robber had carried a Lugar pistol. When asked about the details of the gun, he remembered that it was chrome, not black, even though the officer taking down the information told him that Lugar pistols are generally painted black. But Jerry remembered the gun as chrome, and continued to insist it was so—until film in a hidden camera revealed that the Lugar pistol had in fact been black. Something about the fear of the moment caused him to remember the details incorrectly. That's a common occurrence, though most juries still prefer one eyewitness to a mountain of circumstantial evidence.[4]

Therefore we cannot always trust the words of someone who claims, "I saw it with my own eyes." Anyone skilled in the art of magic knows the importance of misdirection—causing an audience to look in one place while a secret action takes place in another. Magician Harry Blackstone used to put several ducks into a bucket, cover it for a moment with a box, and then at just the right moment have one of his pretty assistants on stage appear to stumble. All eyes turned to the girl for a split second, and in that short span of time a rope would pull the ducks off stage. It was nothing fancy—no trap doors or anything, and it happened right there in front of the audience—but rarely did anyone catch on. They were too busy watching the assistant, though most people would later insist, "I had my eyes on those birds the whole time…They just disappeared!"

Fake psychics, mediums, and channelers have used that same technique to fool people at seances and in shows. Those who watch would swear there could have been no trickery, and over time the "miracle" grows in their mind into something even greater. That is another problem that creates fuzzy facts: Our memories have a tendency over time to create details that were not really there. Psychologists have recently become fascinated with the generation of "false memory" because of a few high-profile cases where parents have been accused by their grown children of childhood sexual assault. But false memory is a common problem; our brains are creative organs that for some unknown reason paint new details into our mental pictures. So a person who "swears" the mind-reader told her all about her childhood might be unintentionally creating additional facts that were not in the original presentation.[5]

People can also be deceived by their selection of facts. For example, stories about Bermuda Triangle disappearances can usually be explained by one piece of information that the writer neglected to mention. The loss of one plane in that area, the Mariner PBM, came to be considered a mystery when it exploded into a fireball for no apparent reason on December 6, 1945. Some people have become convinced it was a time warp, a demonic curse, or some sort of paranormal phenomenon. But that particular plane was referred to as the "flying gas tank" because it carried nearly 2000 gallons of fuel, the fumes were often noticeable inside the hull, and the lighting of cigarettes or the flipping of electrical switches were known to ignite them. Adding that one small detail turns the loss of the plane from a dark mystery into a reasonable, yet tragic, accident.[6] The plane exploded because a spark ignited the fuel on board, not because of some poltergeist.

Most editors and writers attempt to be honest in their presentations, but occasionally stories are complete fabrications. Prominent on the cover of the bestseller *The Amityville Horror* were these words: "A True Story." A movie was made about this supposed haunted house, but investigations by others have revealed the entire affair to be a hoax. Lawyer William Weber, who represented the family in the story, told the Associated Press, "We created this horror story over many bottles of wine that George Lutz (the owner of the home) was drinking. We were really playing with each other. We were creating something the public would want to hear about."[7] Sometimes behind the fuzzy facts of a story there is no story at all. As P.T. Barnum liked to put it, "There's a sucker born every minute."

RESEARCH VERSUS DECEIT

A third reason we find that people are misled is because *science has difficulty discerning between the fake and the real.* Those skilled in the area of para-psychological research usually have no experience dealing with the tricks of con artists and magicians. Numerous scientific studies have supposedly "proven" the existence of various paranormal phenomena. Most of these scientists sincerely believe in their experiments, and many want to believe that they have verified certain powers. But the facts do not bear them out. *In no case, under strict research conditions and with a magician present to detect deception, has anyone been able to demonstrate genuine psychic ability.* This is an important point, since our society has taken it for granted that psychic ability is a fact. Yet for almost 20 years André Kole has made his offer of $25,000 to anyone who could show evidence of genuine paranormal ability, and no one has been able to offer such evidence.

Remember, scientific research is based upon the idea that an individual can perform an operation under controlled conditions in order to discover or illustrate a law. In other words, if a researcher claims he can produce diamonds by putting charcoal briquettes into a vice, he needs to be able to repeat his experiment in a laboratory, not simply show up at a news conference with a diamond necklace. Psychological experiments are a bit more complicated than scientific experiments, for researchers cannot always judge how individuals will respond. For example, if you allow 100 children to view ten hours of violent television programming, then turn them loose in a room full of punching bags, not all 100 children will respond violently. Some were violent before watching the programs, some will become more violent for a short time in response to the programs, and a few will not be affected by the programming at all. So what researchers look for are the common or typical responses of people, measured over an adequate number of participants.

Unfortunately, neither of these types of research seems to be put into use when testing psychic ability. Most experiments cannot be duplicated in other laboratories without widely divergent results. When one famous psychic claimed to be able to discern the numbers of dice that were inside a sealed container in one lab, he was unable to replicate his ability at a second lab (leading us to believe he fooled the researchers in the first place). Tests that initially produce results significantly beyond the laws of probability produce very normal results when controls are tightened. Yet if the individual really had psychic ability, why was it only available at certain times, under certain conditions, with certain people in the room?

The main reason scientists often fail to distinguish between illusion and reality is that *they do not suspect that someone might try to deceive them*. For example, when the McDonnell Laboratory for Psychical Research at Washington University in St. Louis, Missouri, was looking for people with psychic powers, they sorted through a group of applicants until they found two teenage boys who both claimed they had the power to bend metal with their minds. The two boys, Mike Edwards and Steve Shaw, impressed the scientists with their ability to bend spoons, move objects, transmit thoughts to each other, and impress images onto photographic film. Their abilities were so great that a scientific term was coined to describe them: *psychokinete*, a person with the ability to affect matter through mind power alone. For two years the lab tested their powers, verifying their amazing talent.

But those experiments, now referred to as *Project Alpha*, did nothing but prove how easy it is to fool scientists who have no knowledge of conjuring techniques. The two boys were what's known as "ringers"—fakes, sent in to alter the results. They were teenage magicians who had done some reading on mental magic tricks. Though all the researchers counted them as the genuine article, the boys themselves admitted in 1983 that it was all a hoax—*after* the researchers had prepared a formal research paper that claimed to have "proven" the existence of supernatural forces! The McDonnell Lab closed permanently thereafter.[8]

Neither boy meant to cast suspicion on the honesty of the researchers. They merely wanted to show how easy it is for a conjurer to deceive a scientist. The reason so many people are fooled into thinking psychic power is a reality is because *the average person can't detect deception*. The best person to detect a trick is an expert in trickery—a magician, not a scientist. In our opinion most people cannot distinguish between a normal fraud and a supernatural feat because they aren't trained in the field of deception.

As magicians, we take pride in our profession, and we resent those who misuse our methods, designed for entertainment, to lead others to believe they have supernatural powers. Whether they claim it is from God, Satan, or some other source, the bottom line is still the same: Anybody who claims to have psychic ability is deceiving people, and possibly even deceiving himself.

In order to reveal these frauds, a number of scientists and magicians founded CSICOP—the Committee for the Scientific Investigation of Claims of the Paranormal (pronounced "sycop" for short). The organization promotes the careful, controlled testing of those who claim paranormal power, and publishes *The Skeptical Inquirer*, a quarterly journal reporting its investigations. They have yet to find *anybody* who shows evidence of such power.

THE ILLUSION OF TRUTH

A fourth reason people are misled into believing in psychic power is what has been referred to as *the illusion of truth*. The more something gets repeated, the more we are apt to believe it. The repeated exposure to even the most unbelievable ideas makes them more believable. For example, if you're standing in a grocery store and you read a headline trumpeting "Woman Gives Birth to Chimp!" you're apt to laugh it off as another goofy stunt created to sell those tabloid rags. But if you're watching a television show three weeks later, and somebody mentions something about a woman giving birth to a chimp, your mind tells you, "Hey, I've heard about that somewhere!" It's called the "mere exposure" effect, and it's one of the reasons so many people have bought into the lie of psychic powers.[9]

There is an illusion that a few select individuals have tapped into some sort of incredible mental power. It's not the truth, but it has been given the illusion of being true. It seems somehow possible, as though it *could* happen, so people begin to believe it. And once people begin believing something, it is very hard to make them *unbelieve* it. Psychologists refer to that as "belief perseverance"—the notion that it is extremely difficult to eradicate an individual's beliefs. Even when presented with incontrovertible truth, the person is likely to continue believing. That's why someone may read this book and scoff at our arguments, ignoring our research and the truth we present. "Well," you say to yourself, "*some* of those mind readers may be phonies, but *not the guy who read my mind!*" Yet we'll wager that either of us could duplicate any mental feat you've observed.[10] Any demonstration of an alleged psychic power is nothing more than the use of some magical or psychological trick, not a supernatural event.

Unfortunately, the more our information base grows, the more belief there is in the paranormal. Professor Ray Hyman refers to this as "information pollution." You see, information in our society is growing at an incredible pace. There will be more discoveries made this decade than in the previous century. The body of scientific knowledge created in the last 40 years outweighs that made in the last 40 centuries. But with that information comes a percentage of *misinformation*. That is, some "facts" are false; some information is bad. And as we increase the volume of information, we increase the amount of bad information. As Dr. Hyman likes to say, "The worldwide web has an immense amount of information—much of it totally wrong."[11]

Thus in writing this book, we are trying to overcome the illusion of truth in order to present you with the *real* truth. We are attempting to offer wisdom in an area where many believers are getting fooled.

WE WANT TO BELIEVE

Fifth, we think many people are misled simply because they *deeply desire to see and believe supernatural phenomena*. There is excitement when we hear of someone miraculously healed, for that encourages us that we and our loved ones can also experience victory over illness. In the same way, there is an eagerness to know about the future, for that can help us cope with the uncertainties of daily life.

Is it wrong to desire healing or to wonder about the future? Of course not! However, there is a danger when we desire these so much that we become vulnerable to those who would prey on our desires and mislead us for their own benefit. One well-known scientist, the late Carl Sagan, talked about the emotional stakes involved in any examination of the paranormal:

> *In many such cases we are not unbiased observers. We have an emotional stake in the outcome—perhaps merely because the borderline belief-system, if true,*

makes the world a more interesting place; but perhaps because there is something there that strikes more deeply into the human psyche. If astral projection actually occurs, then it is possible for some thinking and perceiving part of me to leave my body and effortlessly travel to other places—an exhilarating prospect. If spiritualism is real, then my soul will survive the death of my body—possibly a comforting thought. If there is extrasensory perception, then many of us possess latent talents that need only be tapped to make us more powerful than we are. If astrology is right, then our personalities and destinies are intimately tied to the rest of the cosmos.... But the fact that these propositions charm or stir us does not guarantee their truth. Their truth depends only on whether the evidence is compelling; and my own, and sometimes reluctant, judgment is that compelling evidence for these and many similar propositions simply does not (at least as yet) exist.[12]

In other words, sometimes people believe in something merely because they *want it to be true,* not because there are any facts supporting it. The notion of psychic power is interesting, even seductive, and it has been portrayed in countless television and movie productions as genuine. But just because we want to believe in something doesn't make it so. In the 1930's, people in Germany wanted to believe that Hitler would bring order and pride to society because he was unabashedly patriotic. But their desire to believe colored their judgment, and within a few years their country lay in ruins.

Of course we, we believe there is a spiritual dimension to life. Supernatural power does exist, and is resident in God. It is not our intention to dismiss all reports of miracles, but neither should we go to the other extreme and assume that all reports of miracles are accurate. Experience has shown us that many reported miracles simply do not hold up under scrutiny. Rather than concentrate on finding such miracles as mind reading, psychokinesis, and foretelling the future, we can benefit far more if we focus on experiencing the supernatural power that God provides for all believers in Jesus Christ. When the Bible talks about miracles such as healing, it is displayed according to God's discretion, not by the manipulations of man. The incredible power that God wants all of us to experience has to do with changed lives, not psychic tricks. We also believe in Satan, and recognize that he desires to deceive people and destroy their lives. However, we do *not* believe he has the power to discern the future or reveal hidden information to people (though he desperately wants us to *think* he can).

SINCERITY AND THE TRUTH

Our research has led us to conclude this final point: *There are far fewer genuine supernatural phenomena than are generally supposed.* For all the smoke, we can't seem to find any fire.

"What about psychic healers?" we're often asked. "Aren't many patients healed?" The truth is, *some* are healed. Doctors have demonstrated, however, that as many as 50 percent of their cases are psychosomatic diseases or illnesses that will improve *without any treatment*, and many illnesses can be healed by the *suggestion* of a cure. Doctors call it "the placebo effect." But when it comes to genuine psychic power, André has yet to investigate a demonstration that didn't prove to be the result of trickery.

And that's only one example. Since 1966, magician and psychic-debunker James Randi has carried around a $10,000 check that he will give to anyone who can demonstrate one paranormal feat under controlled conditions. So far no one has collected the prize. "With all the claims of paranormal power that we see every day in the press," says Randi, "you'd think that I'd have many more people lined up to take the prize. As it stands, just 52 persons have passed the simple preliminaries, only to fail to support their claims to supernatural powers."[13] For all the sincere belief in human psychic ability, there seems to be a total lack of hard evidence.

Of course, we believe there is a spiritual dimension to life. Both of the authors believe in God, and both think that belief is entirely in harmony with psychic skepticism. (Being a skeptic doesn't mean one cannot believe in a divine or supernatural being—one who transcends nature. It simply means that we doubt, question, or suspend judgment on proclaimed truth until it can be verified.) Both of us are willing to accept the idea that supernatural power can exist, so is not our intention to deny all reports of "miracles." But that doesn't mean we're willing to accept that all reports of miracles are accurate. Experience has shown us that many reported miracles simply do not hold up under scrutiny. Rather than concentrate on finding such miracles as mind reading, psychokinesis, and foretelling the future, we can benefit far more if we focus on digging into the details to see what is actually true.

For example, most of us have known a person who seemed to be cured of disease "miraculously." There was no medical reason for the individual's improving health, for some unknown reason he or she simply got better. But stories of medical miracles are often hard to pin down—in fact, most of them, when checked out, were not actually miracles at all.

American culture has been inundated with charlatans proclaiming to have "healing powers." But we've noticed that most people who were "miraculously" cured of a disease did not receive healing from any particular individual…they just got better. So while we do not think it is outside the realm of reason to think God could intervene in our world, at the same time we don't have to assume every claim of supernatural power is genuine. Besides, if God really exists, it is doubtful He needs phony miracle-makers to prop up His reputation.

We won't argue the point of God's existence, since this is not intended as a theology book, however let us state right from the start that we do *not* believe, nor have we ever seen any evidence, that "spirits" (or demons, or sprites, or whatever you want to call them) have the power to discern the future or reveal hidden information to people. So while many religious followers enjoy toying with the idea of a demon pulling out their deep, dark secrets, we don't see, nor have we ever seen, that such an event can occur. In fact, in nearly every so-called psychic or occultic experience we've investigated, we have *never* seen any display of secret knowledge.

Remember, it is very easy to be *sincere* and yet be *deceived*. André was once scheduled to do a series of shows in Mexico. The pilot of his plane did not speak Spanish, and the interpreter did not know much about airplanes, so there were some difficulties en route. The pilot radioed through the interpreter, informing the airport that he had sighted the runway and was preparing to land. But on the ground, the plane was met by a mass of armed soldiers. It seems the plane had missed the *public* airport and landed at a *military* airport! The pilot had been *communicating* with the public airport but *viewing* the military airport (a small mountain between the two airfields caused the problem). The pilot had believed sincerely that he was landing at the right place, but he was sincerely wrong. Similarly, many people follow psychic or spiritual leaders because they are convinced the individual has supernatural powers, but in reality they have been misled.

We have spent most of our lives separating illusion from reality, and we would like to share some of our discoveries. Perhaps it will encourage you in your search for truth—and protect you from being deceived.

CHAPTER TWO

Your New Psychic Friends

Talk with a genuine psychic right now! Call 1-900-321-4000."

When the psychic hotlines first started business, most experts thought they would be a flash in the pan. They would take in big dollars for a few weeks, but the buying public would soon see them for what they are—a bunch of phonies grubbing for dollars—and they would stop calling. The experts were wrong. All three of the major psychic hotlines have grown every month they have been in business. The largest of them, which advertises through television commercials and half-hour infomercials late at night, is now taking in more than $10 million a month.[1]

It isn't just psychic telephone lines that are doing well. Our culture has suddenly embraced anything having to do with paranormal phenomena. Shopping malls across the country are hosting "psychic fairs," in which New Age mystics sell crystals, display occultic art, and offer tarot card readings. In urban centers, exclusive "psi parties" are all the rage. Friends gather in a home and a psychic shows up to read minds, offer personal astrology readings, and give an entertaining show, much like the parlor magician from earlier in this century.

Businesses have also become involved in promoting psychic activities. Many organizations have offered their employees the opportunity to attend training put on by *The Forum* or *Lifespring*, which promote quackery and New Age occultism, and countless business professionals have been influenced by the "enlightenment thinking" of success seminars, self-talk, and the purveyors of the Human Potential movement. Colleges not only offer yoga and the martial arts as physical education classes, but many now give full credit for such psychic-based nonsense as *Erhard Seminar Training*. These classes claim to empower individuals by tapping their innate divine powers and helping them reshape reality as they desire it, thus leading to some sort of mystical illumination. In a study of the Human Potential movement's influence on higher education in the State of California, the *San Francisco Examiner* reported, "Accountants, dentists, administrators, police officers, nurses, pharmacists, MDs, family counselors, and teachers can use the *Lifespring* seminars as education credits."[2]

Lest you think this interest in psychic phenomena is limited to those with too much money but too little sense, keep in mind that tens of thousands have gone to hypnotists to be cured of everything from smoking to snoring, though study after study has revealed that hypnosis offers nothing more than a placebo effect in resolving such problems. True, a placebo may offer help in some situations, but it is more dependent on the attitude of the individual than on the talents of the hypnotist. In addition, the entertainment industry's fascination with psychic power has made believers out of millions of Americans. The inherent mysteries behind *The X-Files* and the love affair with "the force" in the *Star Wars* movies have given rise to a generation who believe that supernatural psychic ability is a fact, not a fantasy. To counter that belief, it is important for us to define our terms and explore the evidence for paranormal activity.

WHAT IS A PSYCHIC?

The word *psychic*, which comes from the Greek word *psyche* or "soul," is defined as a person who is sensitive to nonphysical or supernatural forces.[3] In recent years it has become synonymous with the word *paranormal*—someone who can operate outside the limits of normalcy. The entire field has given itself the name parapsychology, since it studies human abilities outside the normal range of psychology. The common abilities claimed by psychics include:

- *Telepathy*: the ability to communicate impressions of some kind from one mind to another, independent of any known sensory process.[4] This would include thought-reading, revealing details about unknown events, and the ability to implant as well as discern a mental image.
- *Precognition*: the ability to predict the future "without the possibility of inference from present evidence."[5] When a psychic predicts a newspaper headline or foretells what is going to happen to you, he is engaged in precognition.
- *Clairvoyance*: the ability to receive information about physical objects or external events. The word literally means "clear-seeing," so a clairvoyant can allegedly "see" objects even when blindfolded. In the fifties, psychic Joseph Dunninger caused a sensation by driving a car while blindfolded, apparently demonstrating clairvoyant power. A related ability is called *clairaudience*, in which the psychic claims to hear voices offering direction and guidance.
- *Psychokinesis*: the ability to influence objects without using physical energy. Causing spoons to bend, bells to ring, or chalk to write are examples of psychokinesis. Most experts refer to it by the acronym "PK," though popularly it is generally known as "mind over matter."
- *Divination*: the ability to discern the mind of God. Throughout the centuries mankind has wanted to divine the supernatural by casting lots, reading the stars, talking with spirits, and looking for a sign of some kind. Most ancient books are about divination

in one form or another, whether hepatoscopy (reading the entrails of animals), rhabdomancy (reading the direction of dropped arrows), or idolatry (waiting for an idol's guidance). If all that seems like the ancient equivalent of spinning a lottery wheel, remember that in our own day we still have people who put their trust in astrology (reading the stars), phrenology (reading the bumps on the head), and fortune telling (reading palms, runes, tarot cards, and the like).[6]

All of these purported powers can be lumped together under what Dr. J.B. Rhine termed *"extra-sensory perception,"* or ESP for short. A 1993 Gallup poll indicated that two-thirds of Americans believe in ESP. One in three believes in precognition, one in four believes that a person's horoscope "can affect the course of their future," and more than half of American adults believe they have had a psychic experience.[7] Even without evidence of its proof, people *believe* in the existence of psychic phenomena.

A HISTORY OF LIES

The fact that so many people believe in ESP is not surprising, since there has been a plethora of authors and experimenters claiming to have witnessed some sort of mental miracle. For example, parapsychologist Richard S. Broughton has reported that psychics have been able to discern numbers created by random-number generators, and has made a lot of noise about the attempts to influence the fall of dice through psychokinetic power.[8] Sheila Ostrander and Lynn Schroeder caused quite a stir in the American defense community when they wrote a book proclaiming the Soviets had made "significant breakthroughs in psychic research," and were relying on psychic power to gain an advantage over American defense technology.

But these so-called experts have proven themselves to be long on professions and short on particulars. The "experiments" conducted by Broughton have been laughed down by magicians, who can easily explain the tricks that were used to fool those in charge. And the fall of the Iron Curtain revealed that the West was never in danger of Russian psychic powers, since the entire argument was apparently a hoax.

Of course, hoaxes have always played a huge role in the investigation of so-called parapsychology. The first scientific experiments of the modern era were begun in England by the *Society for Psychical Research*, founded in 1882. Their purpose was to investigate paranormal events and offer some sort of rational explanation in terms of science and religion.[9] Their first case involved the Creery sisters—Mary, Alice, Maud, Kathleen, and Emily. Daughters of an Episcopalian pastor, they claimed to share the ability to transfer thoughts from one sister to another. If one girl was given a word to read silently, another could write it on a slate. Sir William Barrett announced that the girls had passed the tests—but seven years later they were caught by a magician familiar with hand signals and codes, and the girls admitted they were frauds.[10]

In the 1930s, Dr. J.B. Rhine founded the Duke University Parapsychological Laboratory, in an attempt to pursue paranormal research from a statistical approach and to move it toward recognition as a legitimate field of study. Rhine was preparing for the ministry when he attended a lecture on spiritualism by Sir Arthur Conan Doyle and became interested in paranormal claims. He created many of the terms and procedures still in use today, and established some legitimate tests for psychics. For example, Rhine would mentally select one of six geometric figures, and the psychic would attempt to identify the selection through telepathy. To test clairvoyance, a deck of cards would be shuffled and the psychic would attempt to identify the top card. Precognition was explored by asking the psychic to predict the order of cards in a deck after being shuffled. And psychokinesis was tested simply by giving the psychic a pair of dice and asking him to roll a particular number.[11]

Rhine was a great believer in psychic phenomena, and tried hard to produce evidence that ESP existed. His first "breakthrough" came with a horse, of all things. "Lady Wonder" was a mare that Rhine claimed could answer questions by pushing over children's alphabet blocks to spell out responses. He published his findings, noting that "the telepathic explanation…by an unknown process" was "the only conclusion possible." His research became all the rage in the scientific community, until a magician, Milbourne Christopher, observed the experiments and pointed out that the horse could never answer questions *unless her trainer knew the answer.* It was a hoax: The trainer was signaling the horse with a movement of her whip. When the horse was tested with the trainer out of the room, "Lady Wonder" could answer no questions. Rather than accepting that explanation, Dr. Rhine concluded that the horse had once possessed ESP, but lost it![12]

Professor Rhine may not have been dishonest, but an investigation into his papers after his death in 1980 revealed that he ignored the many failures he found, trumpeting the few "gifted" psychics he claimed to have located. Unfortunately, by that time no one was paying attention, because his closest colleague, Dr. Walter Levy, confessed to cheating with subjects on ESP tests, and the controls used in their experiments had been shown to be weak.[13]

In the 1940s, Samuel George Soal conducted telepathic experiments with Basil Shackleton that were considered to be extremely credible. But in 1978, researcher Betty Marwick published evidence revealing that Soal had manipulated the results.[14] There have been dozens of similar instances, some in which sleight-of-hand artists have manipulated playing cards, where raw scores were changed to give the appearance of psychic ability, or controls were so weak as to invite fraud. The biggest problem in paranormal experimentation has simply been that failures have been swept under the rug: In every major study, the number of people who *failed* has been artificially lowered to make the occasional successes appear more significant.[15] Sometimes files were lost, others went unreported due to low success rates, and occasionally outright fraud took place.

On June 7, 1989, television personality Bill Bixby hosted a live television special, "Exploring Psychic Powers," in which several psychics attempted to win $100,000 by successfully demonstrating their powers. Even though every participant approved the tests before the show began, no one scored significantly higher in any of the tests than might be scored by chance. The National Research Council, formed at the request of the U.S. Army Research Institute to examine psychic techniques for enhancing human potential, could find no evidence to support any type of psychic ability. They concluded that *no scientific research conducted in the previous 130 years had proven the existence of parapsychological phenomena, and that the best scientific evidence does not justify the existence of ESP or psychokinesis.*[16] There is simply *no* scientific evidence to support the concept of ESP.

FAKES AND FRAUDS

But fakery and fraudulence doesn't stop with the research laboratory. Performers, mediums, and personal psychic readers have also been proven to be phony. On March 31, 1848, sisters Kate and Margaret Fox claimed to hear spirits rapping in their home, and arranged for public meetings and high-priced private seances throughout the country, in which they made the spirits appear to respond to questions. The girls became quite famous, and it was their activities which inaugurated the Spiritualist church movement of the late 1800s. But on October 21, 1888, Margaret admitted in the Sunday edition of the *New York World* that it was all a hoax. She produced spirit raps using the first joint of her big toe, and demonstrated it to 2000 people on the New York Academy of Music stage.[17]

Douglas Blackburn and G.A. Smith were widely reported to share psychic abilities, being able to reproduce each other's drawings. Their case is still heralded as the first "evidence" of psychic power. But in 1908, Blackburn revealed that he had simply drawn a picture on a tablet, then under cover of the table, duplicated the drawing on a piece of cigarette paper. The paper was rolled up and placed into the cap of the fountain pen, which was then handed to Smith. As he took his turn at the table, Smith would pull off the cap, secretly unfold the paper in his left hand under cover of the table, take a quick glance at it, then duplicate the drawing. Such sneakiness is common among those claiming to have supernatural powers.

Helene Petrovna Blavatsky (1831-1891), Russian-born founder of Theosophy, claimed to have psychic powers inherited from Tibetan masters. She wrote several popular books that she claimed were given to her by the ancients, and her most famous spectacle was occasionally having the letters flutter down from the ceiling, as though they had suddenly appeared from another dimension. Unfortunately, Ms. Blavatsky didn't take proper care of her domestic help. Emma Coulomb, Blavatsky's housekeeper, confessed in the *Christian College Magazine of India* that she had helped write the letters, then had dropped them through a crack in the ceiling. The *Society for Psychical Research* examined Blavatsky's claims in 1884 and produced a 200-page report that concluded she was a blatant fraud.

Eileen Garrett (1892-1970) claimed to be one of the greatest psychics and mediums of all time. Her crowning achievement was "communicating" with the dead pilot of airship R-101, a plane that had crashed on its maiden voyage. Garrett gave details of what went wrong that her supporters claimed only the pilot could have known, catapulting her to national prominence. But when investigator Melvin Harris looked at her statements, he found them to be either "commonplace information, easily absorbed bits and pieces, or plain gobbledygook. The so-called secret information just doesn't exist."[18] In 1962 a friend of Garrett's, Archie Jarman, began investigating the situation in order to prove Garrett's power. His 80,000-word report conceded it was all a hoax, and concluded everyone should "best forget the psychic side of R-101; it's a dead duck—absolutely."[19]

In the early 1970s, M. Lamar Keene was a highly successful medium and trustee of the Universalist Spiritualist Association, performing clairvoyance, psychic healings, and psychokinesis. But in 1976 Keene published *The Psychic Mafia*, in which he exposed it all as a fake, conning people into spending money on worthless tricks. Keene summed up psychic powers this way: "Every phase that every medium in the world demonstrates is fraudulent."[20]

Throughout the 1980's, psychic detectives claimed to have aided the police in finding murder suspects and buried bodies. Gerard Croiset received tremendous media coverage for claiming to locate a body in a famous Japanese murder case—until the Japanese police revealed that Croiset had nothing to do with the discovery. Peter Hurkos, a Dutch psychic who claimed he had developed his "powers" when he fell off a ladder onto his head, was another who claimed to have helped the police, this time Scotland Yard and their investigation of the Stone of Scone robbery. Hurkos claimed he had provided the definitive clues for solving the case, and his claims were trumpeted in the press—until a police spokesman denied the whole affair. When investigators found maps and false ID in his vehicle, they realized that Hurkos had been posing as a reporter to solicit information he would later claim he received psychically.

In 1993, Russian psychic E. Frenkel attempted to stop a freight train using his psychic powers. He claimed to have been successful in stopping a bicycle, automobiles, and a streetcar, and newspaper reporters gathered to watch him attempt his greatest feat. Unfortunately, his "powers" seem to have failed—Frenkel was killed when the train ran over him. He is just one in a long line of psychic frauds who have attempted to dupe the public into believing in the existence of paranormal powers.

EVIDENCE VERSUS CONVENTIONAL WISDOM

As we have been writing this book, we have had sharp, educated people say to us, "Surely you don't mean no one has psychic power. ESP is a well-known fact!" Our reply is simple: "It's conventional wisdom, but the facts actually argue against psychic ability." There are some common theories offered to explain psychic powers, but none of them stand up to scrutiny. Consider these common explanations of alleged psychic power:

- *God gives special psychic ability to some people.* This was the argument made by Jeane Dixon and a handful of other "Christian" psychics,[21] but there is no scriptural support for God-given psychic power, particularly the way it is practiced in twenty-first-century America.

- *God gave man psychic power at creation, but it was lost at the fall of man, and only enlightened individuals can regain it.* This would be an interesting theory, if only there were a shred of biblical support for it. Those who have opted to believe this fallacy have opened themselves up to a host of theological problems.[22]
- *Psychic powers are the result of satanic machinations.* This explanation, the most popular with evangelical Christians, is nearly always offered by someone with no background in magic and deception.[23] It presupposes that psychic power is a fact.
- *Psychic powers are latent in some people, but current science does not yet understand them.* This is a nice "out" for those who cannot come up with any better answer, but it ignores the fact that there is no genuine evidence for psychic phenomena. As paranormal researchers Terry O'Neill and Stacey L. Tipp put it, "To date, no one has come up with undeniable evidence that paranormal phenomena exist. . . ."[24] Contrary to the claim that science cannot provide explanations for the paranormal, there are simple explanations for every paranormal event."[25]

Remember, extraordinary claims require extraordinary proof. No matter how widespread the claims of psychic power, it is the quality of evidence that establishes fact, not the quantity. Millions of children believe in the tooth fairy, but their sheer numbers does not make her existence a fact. It is really not our responsibility to prove psychic phenomena is impossible, *it is the responsibility of those who believe in psychic ability to prove it possible,* and to date they have failed to do so.

For example, everyone in America knows the legend of Santa flying through the sky on his magic sleigh with eight tiny reindeer. As skeptics, let's say we wanted to prove that "reindeer cannot fly." In the colorful words of James Randi, "We may assemble one thousand reindeer atop the tallest building in the world and push them off, one at a time, to prove they cannot fly.... Based upon my good common sense, I strongly suspect that we would end up with a large pile of very unhappy reindeer in very poor condition. But what have we proven? We have only shown that *these particular* subjects either could not fly,

44

chose not to fly, or perhaps could not fly on this occasion. We have not shown that there are not eight tiny reindeer at the North Pole who, on one night of the year, can and do fly."[26] Rather than having to prove a negative, it is mandatory for those who believe in flying reindeer to prove the positive—and for those who believe in psychic powers to do the same.

CAN EVERYONE BE WRONG?

Dr. Jerry MacGregor once asked two psychologists to test him for psychic ability. Using Dr. Rhine's tests, *he showed psychic ability on every test.* The researchers were amazed, until he told them he had cheated. They didn't believe it at first, so he described for them how he "fooled the experts."

First, one of the researchers would mentally select a geometric diagram and write it on a board. The choices included a circle, cross, triangle, square, star, and six wavy lines. By *listening* carefully, Jerry was able to discern how many lines were drawn—a circle sounds like one long line; a cross is two lines; a triangle three lines; a square four lines; a star five lines; and six meant wavy lines. He "hit" on 16 out of 25.

Second, a deck of cards was shuffled and he was asked, without looking, to name which cards were on top of the deck. Jerry insisted on cutting the deck, and that was when he added six palmed cards to the top of the deck. "Miraculously," he got the first six right, missed the next three, and decided he "couldn't focus his mental energies on it anymore." It didn't matter—those first six cards astounded the researchers.

Third, when he was asked to predict the order of cards in a deck, he simply switched decks—replacing the researcher's deck with his own memorized deck. He hit 39 out of 52 (and could have got all 52 right—the "misses" were to lend an air of legitimacy).

Finally, he was asked to "see" what numbers would come up on two dice jumbled inside a small index-card box. This was harder, but Jerry had read how a famous television psychic had fooled researchers at Stanford University by catching a glimpse of the dice. Holding the box at just the right angle, he could flip the lid open a bit with his thumb and observe the dice, though it appeared to the researchers seated in front of him that the lid was closed. He "hit" on 13 out of 20 tries. (Jerry would later try the same tests, this time without touching the box, and he had even higher scores. How did he do it? He used an accomplice!)

Lest you think this unfair, *this is exactly what so-called psychics have been doing for years!* James Hydrick claimed to be able to make feathers, pencils, and folded dollar bills move by mind power, until Christian magician Danny Korem revealed that he was simply blowing puffs of air to get them to turn. Hydrick later made a full confession.[27] Uri Geller, an Israeli who took the entertainment world by storm with his alleged psychic feats in the 1970s, claimed to be able to determine the one container out of 20 that was filled with liquid. But when Geller went on the *Tonight Show*, host Johnny Carson, a former magician, stumped him by not allowing him to see or touch the containers before going on air.[28] Kreskin, who never claims supernatural power but obviously leads his audience to believe he has, relies on chutzpah and tricks common to most magicians. Jerry MacGregor once attended a show in which a famous mind-reader "dematerialized" a knitting needle through a pane of glass and claimed it was by mental power—though Jerry was demonstrating and selling that same trick for $25 in the magic shop where he worked at the time!

Before attributing any demonstration of the paranormal to genuine psychic power, it would be wise to keep in mind a principle developed by William of Occam. "Occam's razor" says that man should not make things more complicated than they really are. The simplest explanation is usually the best. For example, when President Ronald Reagan was shot on March 30, 1981, Los Angeles psychic Tamara Rand showed up on CNN, the *Today* show, and *Good Morning America*, broadcasting a tape she claimed to have made months earlier in which she predicted the shooting. For those who doubted her ability to predict the future, the simplest explanation was the best: She was lying. Investigators later discovered that this was exactly the case. Rand had made the tape on March 31, the day after the assassination attempt.[29]

Examples of fraud and deceit go on and on. Dorothy Allison claimed that during the search for the killer of several Atlanta children, she gave the police the name of the muderer, which she had discovered in a moment of psychic clarity. The Atlanta police department is on record as having denied any help from Allison.[30] American Greta Alexander and Holland's Gerard Croiset have made similar claims of helping police solve cases, and both have appeared on popular television shows, but investigative journalist Piet Hein Hoebens has shown their claims to be wildly inconsistent, if not outright fraud.[31] So-called psychics will often bring another perspective to a criminal case, just as any other individual would, but there is simply no evidence that they have helped solve any cases.

One of the common elements investigators have found about psychic sleuths is that they make very broad statements. Since people generally find what they are looking for, it is an easy matter of going back through the psychic's statements after the fact and "discovering" all sorts of important clues to the crime. But the thousands of failures psychics have had in offering help to the police are rarely trumpeted on television programs. It's what magicians call the "Dave Hoy principle."

Dave Hoy was a wonderfully entertaining fraud, who loved magicians but proclaimed to have psychic powers whenever he had a lay audience. He was a master showman, and particularly enjoyed making predictions. Hoy called it "hurling the headlines," and any time he was being interviewed, he would toss out a few "predictions" for the future. "I've hit several hundred of them in the past three years," he once admitted. "In all honesty, I must say I missed several thousand! But people remember the headlines that you correctly predict," and they forget the masses of headline predictions that are wrong.[32] Psychics and psychic detectives will toss out all sorts of general phrases, knowing that some of them will probably come true, and the rest will be forgotten. In other words, if you throw enough garbage against the wall, some of it will stick. That's the "Dave Hoy principle," and it's been working for many psychics in our society.

CHAPTER THREE

The Limits
of the Mind

In the early 1970s a handsome young man with a mop of dark, wavy hair burst into the public consciousness. On television shows and in laboratory experiments, the Israeli bent metal objects such as spoons and keys, fixed watches, recreated drawings without seeing them, predicted the roll of a die in a box, and altered the direction of a compass—all through only the use of his mind, or so he claimed. He appeared on every popular television show, read minds over the radio, and was extremely popular at clubs and upscale parties.

The perpetrator of those feats was Uri Geller, and many people still refer to him as a prime example of the human mind's potential power. He claims that he can receive and send mental images, that he can see things even though his eyes are closed, and that miraculous events occur around him for no apparent reason. Geller has even been written up in science magazines as evidence of ESP.

THE TRUTH ABOUT URI GELLER

Many people feel that most or all humans have latent ESP potential. They refer to numerous experiments which claim to have "proven" psychic power, and particularly to a handful of well-publicized psychic superstars. The most commonly cited example is Geller, who supposedly has demonstrated all four elements of ESP: telepathy, precognition, clairvoyance, and psychokinesis. Geller received much publicity after his powers were tested at the Stanford Research Institute (SRI) in Palo Alto, California, by doctors Russell Targ and Harold Puthoff.

Targ and Puthoff published their findings in a very controversial article in *Nature* magazine, a highly respected scientific journal popular with lay audiences. They wrote that the results of their experiments suggest "the existence of one or more perceptual modalities through which individuals obtain information about their environment, although this information is not presented to any known sense."[1]

The two doctors reported on three experiments. First, Geller was asked to reproduce simple line drawings, "while separated from both the [drawing] and anyone knowledgeable of the material." Results of the 13 separate drawing experiments were mixed. Geller did duplicate one of the pictures, a cluster of 22 grapes. He also was reasonably close on four of the other 12 drawings. On three targets, he "got no clear impression" and refused to submit drawings.[2]

A second series of experiments involved 100 target pictures sealed in envelopes and randomly divided into groups of 20. Geller was asked to associate any envelope with a drawing he made. He expressed "dissatisfaction with the existence of such a large target pool" and refused to associate any of his drawings with specific envelopes. On each of the three days, two of his drawings "could reasonably be associated with two of the daily targets." But the authors concluded, "The drawings resulting from this experiment do not depart significantly from what would be expected by chance."[3]

The third experiment yielded the most spectacular results. After a die was shaken in an enclosed steel box, Geller was asked to identify its uppermost face. In ten tries, Geller passed twice and gave the correct response the other eight times. The authors concluded that the probability of this occurring by chance was approximately one in a million.

Regarding Geller's metal-bending ability, the authors declined comment, saying that they were not able to observe it under sufficiently controlled circumstances to support his claim of psychokinesis.

For all the publicity generated by the experiments, the results were not particularly impressive. In fact the editors of *Nature* expressed concern over the article:

> **All the referees felt that the details given of various safeguards and precautions introduced against the possibility of conscious or unconscious fraud on the part of one or other of the subjects were "uncomfortably vague."**

> **This in itself might be sufficient to raise doubt that the experiments have demonstrated the existence of a new channel of communication which does not involve the use of the senses.**[4]

Author-researcher Martin Gardner examined Geller's most sensational experiment, where he correctly called the roll of a die in a steel box. He pointed out that Puthoff and Targ "describe the die test with a brevity that seems inappropriate for so extraordinary a claim. We are not told who shook the box, where or when the test was made, who observed the trials, how long Geller took to make each guess, whether he was allowed to touch the box, whether there were earlier or later die-box tests with Uri, or whether the experiment was visually recorded."[5]

Gardner correctly concluded that Geller could have cheated in many ways. The only way to rule out the possibility of trickery would have been to have a knowledgeable magician present, or to see a video-tape of all the attempts. "In the absence of such controls for guarding against deception by a known charlatan, the die test was far too casual and slipshod to deserve being included in a technical paper for a journal as reputable as *Nature*," Gardner concluded.[6] It was his assumptions that allowed Jerry MacGregor and other mental-magicians to duplicate Geller's results.

We believe that Gardner and the editors of *Nature* were right to express concern. What most people do not realize about Uri Geller—what he has tried to suppress in his publicity—is that he studied and practiced magic as a youth in Israel. He soon realized that he attracted a far greater following by claiming paranormal powers than he did as a conjurer. In fact, most of what he does would be rather insignificant coming from a magician, so he turned from a magical performer into a mental miracle-worker.

Geller also is a clever opportunist. Friends of André who have observed him say he is a master at taking advantage of a situation. At a table full of silverware and keys, he may bend one, but he rarely announces what he will do, so people don't know what to expect. He uses misdirection and timing to manipulate his audience. In a controlled setting, when asked to bend one specific object without handling it, his powers mysteriously disappear.

DIACONIS AND HYMAN

Persi Diaconis, formerly a professor of statistics at Stanford University, tells a story that demonstrates Geller's methods. Diaconis drove Geller to the airport after he had appeared at Stanford. While waiting for his flight, the psychic expressed disappointment that the professor remained a skeptic, and he offered to provide conclusive proof of his powers. He then asked Diaconis to reach into his coat pocket, grab his keys, and concentrate on a key that could be bent. The professor says, "I opened my hand and the key I was thinking of was bent. For about five minutes I was as badly fooled as I've ever been in my life."

Diaconis solved the mystery by reviewing the trip to the airport. Geller had insisted on sitting in the backseat, where Diaconis' coat lay. At the airport parking lot, Geller had insisted that he bring the coat "in case it gets too cool." The key ring contained four keys, only one of which could be bent easily. When he further examined his coat, he discovered an envelope turned inside out, and each of his pens' tops bent and twisted. Geller apparently had prepared several "proofs" of his powers.

When Geller is confronted by skeptics, rather than substantiate his claims, he often plays the role of a misunderstood genius and puts his opponents on the defensive. Dr. Ray Hyman has observed that Geller is very quick to pick up sensory clues from people. He learns what people expect from him as a psychic, and he doesn't disappoint them. In a casual conversation, one SRI scientist said that psychics seemed to be very sensitive to electronic equipment. An hour later Geller balked at an experiment because a video machine was giving off "bad vibes." "Several times I would ask him a question," Hyman says, "and before he could answer, one of the scientists would butt in and give the answer. Sure enough, when the subject came up again, Geller would rephrase what the scientist had said earlier."[7]

All of this illustrates a point that André often makes in his programs: Even the most intelligent people can be deceived when presented with a phenomenon—no matter how ridiculous—in a serious manner, in an atmosphere where honesty is taken for granted. The sad fact is that scientists are not especially well-equipped to detect fraud. They will go to elaborate lengths to eliminate any possible form of sensory input in ESP experiments, but if they miss even one such form, that avenue must be examined before their conclusions can be verified.

Hyman is in a unique position to verify this point because as a youth he became an accomplished magician and mentalist. The money he made from his mindreading act helped put him through school. After earning a Ph.D. in psychology at Johns Hopkins University, he served as a professor at Harvard before moving to Oregon. He is one of the leading international experts in the investigation of the paranormal.

"It is fairly easy to fool a scientist," Hyman says, "because he thinks very logically. Scientists can cope with nature because nature doesn't change the rules. But an alleged psychic changes the rules. He takes advantage of the way you think and leads you down his path of deception. That's why children are much harder to fool—they aren't as well-conditioned."

INVESTIGATING PSYCHIC PHENOMENA

Project Alpha confirmed that statement. In 1979 Washington University was awarded a $500,000 grant to form a laboratory for psychical research. From among 300 applicants, the only two subjects chosen to study were the two teenage magicians who had been sent in to fool them. The important thing to remember is that the scientists *never suspected that they were set up.* "There is no question that the lab personnel believed that Mike and Steve were actually psychic," wrote Randi after he exposed the project two years later. "It was this belief that made the deception exceedingly easy, and it was clear that, had the two entered the arena as conjurors, they could never have gotten away with all they did."[8]

This leads us to clarify two guidelines for anyone reading about paranormal powers. First, when investigating a potential case of ESP, *assume every other possible explanation first.* The conclusion of ESP can be made only after every other possible natural explanation has been examined and eliminated.

For most people, eliminating all the options is nearly impossible, since many methods are used to obtain information from a person without his knowledge. One is called *cold reading,* or unconscious sensory cueing. That is the ability to learn all sorts of information about a person from studying his or her body language and facial expressions. It looks like "guessing," but it is actually psychology, and a person using it may appear to read minds.

Uri Geller often complains that he can't perform when a skeptic is in the room—and especially if that skeptic is a magician! He is simply using good showmanship and protecting himself when controls become too tight. People usually are sympathetic to that argument because they want to believe in Geller's abilities. But if someone really had psychic powers, we could reasonably expect him to demonstrate them under tightly controlled conditions, regardless of who was present. If nothing else, the monetary rewards would be fantastic. (Such a person could make a financial killing in a place like Las Vegas!)

A second guideline is: *Be wary of statistics.* Geller's chances of calling eight rolls of a die without a miss was one in a million. That seems most impressive, but all it tells you is that it didn't happen by accident. In and of itself, it doesn't prove the existence of ESP. Persi Diaconis wrote about this in *Science* magazine. After reviewing several parapsychology experiments, he observed, "Most often these tests are 'highly statistically significant.' This only implies that the results are improbable under simple chance models. In complex, badly controlled experiments simple chance models cannot be seriously considered as tenable explanations; hence rejection of such models is not of particular interest."[9]

Diaconis went on to examine how statistical data can be drastically skewed if just one or two details of an experiment are altered—for example, if a subject receives unconscious sensory cues. "There always seem to be many loopholes and loose ends," he says in his conclusion. "The same mistakes are made again and again."[10]

Consider the investigations of those who claim they can levitate. For several years, Transcendental Meditation was the rage among young people. But when participation dropped off, the movement, under the leadership of Maharishi Mahesh Yogi, came up with the idea of *teaching* students to levitate—for a substantial fee. This seems to be an ultimate dream of those who wish to use mind power. There is something godlike about being able to defy gravity. The Maharishi claimed that people could levitate through a purified, altered state of consciousness—plus lots of practice. Thousands of students enrolled, paying between $3000 and $5000 each for the privilege of bouncing up and down by means of TM. No one from the program, however, could publicly demonstrate the ability to levitate.

The late Doug Henning, who resurrected magic in the 1970s with his television specials as the "hippie magician," gave up performing to immerse himself in TM. A couple of years prior to Henning's death, when André wrote to find out how he was doing, Henning replied by saying that they were "not quite there" but were all "very close" to levitating, that soon "scientists from all over the world will be coming to study this remarkable occurrence," and that "this phenomenon will create a paradigm shift in the thinking of Western science." Henning's letter was written in June of 1993, but we have yet to hear of anyone actually leaving the ground. (Apparently the followers of the Maharishi are still "not quite there"!)

One of the highlights of André's show is the self-levitation illusion in which he appears to rise and float about ten feet above the stage. It is a most effective illusion, and it baffles audiences even though it is accomplished entirely by natural methods. Again, André has no supernatural powers whatsoever. Since he began practicing magic, André has performed 11 different forms of levitation. In his travels around the world, including five tours of India, he has attempted to find one genuine demonstration of levitation—and has never succeeded. (Sorry, we won't tell you how André does it!) For all the talk about self-levitation, there is no evidence for its reality. We feel confident that if someone had the ability, we would learn about it quickly through the worldwide network of magician friends.

CAN WE REALLY PUT MIND OVER MATTER?

Another "mind-over-matter" experience that has become quite popular in recent years is *fire-walking*. André witnessed his first demonstrations of fire-walking many years ago in India and Sri Lanka. The walk over a 20-foot-long bed of hot coals was attempted only after the participants put themselves into a trance, or following hours of religious ceremonies. Fire-walking occurs in one form or another in cultures as diverse as Greece, Spain, Brazil, Trinidad, Tahiti, Japan, and China. Some of the ceremonies have religious trappings, others serve as a rite of passage, and still others are simply a form of tribal ritual or celebration.

Fire-walking was first brought to popular attention in North America by a Pakistani magician named Kuda Bux. In recent years a number of people have developed seminars built around the fire-walking experience. Jim Parker went through one such workshop in Tucson, Arizona, which included the singing of spirituals, a message about coping with fear, the chanting of a Sanskrit mantra, instruction in the basics of fire-walking, and hypnotic chanting before the big moment when participants walked on a 12-by-6-foot bed of coals sometime after midnight.

After the seminar Parker concluded, "When you look at the experience...closely, you realize that if you can will yourself to walk on a bed of scorching hot coals, you can will yourself to do just about anything you can think of for the rest of your life—*if* you want to and *if* you're willing to take that first step."[11] So for some people fire-walking has become the ultimate self-improvement seminar, since the belief is promoted that those who can conquer the coals can control any kind of fear and pain.

The dynamic Anthony Robbins is currently one of the most popular and successful motivational speakers in America. Every year thousands of people pay tens of thousands of dollars to attend his high-powered, unconventional success seminars. Because of his flair for showmanship, Tony has been a great fan of André's magic and for many years has even included the performance of one of André's illusions as part of his week long "Mastery University" seminars.

But one controversial feature of the Tony Robbins' seminars has been the fire-walk experience which he has incorporated, believing it would help give people confidence to overcome many of their fears. Those who do not understand how and why the fire-walk can be accomplished have often interpreted this feat as being a demonstration of some demonic or occultic power. At the very least it appears to support the notion that one's mind can overcome the material world.

But is fire-walking—actually taking five or six quick steps over hot coals in a couple of seconds—really an evidence of mind over matter? Can it really change a person's life? It's hard to argue with a person's emotional experience in that setting, so no doubt some people find fire-walking meaningful. But as far as it being a psychic demonstration of mind over matter, it lacks credibility. If the mind is that powerful, why is it that we don't see people walking over beds of coals *longer* than 35 feet (supposedly the world record) without getting blisters? Writer Peter Garrison tried to get some answers for *OMNI* magazine.

Part of the research involved close examination of Robbins' "Fear into Power: The Firewalk Experience" seminar. UCLA plasma physicist Bernard Leikind and UCLA research psychologist Bill McCarthy enrolled in a seminar in Southern California. Leikind's theory was that the secret of fire-walking is found in *physics,* not *psychics.* They decided that McCarthy would participate in the seminar while Leikind remained outside to avoid the mental suggestions of the seminar. Then both walked over the coals. Leikind did so twice, the second time over a freshly laid bed of coals. Garrison observed the results:

Psychologist McCarthy noted that the Robbins' fire-walking techniques—turn your eyes upward, clench your fist, breath heavily, chant "Cool moss," and celebrate when you reach the end—involves a number of well-known stratagems for blocking pain. These include repeating a mantra-like phrase, looking away from the source of pain, and focusing attention on an internal cue, in this case a Lamaze-like breathing style.... McCarthy did get burned slightly, but he felt no pain, not even heat, at that time.

Leikind fared better. "Once the coals had been spread out, they cooled rapidly," he says. "Incandescence is a simple gauge of temperature. I saw dark footprints where people's feet had been. Robbins' people claim to be blocking the heat somehow, but to me that meant much of the heat in the coals was being absorbed by the feet. But people apparently weren't getting burned, so I knew there just couldn't be that much heat energy present." In defiance of Robbins' prescription, Leikind looked down, breathed normally, and thought about the coals....

Leikind's walks were not a controlled experiment, and his success was not a scientific proof; it merely put his hypothesis on an equal footing with the mind-over-matter theory. But it is a preferable hypothesis, he says,

*because science does not seek farfetched reasons for
things that can be accounted for by simple ones.*[12]

It should be noted that not everyone emerges from the fire-walking experience unscathed. Some people get blisters on their feet, and some have had to go through counseling because of the depression brought on by their "weakness of spirit." But for those who do emerge unscathed, what is the explanation? One scientific explanation is the "Leidenfrost effect," in which a liquid exposed suddenly to intense heat instantly forms an insulating layer of steam. This is the phenomenon which causes water droplets to dance on a hot skillet without dissolving immediately. The theory is that vaporized perspiration provides temporary insulation for the foot, much as a little saliva allows us to snuff out a candle with our fingertips.

Professor Leikind thinks there's an even better explanation:

*...He views the coals themselves as the principal factor.
He thinks they are neither sufficiently dense and massive nor sufficiently good conductors of heat to burn the
foot during brief contact.*[13]

Laymen, Leikind argues, usually don't distinguish between temperature and heat. The motion of molecules is heat. Temperature is something else. It's analogous to "fullness." A small container can be filled by an amount of water that would barely wet a large one. Similarly, an object having little mass can be raised to a high temperature by an amount of heat energy that would barely warm something more massive....

Leikind cites the act of removing a cake from an oven as an example. You open the oven and thrust in your hand. The air in the oven is at the same *temperature* as the pan, but it does not burn you because it has little *mass*, and therefore contains very little heat energy. The pan, of course, has a large amount of heat energy. If you touch it without a potholder, which is a poor conductor of heat, you get burned.

Though the temperature of incandescent coals is at least 1200 [degrees Fahrenheit], they contain very little heat energy because they are not massive: They are a fluffy, spongy material, as light as balsa.... [Because] carbon is a poor conductor, the heat moves slowly, and the foot is gone before significant transfer has occurred.[14]

André once had the opportunity to watch a well-known Australian fire-walker give a public demonstration of his "powers." The man was scheduled to walk across hot coals placed on the rooftop of a popular shopping center. Unfortunately for the performer, the building had a metal roof and it was a sunny day, so after he walked unflinchingly across the lengthy bed of coals without harm, he stepped onto the hot metal roof and burned his feet so badly he had to postpone the rest of his fire-walking exhibitions!

Our conclusion is that fire-walking is not a dramatic demonstration of spiritual power or "mind over matter." It's a scientific possibility—and in countries where people go barefooted and thus have thick-soled feet, it's really not very impressive.

WHAT ABOUT DEJA VU?

One thing we haven't addressed in this discussion about mind power is the occasional unexplainable *premonitions* that many people have experienced. Almost all of us have had that feeling "I've been here before," or we know a friend or relative who has had a dramatic premonition for no apparently logical reason. Is ESP, particularly precognition, a possible explanation?

André knows of two such experiences in his family. One time his parents were in a movie theater when his mother sensed that his brother was in trouble. Later she found out that he was in an accident at that very moment, but wasn't seriously hurt. Another time André's brother-in-law was driving a car when he suddenly had a tremendous impression that his father had died. He literally had to pull off the road because he was so emotionally upset. When he arrived home, a call informed him that his father had indeed died at the exact moment the feeling had come over him.

Many cases like this are recorded. They are real and are difficult to explain. But they do not prove the existence of ESP because they are onetime, isolated events. No one has demonstrated the ability to use such power in a regular, everyday manner.

Luis Alvarez of the University of California at Berkeley offers a mathematical explanation for what happens. Using a complex statistical analysis, he concludes that events such as this occur about ten times per day around the United States. "With such a large sample to draw from, it is not surprising that some exceedingly astonishing coincidences are reported in the parapsychological literature as proof of extrasensory perception in one form or another."[15]

Psychologists have an even better explanation. "My brother was killed in World War II and my mother had a dream about it the night before it happened," Ray Hyman says. "Both my mother and sister believe it was a prophetic dream, but I see nothing miraculous about it. All three of us had that dream many times. They just don't remember the others because nothing happened to make them come true.

"The current theory of memory is that you tend to remember those things that you can connect to something meaningful. Let's say you periodically have fleeting thoughts of Uncle Moe, but they come and go and you forget them. Then one day you happen to think of Uncle Moe and he calls that evening. You say to yourself, 'I haven't thought about Uncle Moe for years.' You probably *have* thought of Uncle Moe many times, but nothing happened to make those thoughts memorable."

While we're willing to admit that deja vu events occasionally occur in all of our lives, they do not offer hard evidence in support of ESP. Whether it is chance, coincidence, or the comfort of God being evidenced, these sorts of events are not measurable, controllable, or demonstrable. If someone could clearly tell what would happen in the future, or what was happening in a remote location, the possibility of precognition would be more believable. As it is, there is no evidence to suggest these instances "prove" anyone has ESP.

André likes to perform an illusion in which his eyes are covered by two half-dollars, taped shut, then covered with a blindfold. Members of the audience are then invited to test his "second sight" ability. Without touching anything, André can identify the colors of several scarves, describe objects such as wallets and combs held up by spectators, and apparently "read" with his fingertips words written on 3 x 5 cards.

Sound impressive? Would you believe he has the power of ESP? Well, think again. Over the years, André Kole has practiced 12 to 16 hours a day with cards to master the art of finger manipulation. Often his fingertips were raw from the hours of practice—however, they never became so sensitive that he could identify *colors*, much less "see" things or accomplish any of the other amazing feats he apparently can do with his fingertips. How does he do it? It's a *trick!* André freely admits he does not have ESP, and he would strongly rebuke anyone who claims he does. Mindreading is a trick, and anyone who looks carefully at magic and mindreading will come to that same conclusion.

CHAPTER FOUR

Magic and Mindreading

One of the most frustrating things in talking with Christians about the facade of psychic ability is that many believers have accepted this false concept. For example, Dave Hunt, a diligent researcher and author of such significant books as *The Seduction of Christianity* and *Peace, Prosperity, and the Coming Holocaust*, declares, "Materialistic science has traditionally viewed psychic phenomena with suspicion and skepticism. Within the past few years, however, ESP, psychokinesis, telepathy, clairvoyance, and other such powers have been scientifically demonstrated beyond any reasonable doubt."[1] While we have great respect for Mr. Hunt, we would request persuasive evidence for such a claim. Every credible source we have ever come across repudiates this statement.

Dave Hunt is not the only popular author who has accepted the concept that ESP exists. The famous Christian author Hal Lindsey has written, "There is definite, validated evidence that unexplainable phenomena are taking place in various occultic practices. Medical doctors have verified many incidences of supernatural physical cures performed by psychic surgeons."[2] The evidence Lindsey refers to seems to be primarily the word of his sister-in-law, Johanna Michaelsen, author of the *The Beautiful Side of Evil*. This bestselling book has probably done more to mislead Christians toward an unbiblical perspective of Satan's powers than any other in recent memory. It offers no evidence other than the author's admittedly clouded memory, and tells of taking drugs, hearing voices, seeing the vision of an old professor fade in and out of view, and watching a "psychic surgeon" perform what she is convinced are miraculous operations. (However, it should be noted that Ms Michaelsen also claims to have seen ghosts and fairies, and taken a walk with leprechauns.)

The author claims to have inherited her power from a psychic relative, Lulu Hearst—the infamous "Georgia Magnet," a circus performer in the late 1800s who admitted in her autobiography that all of her feats were nothing but simple magic tricks. As people who have spent almost a half-century combined in looking for hard evidence of para-normal activity, we require a bit more definite, validated proof than one person's word. Chapter 12 of this book discusses André Kole's worldwide investigation of psychic surgeons, exposing the deception that *The Beautiful Side of Evil* presents as authentic.[3]

For some reason, many Christians like Hal Lindsey and Johanna Michaelsen just don't seem to believe they can be deceived. But magicians have continually used various methods of deception to produce the appearance of a supernatural effect. The most famous magician of recent years, David Copperfield, has convinced people he can walk through the Great Wall of China and levitate over the Grand Canyon. Copperfield, who has consulted with André on most of his major effects, used seven different methods of deception to cause the "disappearance" of the Statue of Liberty on national television. Surely if a magician can produce such gigantic deceptions, a charlatan can produce the smaller deception of creating the illusion that he has predicted the future or performed psychic surgery.

CONFABULATIONS AND CON MEN

The fact is that magicians understand that an audience wants to believe so badly that *they will sometimes deceive themselves.* Psychologists refer to this as *confabulation*—the tendency of "ordinary, sane individuals to confuse fact with fiction and to report fantasized events as actual occurrences."[4] We all have a tendency to believe what we see and what we are told. Few people tend to check the background facts and test the evidence of the things they see on TV. We also have a tendency to exaggerate—a fact magicians have used for years to boost their reputations.

Another thing that has created a supportive environment for psychic phenomena in this country is the faith we have placed in so-called "experts." The late Dr. Kurt Koch, a famous psychologist who has looked into paranormal events, claimed that "psychic powers as strong as those possessed by Uri Geller come from the sins of sorcery committed by one's ancestors. It would be better if he did not use them, but rather, if he would ask God for deliverance."[5] But Koch believed in the reality of psychic powers because he *observed* a psychic bend spoons and read minds—that is, he believed in what he saw. Koch had no knowledge of magic tricks, never enlisted any magicians to assist him in his investigations, and has been fooled by Christian magician Danny Korem. The "incredible abilities" Koch wrote about can be found on the shelves of any library in the pages of a children's magic book. As Bob Passantino has stated, "Christian bookstores are full of personal stories, testimonies, and experiences...characterized by subjective emotionalism, undocumented assertions, and little or no biblical or theological evaluation."[6]

When André Kole was performing in Germany, Kurt Koch and his associates were convinced he was using supernatural powers—to the point of harassing André on stage during his performances, in hopes of getting him to publicly admit his satanic power. But a magician is nothing more than an actor playing a part. There is no magician on earth who wields any supernatural ability. As André pointed out, "Here is a man who most of the world looked to as being the leading authority on the occult, accusing me, a magician, of having supernatural powers! I was not able to convince him otherwise. That fact alone completely discredits his ability to discern the difference between genuine supernatural power and common trickery."

A similar example was the brilliant scholar Sir Arthur Conan Doyle, author of the Sherlock Holmes novels. Doyle was convinced that the famous magician and escape artist Harry Houdini possessed supernatural powers of "dematerialization." Houdini did everything short of exposing his methods to try to convince Doyle otherwise.

SEEING IS NOT BELIEVING

It is too easy to draw conclusions from faulty evidence. No matter what our conventional wisdom says, seeing is not believing! James Randi summarizes the problems of inexperienced researchers looking at psychics in this way: "Parapsychologists are very much in need of a certain type of expert help. Involved in tests for ESP, precognition, psychokinesis, and other unlikely—but not impossible—abilities, they are frequently faced with human subjects who are sometimes able to deceive them by bypassing controls and outwitting understandably inexperienced and inexpert observers. The field is chock full of examples of this problem, and it is still an active factor in paranormal research."[7]

Therefore, André Kole has come up with some simple experiments to test those who claim to have genuine psychic ability. One of the tests is done by putting a box over the head of the psychic, then writing a simple sentence on a blackboard. If the psychic really had clairvoyant ability, he or she would be able to "see" and recite the sentence. So far *no one has ever been able to recite the sentence, nor even come close*. For example, while André was touring in Russia recently, a Russian psychic insisted on taking this test. André wrote "Billy is a boy" on the blackboard. The Russian's guess: "God loves us." That was a reasonable attempt, since the psychic knew that André is a Christian and was sharing his personal story at his shows, but it was nowhere close to the sentence that had been written.

The weakness of many telepathic tricks is that they rely on playing cards, giving the psychic a 1-in-52 chance of being correct. A much better test that André has used is to simply think of a five-digit number (giving the psychic a 1-in-88,888 chance of guessing correctly). So far no one has ever guessed the number, though occasionally someone will proclaim that he "got one of the numbers correct." It shouldn't be considered a miracle to get one or two of the numerals correct, since there are only ten choices for each number (0-9)!

Using dice as a test of precognition seems rather weak, since the psychic will have a 1-in-6 chance of being correct. A better test is to ask the psychic to predict a number produced by a random number generator. This has been attempted by countless psychics, but the "hits" have never been greater than would be obtained by chance—although in one remarkable case it turns out the psychic had rigged the computer program to produce particular numbers! Of course, why someone with the gift of precognition doesn't simply purchase a winning lottery ticket each week is one of the mysteries of the ages.

The tests that psychics themselves have come up with are far different—and much easier. For example, in the famous "Ganzfeld" experiment, a psychic lies down on a couch with half of a ping pong ball covering each eye (the better to get a "psychic reception"), while the researcher sits in another room drawing a picture. After several minutes the psychic describes the picture he has mentally received. The weakness in this test is that there are relatively few pictures that people will draw—mountains, forests, sailboats, occasionally a stick figure. No one ever draws something way out of the ordinary, like a moose wearing a football helmet while dancing the highland fling. Thus the psychic in a Ganzfeld experiment has a tendency to offer vague descriptions, wait until the picture has been revealed, then point out all the similarities in his description. We once watched a psychic use phrases like "I see water of some sort, and people...there are trees and buildings, though I'm not sure if they're in the picture or just out of reach."

Take a careful look at that wording. By using general terms like "water" and "people," the psychic has given himself a broad range to be able to claim a correct vision. And in the way he mentioned trees and people, he could claim he is right if they are either in the picture or out of the picture. Sure enough, the psychic we observed made all sorts of claims about his accuracy when the drawing was revealed. The actual drawing was of the United Nations building, with flags flying. The psychic claimed that there were buildings with people inside, "just like [he] described," and that the trees he saw must have been the flagpoles. The most remarkable thing to us was that the researcher bought the psychic's explanation rather than showing him the door!

Every psychic or occultic performer has a great advantage over a magician. If a magician's trick doesn't work, the performer is considered an amateur. But if a psychic's tricks don't work, he can always blame his audience. That's why a medium always pleads for the audience's support. Phrases like "My powers will only work if you believe" are common in mental-magic shows. That's also why many mediums ask the audience to send mental messages. If the message works, it appears to validate the performer's abilities, but if it fails, the audience thinks it is their own fault.

The really good psychics learn to take advantage of anything unusual that happens. If a power failure occurs or a car motor stalls, the performer will claim his powers caused it. The best mental performers (for they *are* performers) try to create total chaos on stage. They jump from one task to another, failing at some and succeeding at others, so that the audience has trouble remembering exactly what happened. And of course, lies work extremely well in this context. We have observed a performing medium declare that he had "never touched the spoon that bent," while in actuality he had been holding it in his hands just moments earlier. But the lies that are said aloud and repeated several times are what the audience remembers.[8]

HOW DOES HE DO IT?

One of the best-kept secrets among performing psychics is that *the audience doesn't know what happened before the show started.* We have watched psychic entertainers get all sorts of information from people just by chatting with them before the show began, then "reveal" it to them later in front of the entire audience. Those who don't know that a conversation took place earlier assume the mentalist is reading minds.

There are a few standard tricks that psychics like to perform as "evidence" of their ability. The most famous is spoon-bending, in which the psychic hands a spoon to a spectator, places his finger on the stem of the spoon, and appears to make it suddenly become weak and bendable, to the point that the spoon eventually breaks in two. That alleged miracle has been performed on nearly every major television show, yet it's one of the oldest tricks in the book. All you must do is get hold of one spoon before the show starts and bend it back and forth many times, weakening the metal until it is about to snap. The spoon will look normal, but it will bend with the slightest pressure.

By mixing the weakened spoon in with a bunch of unprepared spoons, then casually selecting the "special" spoon when it's time to do the trick, all the psychic must do is place his finger on the weak spot. The appearance is that the spoon slowly bends one way, then the other, eventually breaking in half. If the psychic has practiced his sleight-of-hand, he can even allow a spectator to choose a spoon, switching in the gaffed spoon as they are getting situated on stage.

The trick is often associated with suggestions like "The spoon feels strong, doesn't it?" and "It's getting warmer, isn't it?" Questions like these are usually asked of women, and nearly always bring a positive response, for few ladies want to upstage the performer. Even if the spoon feels weakened, she won't say anything for fear of embarrassing the psychic. As for it getting warmer, that's just a psychic trick: If the performer tells her it's getting warm, then it must be getting warm, so she goes along with his suggestion.

Some psychics will even try to get away with this sort of thing when confronted by those who know their tricks. Jerry MacGregor was once interviewing a self-proclaimed psychic when he noticed the man surreptitiously bending a spoon under cover of the table. The psychic then brought it up and hid it under his napkin, but when Jerry suddenly reached over and whipped away the napkin, revealing a bent spoon, the performer announced, "How strange! This sort of thing is always happening to me when I eat!"

Key bending is another psychic trick. The small end of one key can be pressed into the hole of another key, thereby creating a fulcrum and allowing the psychic to bend the key under cover of his hands. Later, while rubbing the key lightly with his finger, he'll announce, "Look, the key *just now* bent!" This little lie often convinces people that they "saw" the key bend, when in fact it was bent much earlier. We have also watched them hand back a bent key and exclaim, "Look! It's still bending!" This is utter poppycock, of course. The key hasn't bent any more, but the person holding onto it will usually agree with what the psychic has suggested, later insisting that it bent "while it was in my hands."

Starting broken watches is another common feature for some stage psychics like Uri Geller. Many broken watches will run for a few minutes if they are wound and given a good shake, so there isn't anything miraculous about this trick, but audiences don't know that, and psychics have used that information to their advantage. Having stooges slip in already running watches and claiming to make them start is another common method. Our goal in sharing this is not to ruin the show of a psychic performer, particularly those who are doing it for fun, but to point out that it doesn't require any genuine psychic ability to *appear* psychic. Once, when Jerry was serving as master of ceremonies for a public magic show, a psychic handed him a watch just before the show began and said, "When I ask for a broken watch, hand me this one." The audience had no idea it wasn't Jerry's watch, and if he had told them, he would have looked like a spoilsport.

Changing the hands of a watch is another old standard, though it's the simplest of all. In pretending to wind the watch, the psychic simply pulls out the stem and moves the hands, then places it facedown in a spectator's palm. When the watch is turned over, the hands have "miraculously" jumped forward an hour or so.

What people really want to see from a performing psychic, of course, is mindreading. So the most common trick is to ask a spectator to "draw a simple geometric figure, like a square, then add a different geometric figure inside the first one." Roughly eight out of ten people will draw a circle inside a triangle. Why? Because there aren't that many simple geometric figures to draw. Later the psychic will claim that he asked the spectator to "draw anything that comes to mind." A good psychic will also learn to "arm read," telegraphing what the spectator is drawing. Jerry MacGregor once duplicated five drawings in a row made by a reporter. The reporter wore thick glasses, and his drawings were clearly mirrored in them, so it was one of the easiest bits of "mindreading" he had ever performed—but the reporter was convinced that psychic power was at work, even after being told what had happened!

Determining words is another form of mindreading, and there are countless ways to discern the spectator's word. To begin with, the psychic nearly always asks the spectator to write the word onto a pad of paper. This is so that the stooge in the audience can see what was written and signal the performer, either by sight or by sound. Or the performer might ask the spectator to tear off her sheet, then take back the pad of paper, thereby reading the carbon impression left a few pages down. Or he may force her into selecting a word from a short list, thereby making his job much easier. It's also possible to use a simple radio transmitter, getting signals from a friend in the audience. We have seen hundreds of people walk away convinced that the psychic can read minds, when he did nothing more than employ a few principles of magic. Again, a psychic performer is counting on misdirection, uncritical attention, exaggeration, emotion, and imaginary impressions to create the facade of miraculous powers—the very same things that a magician relies upon!

DECEIVING THE ELECT

Our concern is not just that paranormal powers are a hoax, but that Christians are being duped into believing in them. For example, Christian writer Gary North, author of *Unholy Spirits*, has written that "demon-influenced false prophets would possess the ability to foresee the future" and that "the testimony of the Bible is that occult phenomena are real." Neil Anderson, author of the bestselling *Bondage Breaker*, writes, "I have no question that [the occult] works." Merrill F. Unger, who has produced such important books as *The Unger Bible Dictionary*, believes that "though Scripture condemns magic, it clearly recognizes the reality of its power."[11] And conservative Bible teacher C. Fred Dickason has said, "Occult magic includes demonic forces that actually produce detectable phenomena."[12]

While we admire all these godly men, the problem we have with all these authors is theological: If Satan can produce psychic powers in people, then he can perform miracles, and that is simply antibiblical. A miracle, according to Thomas Aquinas, is described as an event that is beyond nature's power to produce. It requires *supernatural* power to produce a miracle. Contemporary apologist Norman Geisler has defined a miracle as "a special act of God in the world, a supernatural interference into nature, a special divine intervention."[13]

This seems to be the same perspective our Lord had of miracles, for when confronted due to His actions, Jesus replied, "The very work that the Father has given me to finish, and which I am doing, testifies that the Father has sent me."[14] He would later state, "If I had not done among them *what no one else did*, they would not be guilty of sin. But now they have seen these miracles, and yet they have hated both me and my Father."[15] Miracles were a means of attesting to God's power. If something or someone other than God can perform miracles, then the value of miracles for attesting to Christ's divinity is negated.

When Peter preached at Pentecost, he attested that Jesus was "accredited by God to you by miracles, wonders and signs, *which God did* among you though him."[16] Hebrews 2:3,4 indicates that the message of Christ's followers was also authenticated by miracles of God.

The power of Satan, on the other hand, is *deception*, not miracle. If he could really work a miracle, it would suggest that he is divine. That's why 2 Thessalonians 2:9 reads, "The coming of the lawless one will be in accordance with the work of Satan displayed in all kinds of *counterfeit* miracles, signs and wonders." Throughout the Bible, Satan is revealed as deceiving and counterfeiting the work of God, but not matching it. Miracles exist to confirm God's message[17] and to accredit His messengers,[18] and thus Satan cannot perform them nor energize anyone to perform them. It should be noted that Matthew 24:24 is translated this way in the NIV: "For false Christs and false prophets will appear and perform great signs and miracles to deceive even the elect —if that were possible." But the word the translators render as "miracles" is the Greek word *terras*, which is more commonly translated "wonders." Satan can do false *wonders*, but he cannot do actual *miracles*.

The famous commentator R.C.H. Lenski provides a clear explanation of the difference. He notes that Satan can perform "lie-signs and lie-wonders," but they are "derived from what is a lie," thus "producing what is a lie." Lenski goes on to note, "We may translate [Satan's power as] pseudo-signs and pseudo-wonders." That's why pseudochrists shall offer deceiving wonders. "None of these great signs and wonders are real, all of them are deception only…. That is the extent of Satan's power."[19] As the deceiver, he makes things look like miracles, but Satan never delivers what he promises. Andre' has met several people claiming to be witches or warlocks, and they often talk about spells and powers, but they're always a bit short on execution. Satan promised them power, but he lied and failed to deliver. He promises miracles, but he can only offer deceptions.

PHYSIC POWER AND SCRIPTURE

Christians are usually quick to point out supposed examples of psychic power in the Bible, but in our opinion their case is weak. The mention of demonic signs in Revelation, for example, does not refer to actual miracles but to the fraudulent signs that the beast and the false prophet will use to consolidate power. For example, the false prophet will give *breath* to an image of the beast, giving it an *appearance* of life. But, as John Walvoord has noted, Satan has no power over life: "The intent of the passage seems to be that the image has the appearance of life manifested in breathing, but actually it may be no more than a robot."[20]

One Christian writer is on record as saying that "the mediums and spiritists that God warned against in Leviticus and Deuteronomy were not con artists, but people who possessed and passed on knowledge which didn't come through natural channels of perceptions. These people have opened themselves up to the spirit world and become channels of knowledge from Satan."[21] But that argument is extrabiblical. The Scriptures do not attest to the actual power of mediums. In fact, the context of Scripture would suggest just the opposite—that they are fakes. Satan might promise them supernatural power, but Satan is in the business of promising that which he cannot deliver. The mention of divination and consulting idols are always shared in the context of their "knowledge" being false. The prophet Jeremiah warned, "The prophets…are prophesying to you false visions, divination, idolatries [the word literally means "things of no value"] and the delusions of their own minds."[22]

The Bible tells of sorcerers and those engaging in witchcraft being *unable* to tell Nebuchadnezzar about his dream. It ridicules the Babylonians for believing in sorcerers, the Egyptians for interpreting the stars, and the Jews for listening to mediums who "whisper and mutter." Why? Because they are valueless! There is no supernatural power in them.

The most commonly used arguments in favor of satanic power are Pharaoh's magicians, the witch of Endor and the sorcerers referred to in the book of Acts. Pharaoh's magicians used deception to create what appeared to be a snake, but it was an illusion using "deceptive arts," according to the original Hebrew.[23] To teach that Satan could change a dead stick into a living serpent implies that he could create life— something he clearly cannot do. The magicians simply perform a magic trick, as evidenced by their amazement at the later plague of gnats and their response: "This is the finger of God." Similarly, the witch at Endor must have been a fraud, for even she was frightened by the appearance of Samuel. She knew she had no power to communicate with the dead, so when God miraculously made him appear, she was terrified. It was God's power, not Satan's, that brought the words of Samuel to her.

The various magicians in the book of Acts make for a wonderful example of our contention that Satan cannot produce miracles. Some authors, including Hal Lindsey and C. Fred Dickason, argue that Simon the sorcerer actually performed miracles through the power of

Satan. But nowhere in Scripture does it say Simon had supernatural power; it simply says he *practiced magic*. As a matter of fact, the passage argues *against* his having any power, for when he saw Peter doing genuine miracles, he wanted to purchase the secret.[24] Similarly, Elymas the sorcerer is not credited in Scripture with any supernatural power. Instead, he is criticized for being "full of all kinds of deceit and trickery" (Acts 13:10).

The fortune-telling slave girl is perhaps the most commonly used biblical reference to the power of demonic magic. John Ankerberg and John Weldon, wonderful authors and researchers, cite her as proof that "demons work though people by giving them psychic abilities."[27] However, a careful study of the text reveals just the opposite. She certainly was demon-possessed, for the Greek word describes her as having the "spirit of python" within her. That phrase means she was used by the priests of the Delphic Oracle to predict the future. The word literally means "pregnant with a god," or in more modern terms, a "ventriloquist." Here's how the scam worked: The person with the python spirit would mutter unintelligible phrases that were alleged prophecies, then the priests would translate them. The fact that the slave girl earned a lot of money for her masters doesn't mean her predictions were correct, any more than the psychics answering the "900" telephone lines are correct. As far as we know, the only thing this girl got correct was that Paul and Silas were servants of the most high God.

THE LACK OF EVIDENCE

If there is strong evidence that psychic powers were granted to men and women, no one has yet found it. In the words of skeptical inquirer David Marks, "Contrary to the claim that science cannot provide explanations for the paranormal, there are simple explanations for every paranormal event."[25] Of course, that hasn't kept people from believing. Author and speaker Hal Lindsey believes that his sister-in-law assisted a genuine psychic surgeon. It doesn't matter that this psychic surgeon has been proved to be a complete phony—he still believes. Though André Kole has exposed the deceptive methods used by psychic surgeons worldwide, even duplicating the operations on film and national television, many people persist in their belief. Uri Geller, the magician-turned-psychic, has been revealed as nothing more than a handsome trickster with great presentational skills, yet Christian writers and researchers continue to use him as an example of someone relying upon demonic power.[26]

Author Gary North is on record as claiming that American psychic Ted Serios relied on demons for his psychic demonstrations.[27] Serios is the psychic who underwent a series of experiments in "thoughtography"—the ability to imprint a mental image onto camera film. Parapsychologist Jule Eisenbud was in charge of the testing, which was done at various times between 1964 and 1967. During the process, Serios would hold a tube he called his "gizmo" in front of the camera lens, claiming it helped him concentrate. But after three years of testing, a magician exposed how it was done in the October 1967 issue of *Popular Photography*, palming an optical device into the gizmo tube and resulting in the photograph being altered. Serios denied this, but he was strangely unable to repeat his ability without his beloved "gizmo."

Sathya Sai Baba is an East Indian religious leader who claims to be both God and the reincarnation of a renowned Indian holy man. His followers claim he can do miracles, including making jewels appear out of the fourth dimension. Tal Brooke, a former disciple and now president of *Spiritual Counterfeit Project*, insists that Sai Baba is for real. Brooke, the author of several interesting books on why people follow false religious teachers, considers Sai Baba to be "a modern antichrist, empowered by demonic forces" which enable him to work miracles such as levitation, telepathy, healing, and the materialization of objects.[28]

While performing in Bangalore, India, André personally investigated and observed first hand Sai Baba in action. André was able to detect the sleight of hand methods he was using and duplicate the 'miracles' of Sai Baba. One of André's magician friends from India had also located the source of where Sai Baba acquired the watches and jewelry he later supposedly materialized out of thin air. In his book *Sai Baba's Miracles: An Overview*, researcher Dale Beyerstein reveals enough untrue information to prove that Sai Baba is neither omniscient nor omnipotent. He also points out that Sai Baba never resurrected anyone from the dead, as he claims, and that the "proof" of his claims to medical healing are a farce.[29] Sai Baba has refused to allow himself to be tested by magicians, but when we viewed his videotapes (sold by the Sai Baba Book Center), it was also clear that he was using simple sleight-of-hand to produce jewelry.

On August 29, 1992, Indian cameramen videotaped Sai Baba's assistant in the act of slipping a gold chain into Baba's hand just prior to a "materialization" of the chain. Although Sai Baba tried to suppress the videotape, it was shown on Indian television. As the *Illustrated Weekly of India* noted, "It is difficult being a god/man these days."[30]

THE DANGER OF PSYCHIC POWER

If there is no such thing as psychic powers, why does everybody believe they exist? As we have reflected on that question, the answer we have come up with is that Satan wants to deceive people. Keep in mind that Satan is called "the deceiver" in the Bible. In John 8:44 Jesus says about Satan, "When he lies, he speaks his native language." Everything that comes from him is a lie and a deception, aimed at moving people away from God.

Nevertheless, people are fascinated with ESP. Christian author Dave Hunt isolated the real issue when he said, "I believe that the ultimate purpose, the ultimate goal, of psychic power is to validate Satan's lie—the lie that *man is God*. Unless humanity can manifest these powers, they can't really validate what Satan has promised.... As to the various manifestations of *psi*, you could categorize them as attempts to mimic the attributes of God, because they try to appropriate the omnipotence, omniscience, and the omnipresence of God. This is basically the *function* of psychic phenomena, theologically speaking."[31]

Satan wants to destroy mankind, so he encourages people to believe that they can have supernatural power like God. It's the same argument he used with Eve in the Garden of Eden: "You will be like God."[32] The most basic choice every individual makes in this world is who will be God—either themselves or the true God. The devil wants people to be deceived into thinking of themselves as having Godlike powers, so he foists supposed paranormal activity upon them.

All of the recent interest in psychic phenomena is in harmony with the growing New Age movement, which teaches that people can discover God within themselves. The Old World beliefs in monotheism, a natural/supernatural divide, and a definite difference between the temporal world and the eternal world have been put aside. The New Age replaces those beliefs with polytheism, a blending of the natural and supernatural, and a belief in everything as eternal. It's a whole new way of looking at our world and our lives, and it embraces the notion of psychic power as one of the "links" between the natural and the supernatural.

PRINCIPLES OF THE NEW AGE

There are five fundamental principles to New Age teaching: First, it is *monoistic*. That is, New Agers believe that "all is one." The trees are part of us, the dolphins are our friends, and one culture is as good as another. This teaching is in direct opposition to Scripture, which teaches that man was created especially in God's image, was put in charge of the earth, and has a unique relationship with Him. In this regard, the extreme animal-rights and eco-terrorist groups in our society, who are at odds with the Bible. At best they make man nothing more than a "naked ape," and at worst they make him an evolutionary mistake. Unfortunately, it's lunacy. Even a moron can see there is difference between mankind and animals, and there is greater value to a man's life than that of a tree or a cockroach.

Second, New Age teaching is *pantheistic*. That is to say, it teaches the existence of many gods. Not only is all one, but all is God. Thus, when you cut a tree or butcher a cow, you are doing harm to part of God and His order. The science-fiction notion of a "force" is a common illustration of pantheism. Of course, the Bible is clear that there is *one* God, and that we are to worship Him rather than His creation.

Third, teachers of the New Age believe in *gnosticism.* The Greek word *gnosis* means "to know," and those who embrace gnosticism believe that we all have deep knowledge within us that must be discovered and known. Gnosticism was a heresy the early Christian church had to confront, as some teachers began claiming that Jesus Christ had not been on earth in body, but only in spirit, and that His death was unimportant. They considered the physical body "evil," so they were free to engage in all sorts of sexual activity, and their immorality, use of magic talismans, and ever-changing theology caused them to be branded as heretics. Gnostics pretended to be above theological disputes, establishing a dichotomy in the church between those who had "discovered" some deeper truth and those who were "still searching." It was this same belief that fostered the "enlightenment" of the seventeenth century, in which people felt they no longer needed God, for they had discovered truth within themselves. This notion persists today, as the TV screens are full of self-proclaimed shamans wanting to sell the secrets to enlightenment for $499.99 (plus tax). Their basic tenet is that there is some sort of secret knowledge that they've tapped into, are the only ones to have done so, and are therefore smarter than you and me.

Fourth, the New Age teaches the importance of *supernatural contact.* They claim it is through some sort of connection between our natural state and the supernatural world that an individual discovers the deeper knowledge which will help him or her to know God. Psychic powers are a natural fit into this kind of teaching, for they pretend to offer an exercise in paranormal gifting or supernatural contact. The Bible is clear that we do not gain salvation by means of discovering truth within ourselves, but through surrendering our lives to Jesus Christ. Salvation is found in no one else.

Fifth, New Age teachers believe in *networking.* Since they believe all mankind to be one, they generally desire a one-world government which will bring peace to all nations. More than that, they believe they have truth the rest of us do not know, so they can take whatever steps are necessary to bring us into the New Age for our own good. The apostle Paul, in responding to those who reject the true God, wrote:

The wrath of God is being revealed from heaven against all the godlessness and wickedness of men who suppress the truth by their wickedness, since what may be known about God is plain to them, because God has made it plain to them. For since the creation of the world God's invisible qualities—his eternal power and divine nature—have been clearly seen, being understood from what has been made, so that men are without excuse.

For although they knew God, they neither glorified him as God nor gave thanks to him, but their thinking became futile and their foolish hearts were darkened. Although they claimed to be wise, they became fools and exchanged the glory of the immortal God for images made to look like mortal man and birds and animals and reptiles.

Therefore God gave them over in the sinful desires of their hearts to sexual impurity for the degrading of their bodies with one another. They exchanged the truth of God for a lie, and worshipped and served created things rather than the Creator....

Furthermore, since they did not think it worthwhile to retain the knowledge of God, he gave them over to a depraved mind, to do what ought not to be done. They have become filled with every kind of wickedness, evil, greed and depravity. They are full of envy, murder, strife, deceit and malice. They are gossips, slanderers, God-haters, insolent, arrogant and boastful; they invent ways of doing evil; they disobey their parents; they are senseless, faithless, heartless, ruthless. Although they know God's righteous decree that those who do such things deserve death, they not only continue to do these very things but also approve of those who practice them (Romans 1:18-25,28-32).

God's word is clear that New Age teaching is wrong, and therefore we must understand that those things which promote the New Age, including psychic phenomena are dangerous.

Rather than recognizing the genuine differences between, say, Muslims and Jews, the proponents of the New Age claim that everyone is right. This is so intellectually inane that it's downright laughable.

In the popular movie *Ghandi*, the wise one is once asked why he can maintain peace among both Hindus and Muslims. The character in the movie replies, "I am a Hindu...I am a Muslim...I am a Christian...I am a Jew!" When people heard that speech in theaters, they sometimes burst into spontaneous applause. It's rousing, and it sounds good—we'll all be at peace if we believe everything. But the actor playing Ghandi might as well have cried out "I am an Imbecile!" because some of those things he mentioned are mutually exclusive. A Christian believes Jesus is the Messiah—something that Jews clearly reject. A Hindu holds to a belief in reincarnation—something all those other religions specifically teach against. So while it sounds somehow friendly and polite to believe all things, it is intellectually impossible. To believe in one thing means you must reject some other things as false.

This embracing of New Age beliefs, which is all the rage in Hollywood, is nothing more than ancient religious beliefs dressed up in a spacesuit to make them look modern. Contrary to popular belief, it isn't true. You may very well agree with some of their goals. But neither their goals nor their accessibility through the media make them true. More than that, their clear inference that they have truth the rest of us do not, and that they can take whatever steps necessary to bring us into their proclaimed "New Age" for our own good, is nothing short of scary.

CHAPTER FIVE

Make Big Money: Become a Psychic!

The ads are slick and tempting. A young woman looks into the camera and says, "I never would have believed it! All I had to do was call and tell the psychic my name and my birthday, and she started giving me incredible insights. She answered my questions about my relationships, my school, my career. I used to be a skeptic, but she made a believer out of me. I'm definitely going to be calling her again!"

Then she smiles warmly, surrounded by a group of caring friends, standing outside the crowded gates of a psychic fair. Her amiable disposition and obvious sincerity are effective, for it makes you think, "Well…it *could* be true."

So you pick up the phone and dial. It's late at night, so no one will know. You feel rather silly calling to talk to somebody you don't really believe in, but there's something about the innocence and the genuineness of the people in the commercial that win you over. Besides, there's an 800 number that promises you a free five-minute call, so there's no harm done.

The tape-recorded message you hear is basically another commercial, suggesting that you can find help, friendship, and supernatural assistance simply by calling a psychic. You're told that the company carefully selects those who work for them, that they've all demonstrated psychic ability, and that the whole thing is risk-free: If you don't like your psychic, you can get your money refunded. The whole thing sounds pretty easy, and besides, lots of other people have called, so you give it a try.

THE TRUTH ABOUT PSYCHIC HOTLINES

In researching this book, we called some psychic hotlines, talked with a representative from the headquarters of a psychic hotline, and interviewed someone who works as a psychic. Nothing we discovered dissuaded us from our conviction that the psychic hotlines offer no supernatural help to callers.

The first hotline we called was answered by a machine that offered a long message, so we were already out almost $16 before we actually *talked* with anybody. That person asked for Jerry's birthdate, then started warning about "the health concerns of yourself or someone close to you." This is a common introduction, since nearly everybody either has a physical question or knows someone who does. The psychic then went on to encourage Jerry in his career decisions (he has been a writer for years), hint that he is having relationship difficulties (he has been married for 20 years), and tell him that he "enjoys life and likes people." It was all very general stuff that could have come from any "cold reading" script, and it went on for about ten minutes. The cost: $35.91.

The second hotline we dialed was much more detailed, as the psychic asked for a birthdate and followed it with a tarot card reading—a special deck that psychics claim can be used to predict the future. She also talked about health and career concerns, though she added some specific details: Stay away from the color red, and take that trip he's been putting off. This reading was far more mystical, and the psychic talked uninterrupted for much of the time. The charge: $47.88.

The third hotline was quite similar to the second, with a psychic doing a reading based upon Jerry's astrological sign. Unfortunately, she was using a script we had already uncovered on the internet. When specific questions were asked ("What should I do about my car?"), the psychic seemed totally flustered. However, she came back with some nice words about Jerry doing better financially very soon. She must not have been talking about his credit card, however, since this call cost $38.87, for a total of $122.66 spent in just 34 minutes.

Indeed, one of the scariest things about the psychic hotlines is the speed at which callers rack up charges. A friend of André has been helping a lady who lost $23,000 to a psychic hotline, and we just learned that James Randi is currently assisting a woman who owes $450,000 to various psychic networks. On top of that, a majority of the psychic telephone services are hosted by African-Americans (Dionne Warwick's *Psychic Friends Network*, LaToya Jackson's *Psychic Network*, Philip Michael Thomas' *Network*) in a crass attempt to draw inner-city black callers. Following the lead set by the gaming industry, they want to attract people who have an interest in improving their lives, but who often cannot afford to throw their money away on this sort of nonsense.

In recent months the government has stepped in to try to regulate some of the worst abuses. Some of the hotlines have significantly shortened the instruction and waiting time, there are warnings given when someone has been on longer than 20 or 30 minutes, and the advertisements generally have added the words "For Entertainment Purposes Only." However, that doesn't make the psychic hotlines any better or any more believable.

The office manager at one of the hotlines said he would talk with us provided we did not use his name or identify which company he worked for. He told us 10 percent of each call goes to the psychic, 25 percent to the phone company, 30 percent to advertising, and the rest to the company, though he also admitted a high percentage of people run up high phone bills and then will not pay them. This man also claimed that they try to screen for people with actual psychic abilities, though he added that "the company discourages psychics from being too specific" with people. It's understandable why they wouldn't want a psychic to be too specific—they don't want to be held liable should something go wrong.

MEETING A PSYCHIC

Yvonne (not her real name) lives in Eugene, Oregon. She has taken some graduate courses in counseling, and has had an interest in helping people, so for nearly eight months she worked for two of the psychic networks. Yvonne paid to have a special phone line installed, and would answer calls from people all over the country each evening. She soon discovered that people who get the hotline numbers from print advertisements call in the evening, between 6 p.m. and midnight, while those who get the phone numbers from television commercials call between midnight and 4 a.m. By signing up with one print-based hotline and one TV-based hotline, Yvonne kept herself busy six nights a week.

The company told her an average call ought to last about ten minutes and that she should receive roughly 24 calls in a 24-hour period, and that if either of those numbers went down, she would be dropped from their network. Yvonne was given a script to follow by each of the two networks, and was instructed to always give a general reading first before allowing the caller to ask questions, since that keeps them on the phone longer. One of the networks instructed her to encourage callers to sign up for a newsletter, so that the caller was also charged while she was making her sales pitch. And Yvonne told us that before she could begin working she had to sign a waiver absolving the network of any responsibility, should someone take her advice and experience a disaster. In other words, she made 39 cents per minute and was liable for anything bad that occurred.

Upon getting her first calls, Yvonne discovered something important: Her callers didn't want advice; they wanted supernatural insight. "If they were in bad health, they wouldn't listen to me when I told them to go see a doctor," she told us. "I had to pretend the cards *revealed to me* that they ought to see a doctor." C. Eugene Emery, writing in *The Skeptical Inquirer,* interviewed another former psychic hotline worker who said much the same thing:

> When women called to ask if they were pregnant, Cook
> [the psychic] tried to get them to contact Planned
> Parenthood for a pregnancy test. Most rejected her
> advice. They "weren't about to do something so cheap
> and commonsense unless I told them I read in the cards
> that they should go to the doctor.... "

> One of her callers, who refused to accept his divorce,
> violated a restraining order on the advice of a psychic on
> the hotline. He was arrested. He said he was calling from
> jail. Cook said, "When I told him to discount everything
> the previous 'psychic friend' had told him, he wasn't buy-
> ing it at all. [It wasn't] until I told him I had read in the
> cards that the previous psychic had made a terrible mis-
> take in computing his astrological chart because of a
> power failure that had damaged her equipment with a
> power surge, was he willing to take my advice, the advice
> of his counselor, his mother, and the prison chaplain" to
> read and abide by the restraining order....

> Tonia wanted to know whether her husband was going to
> beat her. Cook tried to convince her to call the emer-
> gency number 911. She also gave Tonia the names of
> churches that might provide counseling. The woman's
> reaction: "I called for a *reading!* I want my *reading!*" So,
> Cook says, she concocted a tarot reading to back up her
> recommendation.[1]

Emery goes on to note that the reason Tonia's husband was angry was because she had rung up a $5000 phone bill talking to psychic counselors. Of course, the most interesting thing we discovered in talking with psychics is that none of them had to actually prove they were psychic to get the job. Yvonne had to give a psychic reading to a staff member over the phone. Cook simply had to verbally affirm that she had psychic ability. When ABC Television's *Prime Time Live* sent a college student with no psychic ability to interview, he was hired on the spot as a hotline psychic. And Emery says, "One self-proclaimed psychic I know who auditioned for the network said she was told by a company representative that psychic abilities didn't really matter."[2]

BECOMING A PSYCHIC
FOR FUN AND PROFIT

In surfing the internet, we discovered several manuscripts for pseudopsychics, and even some helpful guides for starting your own psychic hotline. One of them, *How to Work the 900 Number Psychic Lines*, by Bruce Daniel Kettler, explicitly details how to go about getting hired as a psychic. Kettler is obviously a believer, repeatedly exclaiming, "You are psychic!" but offering no evidence to support his contention. His handy guide covers everything from purchasing an extra phone to creating your pitch.

He claims that most callers to psychic lines have the same concerns: health, death, disease, divorce, cheating, relationships, money, jobs, decisions, and destiny. He also notes that a psychic will occasionally run into a skeptic or religious fanatic who refuses to believe, but he spends most of his time dealing with the practical aspects of the job: how to keep people on a long time, how to "sound sincere," and how to pick good lottery numbers. (Kettler doesn't say why someone who can pick winning lottery numbers is answering phones for 39 cents a minute.) However, his advice for all psychic-wanna-be's is to learn tarot cards, astrological signs, and how to read people. We find it fascinating that none of those three things rely on psychic ability, but on *intuition*.

All of us have experienced flashes of intuition, in which we get an insight or a gut feeling, or else our instincts tell us something is happening. Sometimes our intuition proves useful, and other times it comes to nothing; the entire notion of intuition is such a nebulous, intangible concept that it is hard to define in a satisfactory manner. Yet it is an important part of psychic reading, and of New Age thinking in general. *Webster's* defines intuition as "knowledge, conviction, or cognition attained without evidence of rational thought and inference." For example, a mother seems to intuitively know that her child is lying. A streetwise young man might intuitively sense that he is in danger. A businessman heading toward a meeting can sometimes intuitively determine what his client needs. There is nothing supernatural or magical about intuition. It is often based on instincts. The mother recognizes behavior patterns in her child that suggest he is not telling the truth. The streetwise young man picks up subtle clues from his environment to tell him something is wrong. And the businessman relies on his accumulated experience to help him determine which course of action to follow.

A woman posing as a psychic does the same thing. She recognizes that people experiencing similar events share the same problems. So when the psychic talks to college age women, she is smart enough to focus on two things: guys and grades. When she is talking with a man in his thirties, her focus changes: career, money, and relationships. Somehow intuition has been confused with psychic power. New Agers have a tendency to confuse luck and a good old educated guess with precognition and clairvoyance. *Harper's Encyclopedia of Mystical and Paranormal Experience* even claims that "intuition invariably proves to be right."[3]

This, of course, is total balderdash. Intuition has never proven itself infallible, nor even particularly regular. It can be fleeting and unreliable. Sometimes it's just plain wrong. Humans have a tendency to remember the few times their intuition was right, and forget the many times their intuition was wrong. That's why we read in the paper about the waitress who won a million-dollar lottery when she "just had a hunch" that she should use her birthday and anniversary numbers, but we conveniently forget that for every one winner there are a million other people who had hunches about numbers that proved false. Yet psychics *must* rely on their intuition to help them pretend to "see" the customer and the future, so most have a tendency to talk about intuition as though it were "psychic power."

Dr. Frances Vaughn, president of the Association of Transpersonal Psychology, writes of developing psychic ability by encouraging people to follow their intuition. "Learning to use intuition is learning to be your own teacher, and getting in touch with your own inner guru," according to Vaughn. "ESP, clairvoyance, and telepathy are part of the intuitive function…. Many believe that everyone has the potential for psychic experiences and that these represent a type of intuitive knowing."[4]

But there is danger in leading one's life solely on intuition. When we disregard wisdom and critical thinking to trust in our intuition, we open ourselves up to guidance from feelings and other forces. Dr. Vaughn goes on to suggest that intuition is a way to contact a realm of infinite knowledge, and *Harper's Encyclopedia of Mystical and Paranormal Experience* says that "intuition is integral to all forms of divination and psychic consultation."[5] This is where the Christian has to be discerning, for while we believe psychics are utter frauds, we also recognize that Satan uses them for their purposes. That is, we do not think most psychics who claim to predict the future ware demon-possessed, but the *devil surely has deceived and influenced their thinking*, and through them he will try to deceive and influence us also. Thus the entire flow of culture toward New Age thinking has led us away from God and His truth. While we don't think anyone working on a psychic hotline has supernatural power, it is clear that the devil has tricked some of them into *thinking* they have psychic power, so they are without question under Satan's leadership.

That fact has some scary implications for our society. As business and education embrace intuition and psychic power, critical thinking gets marginalized. Belief in psychic abilities, regardless of the fact that there is no proof they exist, has almost become redefined as something normal—something everyone has within him. Examples abound: Business courses use textbooks like Weston Agor's *Intuitive Management* and Mihalasky and Dean's *Executive ESP*. Counselors rely on the writings of Carl Jung and Sigmund Freud, who claimed to get their principles from spirit guides. Educators espouse learning concepts that come from channelers, mediums, and those who worship the created rather than the Creator, talking about "applied psi" as a principle for all disciplines:

> By 1984 *applied psi* had become an informal part of at least twenty-eight fields: archaeology, agriculture and pest control, animal training and interspecies communication, contests and gambling, creativity, education and training, entertainment, environmental improvement, executive decision-making, finding lost objects, future forecasting, geological exploration, historical investigation, investigative journalism, medicine and dentistry, military intelligence, personnel management, police work, psychotherapy and counseling, safety inspection, scientific discovery, social control, and weather prediction.[6]

Using intuition or alleged psychic power to further our knowledge of a subject appears rather unscientific in light of the scarcity of evidence for its existence. But relying on some sort of intuitive power is nothing more than a New Age religious worldview, and Christians should reject that thinking as downright antibiblical.

PSYCHICS AND SPIRITISTIC INFLUENCE

When people try to develop their psychic powers, they open themselves up to all sorts of deceit and occultic influences. The individual who wants to become psychic must abandon the normal functioning of the mind in order to try to contact the spirit world. Not only does the Bible specifically forbid this practice, but it is a departure from the physical and mental experiences we normally go through to develop new talents.

Take for example the development of musical talent. If a woman wants to develop her ability to play the piano, she simply starts practicing hours every day. If a young man wants to learn woodcarving, he makes sure he has the right tools, then goes into his shop and starts hacking away at a piece of wood. But if someone wants to become psychic, he rejects this sort of physical or mental practice and instead begins interacting with weird religions, phony teachers, and demonic forces. But, as John Ankerberg and John Weldon put it, "developed" is probably not the right word to use.

> It is more appropriate to say psychic powers are increasingly *encountered* in various ways and then utilized, rather than to say they are developed. In the context of this discussion, a term like "psychic development" is misleading. Intuition cannot be developed because it cannot be controlled by the human will.... Psychic powers are consistently associated with spirits; intuition is not. This is why "developing" intuition leads so often and so logically to involvement in the psychic and spiritualistic realm.[7]

After nearly forty years we have yet to find anyone who has had any genuine psychic ability. On one end of the spectrum are the psychic entertainers who know they do not have any genuine psychic ability, who use magic tricks for entertainment purposes, creating the illusion of having special psychic ability. At the other end are those involved in metaphysics and the occult, who have been deceived into believing they have been given or developed some special psychic power. This again points out one of the most important facts about the way Satan works: He promises people they will develop supernatural psychic ability, but he cannot deliver it. That's the reason we find psychic and occultic practices to be, not just phony, but dangerous. History has shown that those who get involved in seeking psychic powers invariably end up in bizarre religious entrapments. There is a clear link between trying to develop clairvoyant or precognitive ability and a reliance upon demonic guidance. That is why so many psychics eventually move toward channeling—an even more overt form of demonic activity.

If you look through the literature of those claiming to have psychic power, you will find that they often talk about surrendering to a spirit's control, and they admit that a spirit is the "source of their power." In truth, *they don't have power!* Some of them think they do, but they have become the foolish victim of Satan's trickery. If they continue down that path, some may even become possessed by demons, allowing the demon to speak through them. However, it is important we remember that, even in a case of demon possession, the individual will not develop supernatural ability. *The demon cannot give the person power to see into the future, or to levitate, or to read minds.* He may *claim* he can give that power, but he will never deliver it. If Satan could, it seems reasonable that somebody, somewhere, would have been able to validate that sort of ability.

Keep in mind that there is no biblical example of a demon giving someone the power to read minds or levitate. Occasionally the possessed person was given great strength, but even then it was super*normal* and not super*natural* strength. That is, the possessed man of the Gerasenes had the power to break chains, but he did not have the power to give life, calm storms, heal disease, or feed 5000 people with five loaves and two fish. He had super*normal* power, but not super*natural* power. Perhaps we need to identify the different between supernatural and supernormal power. There are many documented cases of people developing supernormal strength—like the mother who lifted a car off her son, or the man who climbed a sheer wall when being chased by a bear. But those feats were done with muscle and adrenaline, not demonic power.

To expect that demons can give someone precognitive ability is to suggest they are able to predict the future accurately, and that doesn't seem to be the case (if so, they surely would not have urged the crowds to crucify Jesus!). Demons seem to be able to plant thoughts in our mind in some way, but there is no evidence that they can read akll our thoughts, let alone convey them to someone else. And demons are not omnipresent, so they cannot know what is going on in other parts of the world in order to reveal it to a psychic.

Thus the popular notion among many Christians that demonic power is behind psychic ability contains both truth and error. Satan is promising people psychic power, and he is perpetrating lies about the nature of knowledge and salvation, so he is definitely the source of psychic claims. But he cannot actually give supernatural power to an individual; that ability is retained by God alone. As a matter of fact, the whole notion of demons giving people supernatural abilities just doesn't fit the pattern of Scripture nor the examples of history. All demons can do is help people create false signs and wonders, in order to deceive others and entrap them into more lies.

KEEPING FAITH AND BELIEF IN BALANCE

Once, when André was being interviewed for a story on an alleged psychic, the reporter couldn't understand why he wouldn't believe in psychic powers. "But...can't you just take it on faith?" the reporter wanted to know. "Do you have to have evidence for everything?"

André's answer was plain: "Of course I do. In order for me to believe someone is psychic, I need some sort of tangible proof."

"But what about your faith in God? Doesn't that require proof?"

André's answer was instructive: "*I already have proof in God.*"

Consider André's story: He has performed in more countries of the world than any other magician in history. He has appeared on national television in 47 different nations, is considered one of the leading inventors of magical illusions in the world, and has spent his life investigating mysteries and claims of the supernatural. That makes him uniquely qualified to evaluate the claims of Jesus Christ.

As a young man, André was impressed with the impact of Christ's miracles. Jesus was able to perform things far beyond anything a magician can accomplish today, and He did it without any modern technology or elaborate equipment. Indeed, it would take millions of dollars and tons of equipment to "duplicate" some of the miracles Christ performed. He fed 5,000 people with five loaves and two fish. He walked on a raging sea, healed the sick, and turned water into wine. He even raised people from the dead. His miracles were witnessed by thousands, confirmed by the doctors and scholars of His day, yet no one has ever been able to come up with an alternative explanation for Christ's power. He could do miracles, and the fact attests to His divinity.

Not only that, He fulfilled clear prophecies about the coming Savior. Hundreds of prophecies had been written in the Old Testament Scriptures, predicting details of the Savior's life, and Jesus fulfilled them all. It would be impossible for a man to arrange those types of details in his life.

In looking at the evidence the only conclusion André could reach was that Jesus was who He claimed to be: *God in the flesh*. All the evidence points to it. His disciples certainly believed that, for they were willing to go to their deaths preaching the truth of Jesus Christ.

There was one other piece of evidence which persuaded André to establish a personal relationship with Jesus Christ—the lives of the Christians he met. They had peace with God, joy in their hearts, and meaning in their lives. When André began reading the Bible to find out what made these people different, he found out that Jesus had forgiven them of their sins. A Christian is simply an individual who has turned his or her life over to Christ, and God dwells in their heart. Rather than being a long list of "do's and don'ts," the Christian life is an expression of faith toward a God who longs to save us. By turning his life over to Jesus Christ, André found forgiveness, peace and purpose.

COMPARING CHRIST AND THE PSYCHICS

If a psychic could simply demonstrate his abilities in a way that is verifiable, we would recognize his supernatural powers. That is, he must be willing to duplicate in a research setting his supposed powers, before a committee of magicians and experienced psychic researchers, and the demonstration must be on videotape. But no psychic has ever been able to do so, and everyone who has tried has been proven a fraud. Therefore, until someone can prove their existence, there is no reason to believe in psychic powers.

On the other hand, we think there is a multitude of evidence to believe in God. When you read the descriptions of Christ's miracles, and recognize the number of people attesting to their genuineness (even His enemies granted that Jesus could do miracles), you are left with the conclusion that He must be divine. André has been able to duplicate some of the miracles of Jesus in a small way, like walking on water—but only with tons of equipment, and André is always quick to point out that these are not miracles. They are a demonstration for entertainment, and their very existence is evidence that Jesus must have performed actual miracles.

Some people have accused us of not believing in miracles or the supernatural, but this is a ridiculous charge. We believe in God's supernatural power to move beyond the bounds of nature and Christ demonstrated miraculous ability over the natural world: His ability to calm a storm, make a blind man see, and raise Lazarus from the dead attest to the miraculous power of God. We simply don't believe the demons have that same power, nor that they can transfer that power to humans.

Compare, for example, the claims of a psychic surgeon to those of the Lord. When one of the psychics claimed to have cured Jerry's grandmother of cancer, he offered no evidence other than his word. The grandmother died a year later, so the evidence suggests the psychic was a fraud. However, when Jerry's pastor was diagnosed with cancer last year, hundreds of people began praying for his healing. The doctors had biopsied two cancerous lesions in the pastor's colon, so the people in Jerry's church were praying specifically for the Lord to take the cancer away. When surgery was performed, the doctors found all the cancer was gone, even though the medical records proved it had been evident just two weeks earlier. The surgeon admitted he didn't believe in prayer, but he had no other rationale to explain what had happened. In short: The psychic surgeon failed to heal, so there is no reason to believe him, but the Lord miraculously healed the pastor, so Jerry can put his faith in God. It requires faith to believe that God healed Jerry's pastor, but it does not require any faith to believe the man is now cancer-free.

Others might think we have minimized the reality of demons. This we also deny, since we readily admit that Satan is behind the deception of most alleged psychic power. We do, however, believe that Christians have begun to cede far too much power to demons. Satan doesn't rule our lives; God does. We have no fear of the devil or his minions, for He who is in us is greater than he who is in the world. Our concern is with those who proclaim all sorts of powers as coming from Satan. If there were stronger evidence to believe in them, we would. As it is, we do not, and we are not alone in our beliefs.

A recent example of what we're talking about is the famous case of James Hydrick, a troubled young man who claimed to have all sorts of supernatural powers. He could make pages turn and cause lights to sway, and he purported to be in touch with mystic powers. But Danny Korem, an investigative reporter and lifelong magician, examined Hydrick's claims. What he found was a young man who could con people and use coincidences to his advantage. When confronted with the truth, Hydrick made a public confession, admitting that none of his supposed psychic powers were real. Danny Korem concluded:

I personally have yet to meet or hear of someone who actually has psychic powers. By psychic powers I am referring to something the brain can do in and of its own ability, like reading someone else's mind or moving objects without touching them. It's important to understand that when we talk about psychic powers, we're talking about human powers and not supernatural powers. You see, when I began investigating the possibility of human psychic abilities, I didn't have any preconceived ideas one way or the other. I simply didn't know if such a thing existed.

Scientists, however, who have spent millions of dollars over the last fifty years to find real human psychic powers, have come up empty-handed. They have yet to find even one case of real psychic ability.[8]

Psychics are trying all sorts of ways to deceive us into believing they have power. They try to predict the future, talk with the dead, gaze at the stars, channel a spirit, and make all sorts of wild accusations. In the rest of this book we'll explore the various other avenues psychics are using to deceive and manipulate people.

CHAPTER SIX

Can We Know
the Future?

- Several major American cities including Boston soon will be destroyed.[1]
- The Civil War will be the start of a global conflict.[2]
- The moon is inhabited by a people of uniform size, about six feet in height.[3]
- In a few years, the people of the United States will be destroyed by pestilence, hail, famine, and earthquake.[4]

All of these prophecies were delivered between 1832 and 1837. They sound absurd now, yet the man who proclaimed them was a respected religious leader whose followers now number in the millions. He is just one example of why we must be wary of modern-day prophets.

Millions of people spend their money in the belief or hope that they can satisfy their curiosity about the future. They use tarot cards,

99

palm-reading, and astrological charts to help them plan their lives. But are modern-day prognosticators legitimate? Can anyone predict the future?

TOOLS OF THE PSYCHIC TRADE

Mediums and psychics who claim to be able to predict the future use a few basic gimmicks to lend an air of legitimacy to their methods. One of the most common tools is a deck of *tarot cards*, which they shuffle and deal out onto a table, then use to attempt to divine future events. Some of the top tarot readers get up to $300 for a one-hour reading, in which they'll talk about your money, career, love life, and lifestyle options.

The tarot deck is an occultic tool dating from at least medieval times, though some researchers believe similar decks were used before the time of Christ. The modern deck has 78 cards, decorated with a variety of mystical characters, symbols, and diagrams. Of these, 22 have characters on them (these are called the "Major Arcana"), and there are 56 suit cards, from which was derived a regular deck of playing cards. The premise behind a tarot reading is that the cards, when dealt face up, will form a pattern that will reveal your future.

Another popular tool that psychics use to predict the future is a crystal (the old crystal ball has been dumped for the environmentally friendly crystal rock of the nineties). This method, called *scrying*, demands that the psychic go into a trance as he or she gazes at the crystal in order to see visions of the future. The cost of crystals has skyrocketed in the past ten years, due to the many claims that they contain magic powers for precognition, healing, and paranormal empowerment. Psychics have also used coffee grounds, tea leaves, bowls of water, mirrors, and animal entrails in scrying, and they all work equally well—which is to say, not at all.

In an attempt to prove their claims that crystals have mystic power, many psychics have begun doing science tricks with crystals. James Randi explains:

*One of these is the **piezoelectric effect**, which simply means that when certain crystals such as quartz are squeezed, a small electrical signal is given out. When, conversely, an electrical signal is applied to the crystal, it expands or contracts in response. There is nothing at all mysterious about this phenomenon, and it is fully explained within the parameters of basic physics, but it has been pressed to serve the theories that amateurs publish in the [paranormal] literature asserting that crystals give out some sort of vibrations that psychics can detect. Simple tests of the claim have been designed and carried out. In every case, it has been shown that the claim is spurious.*[5]

Palm-reading is another means of predicting an individual's future by interpreting the shape of the hands, fingers, and palm-lines. Like any other tool, it is highly interpretive, so that one palmist may offer a completely different reading than another. Over the centuries, psychics have also claimed to be able to "read" an individual's future by examining the foot, face, iris, reflexes, and bumps on the head. All of these satisfy the human need to find meaning in some sort of natural pattern, but none has been shown to be correct or effective.

The *Ouija board* is one more precognitive tool that psychics claim will reveal secrets about a person's character and future. It consists of a small, heart-shaped board on three casters, called a *planchette*, resting on a larger board containing the letters of the alphabet and the words "yes" and "no." The psychic and the client place their hands on the planchette, which is allegedly moved by supernatural forces to answer questions and spell out answers. The planchette is actually moved about by ideomotor action, in which one or both of the participants guides it toward a desired response. Although some people believe in the Ouija and swear they "never pushed the planchette," all it takes to disprove this gimmick is to blindfold the operators, which changes the responses into gibberish. The same is true of those who use pendulums.

In recent years there has been a revival of interest in *numerology*, in which the psychic translates your name and birthdate into a number, then offers a reading based upon that number. The main problem with all of these tools is that they ultimately rely upon what is called *cold reading*. Cold reading is a combination of psychological concepts and common sense, in which the psychic essentially gives information back that the client unknowingly has given him. The psychic starts with a pre-prepared character assessment that is general enough to encompass approximately 85 percent of the population, saying things like "You have many acquaintances but few close friends.... People frequently call on you for advice.... You have a tendency to worry at times.... You tend to put off jobs that must be done but that don't interest you...." Then he begins tailoring his words in response to the visual clues given by the customer. Magicians have used cold reading in stage shows to demonstrate "mindreading" skills for decades.

Ray Hyman, who helped pay for his college education with his nightclub mentalist act, explains the process:

> *The cold reader basically relies on a good memory and acute observation. The client is carefully studied. The clothing—for example, style, neatness, cost, age—provides a host of cues for helping the reader make shrewd guesses about socioeconomic level, conservatism or extroversion, and other characteristics. The client's physical features—weight, posture, looks, eyes, and hands—provide further cues. The hands are especially revealing to the good reader. The manner of speech, use of grammar, gestures, and eye contact are also good sources. To the good reader the huge amount of information coming from an initial sizing-up of the client greatly narrows the possible categories into which he classifies clients.*[6]

After his stock spiel, the cold reader begins to address the client's problems and watches the reaction to determine whether or not he's on the right track. He also has to be a good listener, and many times takes what he has heard and rephrases it to make it sound like a fresh revelation. Fortune-tellers have learned that most clients already have decided what they want to do, and simply want support to carry out their decisions. General and ambiguous statements can be taken to mean whatever the client wants them to mean. That causes the predictions to seem more accurate than they really are.

Whenever people claim to have psychic ability to predict future events, we like to apply four basic tests: 1) How specific are their predictions? 2) What percentage of their forecasts are accurate? 3) Do their lives back up their claims? 4) What is the source (or claimed source) of their information?

HOW SPECIFIC ARE THE PREDICTIONS?

One of the biggest problems we have with so-called psychics is their inability to be specific about the future. Psychic superstar Jeane Dixon was perhaps best known for predicting the assassination of President John F. Kennedy. *Parade* magazine reported, "As to the 1960 election, Mrs. Dixon thinks it will be dominated by labor and won by a Democrat. But he will be assassinated or die in office, though not necessarily in his first term."[7]

This is a classic example of vagueness that can, in retrospect, look like an accurate hit. Mrs. Dixon predicted that a Democrat would win, but her chances of being right were 50/50. She was careful not to say *who* would win, since this was three years before any serious campaigning started. And it wasn't a huge risk to predict that the president would die in office. Already three had done so in the twentieth century, and many observers saw a cycle: The president elected every 20 years from the year 1840 either had been assassinated or had died while in office (thanks to President Reagan for ending that alleged "curse"). Mrs. Dixon wasn't willing to state *how* the president would die, whether or not it would be an assassination, or even approximately when it would take place. If the president served two terms, she had eight years for her prophecy to be fulfilled. So her most spectacular forecast really wasn't all that impressive.

But that is how modern prophets work. Right now, André is willing to make some "prophecies" similar to that of many seers. He can tell you with a high degree of confidence that within the next 12 months:

+ A major earthquake will take place, killing more than a hundred people.
+ A major world figure will die in office.
+ A major technological breakthrough will amaze the world and change our lives.
+ It will rain a lot in Oregon.

It doesn't take a prophet to make these kinds of predictions. It only takes a good observer, someone aware of what is happening around him in the world.

One of the most popular prophets over the last few centuries has been the sixteenth-century seer Nostradamus. At age 50 he began composing vague quatrains (four-line verses) which he said were predictions. He divided the more than 900 verses into groups of 100, with each grouping representing a century. The prophecies contained elaborate symbolism and codes that Nostradamus admitted could not possibly be understood until after the events they predicted. That has led to several interesting interpretations over the years. For example, in World War II the Allied forces and the Germans used the same verse to prove opposite conclusions. A. Voldben in his book *After Nostradamus* writes about the prophet he praises:

> *The quatrains are strewn about without any order in such a way that even if the beginning were found it would not be possible to continue them in the right order. They are usually vague, involved in the confused language of sybilline oracles, some literal and some symbolic. So much so that in the confusion between literal and symbolic, one is left*

hardly understanding anything at all! If some are easy to understand, others are incomprehensible. He writes in the French of his day, mixed with Latin words with others made up by him and his own anagrams.[8]

Again, his prophecies were neither specific nor understandable. Surely if somebody had the power of precognition, he or she could be specific about what the future held. It makes you wonder why people still diligently study his work. Yet Nostradamus is extremely popular today, especially on university campuses, and every December his name gets dragged out by the tabloids as they prepare more "amazing prophecies" for the coming year.

WHAT PERCENTAGE IS ACCURATE?

Our second question logically follows from the first. How *accurate* are the specific prophecies of the individual who claims to have the gift of precognition? In promoting their forecasts, today's prophets proudly recall their hits, while hoping that people will forget or ignore their misses. Unfortunately, the public generally complies.

When specific, verifiable predictions are made, it is relatively simple to go back and check the record. F.K. Donnelly, associate professor of history at the University of New Brunswick in Canada, reviewed the predictions that 21 psychics made in the 1975 edition of *The People's Almanac*. The seers included Malcolm Bessent, David Bubar, Jeane Dixon, Irene Hughes, and many other well-known psychics. Donnelly evaluated their predictions over the course of seven years. Here is what he found:

Out of the total of 72 predictions, 66 (or 92 percent) were dead wrong. Among the favorites in this category were those that China would go to war with the United States (predicted 4 times) and that New York City would soon be underwater (predicted 3 times). My favorite inept prognostication comes from the Berkeley Psychic

Institute, which predicted a war between Greenland and the Soviet Union over fish. Since nuclear weapons were to be used, this was to be very sensibly fought in Labrador in May 1977.[9]

Of the six predictions that were not wrong, two were only partially right or vague. Two others were not exactly graphic evidence of psychic power: Russia and the United States would "remain as leading world powers," and there would be no world wars between 1975 and 1980. Donnelly concludes, "Even if we were to accept that four (or 6 percent) of the 72 predictions were correct...a further problem remains. Since we do not know which of the 72 predictions will fan into the six-percent category, then of what use is this? Who among us would take the advice of a tipster with a track record of being wrong more than nine times out of ten?"[10]

It's easy to evaluate Jeane Dixon's track record. Here are just a few of her prophecies that you probably don't remember:

- Russia would be the first nation to put men on the moon. (Unless the Soviets kept it a secret, it was the United States.)
- World War III would begin in 1954. (We must have missed it.)
- The Vietnam war would end in 1966. (It didn't end until 1975.)
- On October 19, 1968, she predicted that Jacqueline Kennedy was not thinking of marriage. *The next day* Mrs. Kennedy married Aristotle Onassis. (Oops.)
- In 1970 she predicted that Castro would be overthrown from Cuba and would have to leave the islands. (As of this writing, Fidel is still in Havana.)

These are just a handful of many examples. The problem is that people remember only her successes. When you compare Mrs. Dixon's hits with her misses, you find that her percentage of accuracy is most unimpressive.

We opened this chapter with four prophecies made by Joseph Smith, founder of the Mormon Church. Smith claimed to be a prophet of God, and in the course of 18 years he made 64 specific prophecies. Only six of them were fulfilled—fewer than 10 percent. Many of his proclamations dealt with the future of his church. For example, in August of 1831 he stated that God had told him, "The faithful among you shall be preserved and rejoice together in the land of Missouri."[11] In September of 1832 he stated that the city of Independence would become the "New Jerusalem...even the place of the temple, which temple shall be reared in this generation."[12] Six years later the Mormons were driven out of Independence. No temple was built there. Eventually they were driven from Missouri and settled in Utah.

We could cite many other prophecies Smith made that were just as faulty. He predicted the return of Jesus Christ to earth by the year 1890, he claimed Indians converted to Mormonism would turn white, and he proclaimed that the United States would be utterly destroyed if there was not redress for the wrongs committed against Mormons in Missouri. None of these were fulfilled. Unfortunately, that hasn't kept millions of people from believing Joseph Smith was a genuine prophet.

WHAT DO WE LEARN FROM THE PSYCHIC'S LIFE?

It is important to look not only at the *words* of the psychic, but at the *works* of the psychic. Evaluate the lives of the persons making psychic claims. The most revealing article about Jeane Dixon was in the *National Observer*. The author, Daniel St. Albin Greene, spent weeks investigating her. "What gradually emerged," Greene wrote, "was a portrait of neither saint nor charlatan, but of a beguiling enigma whose real identity has been absorbed by the myth she herself created."[13] Greene examined the chapters in Jeane Dixon's life that she had tried to suppress. It turns out that legend, not reality, made Mrs. Dixon's career, and it is a legend of her own making. "All the public knows about Jeane Dixon is what she has said."[14]

The article examined the claim that Mrs. Dixon has never used her "God-given gifts" for personal profit. In fact, her book royalties and revenue from her syndicated columns were paid to a company that Mrs. Dixon and her husband owned. Sponsors of her speeches donated money to a charitable foundation run by her. The foundation, "Children to Children," actually had distributed less than 19 percent of its income to the purported recipients.

Most of the information about Mrs. Dixon's background is found in the book *A Gift of Prophecy: The Phenomenal Jeane Dixon*, by Ruth Montgomery. A detailed check of records revealed that much of her earlier biographical material was fiction. A total of 14 years, including a former marriage, had disappeared from her past.

> *If nothing else, the purged 14 years constitute a credibility gap that undermines the whole foundation of the Jeane Dixon story as told by Mrs. Dixon. Rereading the biography of her pre-Washington period in the new time frame, one must constantly choose among three possibilities: each incident that Mrs. Dixon says took place when she was a child prodigy in California either 1) actually occurred many years earlier in the Midwest; 2) happened when she was in her 20s or 30s; or 3) never happened at all.*[15]

Such revelations severely damage her credibility. The same could be said about Joseph Smith. The Mormon Church stands or falls primarily on the reputation of this one man, but a careful examination of Smith's life reveals many disturbing facts. Perhaps most damaging are the various versions of his first "vision," in which he says that God the Father (and/or Jesus Christ, an angel, or a pillar of light, depending on the version) appeared to him when he was 16 years old (later amended to when he was 14 years old). In this version Smith was told that all churches were wrong, and that "all their creeds are an abomination in His sight."

Fawn Brodie states in the supplement of her meticulously researched book, *No Man Knows My History: The Life of Joseph Smith the Mormon Prophet:*

> *One of the major original premises of this biography was that Joseph Smith's assumption of the role of a religious prophet was an evolutionary process, that he began...using the primitive techniques of the folklore of magic common to his area, most of which he discarded as he evolved into a preacher-prophet. There seemed to be good evidence that when he chose to write of this evolution in his History of the Church he distorted the past in the interest of promoting his public image as a gifted young prophet with a substantial and growing following. There was evidence even to stimulate doubt of the authenticity of the "first vision," which Joseph Smith declared in his official history had occurred in 1820 when he was fourteen.*[16]

Numerous points darken this man's integrity. The 1835 edition of *Doctrine & Covenants* condemned fornication and polygamy and admonished, "One man should have one wife; and one woman but one husband; except that in the event of death when either is at liberty to marry again." Those words became a problem for Joseph Smith as he had affairs with more and more women. Finally he received a "new revelation" in 1843, giving God's blessing on plural marriages. The earlier command simply disappeared, without explanation, from later editions of *Doctrine & Covenants*. As best as Brodie can determine, Smith had 48 wives when he died in 1844.[17]

There are many other reasons to doubt *The Book of Mormon*. Joseph Smith was, early in his life, a conjurer, who was charged with being disorderly and "an impostor" for claiming to be able to divine hidden treasure. At the age of 22 he claimed to have unearthed some plates of gold which bore "revised Egyptian hieroglyphics." Though he had no training in languages (plus the fact that *there is no such language*), that didn't stop Smith from claiming he also had two special instruments with enabled him to dictate a translation from the plates, which tell a story of Jesus Christ appearing to supposed Native American tribes. Smith said of this book, the keystone of his religion, that it "was the most correct of any book on earth,"[18] yet since its first printing in 1830 there have been 3913 changes! (Though some Mormons will deny this, these have been thoroughly documented by Jerald and Sandra Tanner, who marked all the changes on a photo reprint of the original edition.) There is absolutely zero historical or archaeological evidence to support Smith's writings, no one else ever saw the golden plates, and some members of his original dictation team later denounced Smith as an utter fraud—yet some people still regard Joseph Smith as a man who could predict the future.

Researchers Josh McDowell and Don Stewart have summarized the problem with *The Book of Mormon:*

+ No *Book of Mormon* cities have ever been located.
+ No *Book of Mormon* names have been found in New World inscriptions.
+ No genuine Hebrew inscriptions have been found in America.
+ No genuine Egyptian inscriptions (nor anything similar to Egyptian) have been found in America which could correspond to Joseph Smith's "reformed Egyptian."
+ No ancient copies of *Book of Mormon* scriptures have been found.
+ No ancient inscriptions of any kind in America which indicate that the ancient inhabitants had Hebrew or Christian beliefs have ever been found.
+ No mention of *Book of Mormon* persons, nations, or places have been found.[19]

Why be concerned with such details? Because a person who claims to be a prophet creates for himself a high standard. By stating that he has divine revelations, he opens himself to scrutiny to see if his *life* supports his claims. J. Edward Decker, a former leader in the Mormon Church, writes, "A lie is a lie, is a lie, and when it comes out of the mouth of a man proclaimed to be a prophet of God, that man is sent not of God, neither has God commanded him."

WHO IS THE PROPHET?

A favorite trick among magicians is to make a prediction of future news headlines—the winner of an election, the World Series champion, a winning lottery number—and seal it inside an envelope. The envelope is then given to someone to hold, and locked inside a safe. The more secure it appears, the better. It is best to have 24-hour security to verify that no one tampers with that safe. Of course, after the result is known, the envelope is opened amidst great fanfare to reveal that the magician had correctly predicted the event.

Many books explain methods to accomplish this trick. Elaborate paraphernalia, some costing thousands of dollars, can help successfully create this illusion of precognition. Some inexpensive methods also do the trick, such as one André used one night during his show: When *Dallas* was one of the most popular shows on television, he correctly predicted who would shoot J.R. two hours before that famous episode was due to be aired on local television.

The audience was amazed, as this was one of television's best-kept secrets. CBS had filmed several versions, so even the cast didn't know who the culprit was until it aired. But the audience didn't know that backstage André had an open phone line to a friend on the East Coast. Of course, East Coast viewers would learn the answer three hours earlier than those in the West, where André was performing. Mystery solved!

Some psychics claim that they have the God-given gift of prophecy. Jeane Dixon had always made this claim. But if indeed she had a gift from God, then the Lord must make an awful lot of mistakes, for her track record was pretty weak. The facts are conclusive that she had no gift of prophecy. The Bible makes it clear that one evidence of a genuine prophet is that he (or she) *never makes a wrong prediction*. "You may say in your heart, 'How shall we know the word which the Lord has not spoken?' When a prophet speaks in the name of the Lord, *if the thing does not come about or come true, that is the thing which the Lord has not spoken*. The prophet has spoken it presumptuously; you shall not be afraid of him."

SEEKING THE TRUE PROPHET

Evidently people feel a need to know something about their future. God understands this need. That is why it is important to understand one more principle: *We need to evaluate all prophecies in the light of Scripture.* The Bible clearly warns us about following after false prophets, sorcerers, diviners, mediums, and the like. In the book of Isaiah God warned, "Let now the astrologers, those who prophesy by the stars, those who predict by the new moons, stand up and save you from what will come upon you. Behold, they have become like stubble, fire burns them: they cannot deliver themselves from the power of the flame."[22] Jeremiah gave a similar warning: "Do not learn the way of the nations, and do not be terrified by the signs of the heavens, although the nations are terrified by them; for *the customs of the peoples are delusion*."[23]

God laid down strict regulations concerning prophets. First, genuine prophets were to point people to the one true God. Joseph Smith failed here because he declared that there were many gods.[24] Second, a genuine prophet cannot utter even *one* false prophecy. Prophets of the Bible told short-term and long-term prophecies, and the fulfillment of their short-term predictions validated their long-range prophecies. Third, the purpose of prophecy is to cause people to obey God's commands and to believe in His Son, Jesus Christ. If a supposed prophet says things to move people *away* from God, you can be sure he or she does not have the gift of prophecy.

The Bible contains numerous prophecies, and already many of these have been fulfilled. More than 300 of them concern the Messiah, all fulfilled by Jesus Christ. Other prophecies concern the end times, and you can find many excellent books to explore those prophecies. But it is important to realize why God gave us these words: They are not intended to satisfy our curiosity, but to help prepare us for the future, and to encourage and comfort us.[25]

Christians must be cautious of those who boldly claim to have inside information from God. There have been a few popular evangelists who gave dramatic revelations of information about individuals in their audiences—addresses, names of their doctors, specific ailments—as a basis for making bold pronouncements concerning God's will for their lives. They are not speaking for God, yet some Christians cling to every word they say as if it were the word of the Lord. We must be careful, for we do not want to miss the time when God does speak through His servants. Yet we must make sure that the one who claims to speak for God can indeed verify that claim in the manner God has prescribed in the Bible.

CHAPTER SEVEN

Talking with the Dead?

During the mid-1800s, dozens of spirit mediums traveled around the United States and England and demonstrated their supposed powers, attracting large crowds. One of the most popular was a slender Irish blonde named Anna Eva Fay. She sat inside a large, custom-made cabinet, her wrists securely bound behind her with strips of cloth and tied to a harness ring attached to a post in the rear of the cabinet. When the curtains were closed and the spirits summoned, musical instruments were played, various objects were tossed about, nails were hammered into a block of wood, and dolls were cut out of paper. These activities were supposedly evidence of spirits. The spectacular performance concluded when the "spirits" took a knife and cut Mrs. Fay's cords.

The effect was so astounding that thousands of people flocked to see her demonstrations. An eminent scientist, Sir William Crookes, tested Mrs. Fay, having her place her hands on brass handles that led to a galvanometer. The tests would show if Mrs. Fay's hands came off the handles during her time inside the cabinet. While the galvanometer showed no break in the current, the mysterious manifestations continued, leading the scientific researchers to declare her a legitimate medium. Anna Eva Fay became known as "the indescribable phenomenon" and the curtained cabinet as "the spirit cabinet."

Years later, her assistant, Washington Irving Bishop, exposed the spirit cabinet to a newspaper. Mrs. Fay was a fraud, who performed her feats using clever trickery. She later admitted this in interviews with Harry Houdini, and she was the first woman inducted into the Magic Circle of London, a prominent club for magicians. Yet people *continued* to flock into large theaters to see her amazing performances, thinking them real!

ANDRÉ KOLE AND THE SPIRIT CABINET

Before her death, Mrs. Fay's secret was passed on to a man from Ireland who later came to the United States, where he and his wife presented the spirit cabinet for the paying public. Before their death they taught it to their son, Harry Willard, who presented it with his wife for nearly 50 years. "Willard the Wizard" taught it to his daughter Frances, who continues to perform the spirit cabinet around the world with her husband, Glenn Falkenstein. In the 1970s André Kole made exclusive arrangements for Frances to train his wife, Aljeana, to present the various kinds of spirit manifestations.

For several years they invited members of the audience onto the stage to help tie Aljeana's hands with linens strips, then nail them to a post. Next, while Aljeana was supposedly in a trance, André closed the curtains on her. Immediately a tambourine played and a basket flew over the curtain. The curtain was closed for less than ten seconds before being reopened, revealing his wife slumped in the same position, her hands still firmly tied and nailed. Then a member of the audience was invited to stand blindfolded inside the curtain. Soon after the curtain was closed, the participant came running out of the cubicle, a bucket over his head, his shoes removed, and his coat on Aljeana, *whose hands were still tied and nailed to the post.*

André included this unique presentation in his performances throughout the world until Aljeana's death, in 1976. It was entertaining and got a lot of laughs, but it also showed how easily people can be deceived. His wife had no power to contact the spirits. Everything she did was an illusion, created exclusively by physical means. It was an excellent trick, but it was still just a trick.

There were those who accused André and Aljeana of being in league with the spirits, but the entire point of the performance was to reveal there was *no spirit activity involved.* People at seances and other spirit-related events are being tricked into thinking they are communicating with spirits, when all they're doing is being entertained by conjurers.

THE SPIRITUALIST MOVEMENT

Modern belief in communication with the dead, or *spiritism,* began in America in 1848 in the little town of Hydesville, New York. People claimed to hear mysterious knocking sounds in a farmhouse owned by a middle-aged couple named Fox. Margaret Fox (age 15) and her younger sister, Katherine (who was 12), began asking questions of the "spirit" inside the house, and answers came as distinct raps, apparently from inside the walls. For example, when one girl held up four fingers and asked, "How many fingers?" they heard four raps. Through their questioning, they revealed that the originator of the noises was the spirit of a man murdered in the house several years before. The story spread, and people from all over the country came to see this remarkable phenomenon.

On March 31 the following year, the noises became so distracting that the family was forced to move from their home, but the rappings mysteriously followed the girls. A much older sister, Leah, arranged for an exhibition at the Corinthian Hall in Rochester, New York, and that led to a lengthy tour of the United States. For 40 years the Fox sisters traveled throughout the world, making a great deal of money demonstrating this spirit's communicative powers. The mysterious rappings followed them wherever they went, and though they were examined by leading doctors, scientists, and preachers, no trickery was discovered. After one seance in 1871, Sir William Crookes (the same person who insisted that Anna Eva Fay was genuine) announced: "I have tested [the girls' raps] in every way that I could devise, until there has been no escape from the conviction that they were true objective occurrences not produced by trickery or mechanical means."[1]

Then in 1888, after a drinking binge, the girls confessed that it was all a fraud. They had started the rappings when they were just 8 and 11 years old, by tying a string to an apple and bumping it on the floor at night to scare their superstitious mother. She did not suspect trickery, since her children were so young. When she called in her neighbors, the girls found a more effective method for producing the raps: They snapped the joints in their toes, in much the same way as you crack the knuckles in your fingers. In the quiet darkness of a seance room, where a wooden floor served as a sounding board, those raps proved very effective.

The confession by Margaret Fox appeared on September 24, 1888, in the *New York Herald*. Among other things, it said:

> *As far as spirits were concerned, neither my sister nor I thought about it. I knew there was no such thing as the departed returning to this life. I have seen so much miserable deception that every morning of my life I have it before me. That is why I am willing to state that spiritualism is a fraud of the worst deception. I trust that this statement, coming solemnly from me, the first and most successful in this deception, will break the rapid growth of spiritualism and prove that it is all a fraud, hypocrisy, and delusion.*[2]

Both Katherine and Margaret admitted they were frauds, both attempted to continue lecturing on the topic of spiritualism, and both died as penniless alcoholics. *Despite their public confessions, the growth in spiritualism continued to mount.* Their followers announced that the ladies must have been forced into lying about their abilities, and continued on "as if the confessions of the Fox sisters had never happened."[3]

Through the rest of the nineteenth century, and well into the twentieth century, interest in spiritualism grew. With it came more and more magicians, who saw a way to make money by using many of their conjuring tricks. But along with that interest came a few people who recognized the danger of people believing in deception, and who were committed to revealing the truth about spiritualism.

The great magician Harry Houdini was probably the individual most responsible for exposing fraudulent mediums. During the final years of his life he was consumed by an obsession to find a genuine medium who could contact his mother. Shortly before her demise, the family had been rocked by scandal. His brother Nat's wife had left her husband to marry another brother, Leopold. Houdini could not forgive Leopold and told his mother that he looked to her for guidance on what he should do. He was performing in Europe when his mother died, and during her final hours she had tried to give the family by her bedside a message for her son, but could not get the words out.

Houdini always wondered what his mother was trying to say. Did she want him to forgive his brother? He often visited his mother's grave, begging her to tell him her last words. Spiritualists believed in communication with the dead, but Houdini found that all the mediums he met were frauds. He determined, however, that if a genuine medium existed anywhere in the world, he would find him.

During his remaining years, Houdini attended some 5000 seances. In many of them, ghostly whispers claimed to be his mother. But there was always one problem: The voices were in English, and his mother never spoke English. As a result, Houdini became very bitter against charlatans impersonating his dear mother, and he began an all-out campaign to expose fake mediums and their methods. He lectured about spiritualism around the country, demonstrating common techniques used by mediums, such as table levitation, the playing of musical instruments, and writing on blank slates. Houdini offered a $5000 prize to any medium who could produce an effect that he could not duplicate. No one ever collected the prize.

Harry Houdini wrote two books about his study, revealing the results of tests with the best-known mediums and disclosing the techniques they used to gather information and perform various feats. In his book *A Magician Among the Spirits* he concludes:

> *To my knowledge I have never been baffled in the least by what I have seen at seances. Everything I have seen has been merely a form of mystification. The secret of all such performances is to catch the mind off guard and the moment after it has been surprised to follow up with something else that carries the intelligence along with the performer, even against the spectator's will. . . .*

> *I have said many times that I am willing to believe, want to believe, will believe, if the spiritualists can show any substantiated proof, but until they do I shall have to live on, believing from all the evidence shown me and from what I have experienced that spiritualism has not been proven satisfactorily to the world at large and that none of the evidence offered has been able to stand up under the fierce rays of investigations.*[4]

CONTACT WITH HOUDINI?

Shortly before his death, Houdini and his wife, Bess, made a pact that whoever died first would attempt to contact the other with these words: "Rosabelle, answer, tell, pray, answer, look, tell, answer, answer, tell." The words following "Rosabelle" were a code that spelled out the word "believe." On Halloween of 1926, Houdini died of a ruptured appendix. Two-and-a-half years later a young medium named Arthur Ford sent to Houdini's widow a one-word message, "Forgive," supposedly from Houdini's mother. A message from her husband followed, with the predetermined words in the correct sequence.

Two days later Bess met with Ford and heard her husband supposedly speak to her through the medium. News of the event spread quickly, and the next day newspapers blared headlines that Houdini had returned from the dead. The great magician's widow signed a declaration that read: "Regardless of all statements to the contrary, I wish to declare that the message, in its entirety and in the agreed-upon sequence, given to me by Arthur Ford, is the correct message prearranged between Mr. Houdini and myself." The statement was cosigned by three witnesses.

But was this genuine evidence of Houdini's return? Skeptics doubted it and found ample reason for their suspicions. Raymond Fitzsimons, in his book *Death and the Magician*, tells how a close friend of Houdini and his wife exposed the fraud to the widow:

> Joe Rinn heard the news and decided that the whole affair was a spook trick to end all spook tricks, a trick that must be exposed. Bess was convinced of the truth of Ford's seances, so Rinn and other friends of Houdini's reminded her of certain things which in her emotional state she had forgotten. Ford's message from Houdini's mother had included the evidential word FORGIVE, but the Brooklyn *Eagle* of March 13, 1927, a year before Ford's seance, had quoted Bess as saying that any authentic communication from Houdini's mother would have to include that word. Ford could have read this. She was also reminded that the code words used had been printed in Harold Kellock's biography of Houdini, published the previous year, on which she had collaborated. Bess admitted that she had not recalled these things. But at the time of the seance she had been sick with influenza and emotionally run-down.[5]

Later Bess retracted her statement about Ford, and to her dying day maintained that she had not received any communication from her late husband. Yet the controversy over spiritualism still rages today.

Millions of people believe that contact with the dead is possible, and they spend millions of dollars to communicate with loved ones through mediums.

MORE FORD FAKERY

After numerous exposures of fraudulent tricks used in seances early in this century, mediums devised safer techniques. Mentalists like Arthur Ford became more prevalent. In his type of seance, the medium usually goes into a trance and his or her body comes under the control of a spirit. The spirit passes messages from other spirits, through the medium, to the sitter. In order to authenticate the communication, the spirit relates seemingly insignificant details that only the sitter could know or verify. Ford supposedly became controlled by a spirit named Fletcher, who had been the son of a wealthy French-Canadian family, but had died suddenly in 1918 while attending college.

In his book *The Spiritual Frontier*, William V. Rauscher, an Episcopal priest, compares the discussion at a seance to a phone conversation with a very poor connection, in which the operator serves as a go-between. The problem is to determine if your friend on the other end of the line really is who he says he is. To prove that the communication is genuine, the medium relates what appears to be trivial details. This information, which the client believes the medium could not possibly know, "proves" that contact with the deceased loved one or friend has been established. The argument sounds good on the surface, but ample evidence shows that many mediums keep extensive files about their clients.

In 1967, Arthur Ford conducted perhaps the most famous seance in history. The event was shown live on network television in Canada and involved Episcopal bishop James Pike. During the seance, Ford supposedly received communications from Pike's son, who had committed suicide in February 1966. Pike was convinced that Ford could not have obtained the facts he gave by any other means, thus supporting his belief in Ford. This single event not only caused a sensation, but it renewed an interest in spiritualism across North America. The conventional wisdom was that Arthur Ford was a genuine medium.

But in his book *Arthur Ford: The Man Who Talked with the Dead*, Allen Spraggett told about his shocking discovery after Ford's death:

> William Rauscher and I, researching this biography, were sifting through Arthur Ford's private papers. Several boxes bulged with the medium's personal letters, diaries, books, newspaper and magazine clippings, scrapbooks, even his income-tax returns.... We knew that we had not inherited all Ford's papers; an unknown amount of personal material had been destroyed by a former secretary shortly after the medium's death, presumably on his instructions. . . .
>
> Bill Rauscher was holding a newspaper clipping and, as he scanned it, his face clouded over.
>
> "What's wrong?" I asked.
>
> Without a word, he handed me the clipping.
>
> It was an obituary, undated, from the *New York Times*. The headline told me why Bill Rauscher was disturbed; it read: BISHOP BLOCK, 71, IS DEAD ON COAST.
>
> In the Ford-Pike seance, one of the purported discarnates who communicated on television, in a manner that James Pike found peculiarly convincing, was his Episcopal predecessor, the Right Rev. Karl Morgan Block, late Bishop of California.
>
> As I read the obituary my disturbance increased. The Block communicator had mentioned several small—even trivial—details which Pike considered especially evidential since their very triviality seemed to rule out the possibility of prior research by the medium. The details Pike found impressive appeared to be too obscure, too idiosyncratic,

> *to be accessible to research. However, every one of these*
> *supposedly unresearchable items was mentioned in the*
> *New York Times obituary.*[6]

Later the researchers discovered further evidence that most, if not all, of the information Ford gave in his TV seance was obtained through personal research, primarily newspaper accounts. While Spraggett and Rauscher say that this evidence does not discount the fact that Ford was a genuine medium, the truth is that Ford's two most famous seances, at the beginning and the end of his career, are shrouded in suspicion.

HOW THEY DO IT

One of the most damaging revelations against spiritualism was made by a very successful medium, Lamar Keene. In his book *The Psychic Mafia*, he details how he conned hundreds of people into believing that he had supernatural powers. He tells of lifting tables with the toe of his shoe or simply by applying pressure with his fingertips, causing rapping sounds, using an accomplice to make things appear, and creating an entire room filled with secret devices designed to cause eerie manifestations. Keene admitted that everything occurring inside the dark, curtained room was a fake—a trick to cause people to believe, giving the psychic power over them and access to their money.

Lamar was raised in a Baptist family, and for a time considered entering the ministry. However, in his twenties he was introduced to spiritualism by a friend, and together they attended a large spiritualist church. After a little more than a year, the pair launched into their own work, half-believing they had genuine, though undeveloped, psychic power. Keene and his friend quickly learned that to develop a following, they needed to give people tangible manifestations of the spirits. They soon discovered how to do this through a national information network. Mediums kept extensive files on their subjects, and by using this network they could obtain accurate information quickly about a visitor from any part of the country.

Many mediums add physical manifestations to their messages. Keene was adroit at dropping personal trinkets into the laps of sitters, but he relied primarily on the quality of his information, which was culled from newspaper clippings and pilfered from the wallets and purses of unsuspecting clients.

James Randi tells about an interview with Keene shortly after his startling revelation:

> I interviewed him and discovered that he knew little about the more subtle methods of chicanery. He explained to me that he didn't need to know much. Anything he did would serve to convince the faithful, he said. They fell for the most transparent ruses, many of which were thought up on the spur of the moment, and he and his fellow charlatans laughed themselves silly, at the end of an easy day's work, as they recounted how simple it had been.[7]

It is interesting that Keene's book was named *The Psychic Mafia*, for after his defection from spiritualism, his former friends threatened to kill him. One night several shots were fired from a passing car. Keene was wounded in the stomach and recovered only after a long hospitalization.

Some Christians continue to believe in the power of mediums. Ben Alexander, a fine Christian man with a spiritualist background, likes to tell about the many seances he attended while a young man in England. He was particularly interested in "ectoplasm," a glowing substance that supposedly leaks out of the medium and takes the shape of a man.

> It looked like a person from the ancient past. It had on a white robe...around its legs were something that looked like graveyard wrappings.... Attached to it was a long piece of white ribbon or robe formed from ectoplasm which stretched back under the curtain.... [Later]

the form in front of me began to sink through the floor.
First the legs disappeared, then the trunk, and lastly the
neck and head. The white ribbon then went back under
the curtain.[8]

Mr. Alexander truly believes in the reality of this sort of activity, but his belief has blinded him to the fact that several mediums have described how to fake that very activity. LaMar Keene tells of dressing himself in black (rendering himself invisible in a dark room), unrolling a piece of chiffon, and manipulating it until it eventually enveloped him. "What the sitters saw was a phenomenon: a tiny ball of 'ectoplasm' sending out shimmering tendrils which gradually grew or developed into a fully formed spirit."[9] Interestingly, one Christian writer who believes in ectoplasm, Raphael Gasson, was once allowed to touch the dreaded stuff. His description: "The substance appears to be like something between cheese muslin and a sheet of fine linen."[10] That caused no end of laughter with Keene, who explains that he often used cheese muslin to create his "ectoplasm"! As for the spirit sinking into the floor, famous fake Tony Corinda describes how to do that in his classic Thirteen Steps to Mentalism by simply stuffing the cloth into a black bag. It may sound like "a laughable heap of nonsense, but paraded in the gloom of the seance room, it is the ultimate in spookery."[11]

About a dozen companies in the United States specialize in building intricate props that spiritualists use in their performances. Several of these companies have extensive catalogs of items they stock or can build. Most also have a section listing books about spiritualistic tricks. Recently André went to the shop of a man who was doing some work for him. That manufacturer was also building a "spirit skull" for one of his other clients, a witch doctor in Africa. A person could whisper a question into this apparently normal skull, and a voice, supposedly from the spirit world, would answer in a mysterious whisper from within. At one time such items were very popular with spirit mediums, but now most people in the United States know what can be accomplished through electronics. One can only imagine, though, how such a "miraculous" demonstration of the witch doctor's powers would astound superstitious natives in Africa.

PEOPLE STILL BELIEVE

Despite such obvious frauds, people still ask, "Do the dead return?" Though there is no hard evidence to suggest that anyone has ever contacted the dead, and despite the fact that every famous incident has been shown to be a hoax, people still believe in the possibility. In 1927, a Boston medium named Margery Crandon was put through a number of strict tests, and produced a thumbprint in dental wax that she swore was made by her spirit guide. "This was heralded by the press as definitive proof of her validity and of the genuine nature of spiritualism. Unfortunately for this breakthrough in human knowledge, the print turned out to be that of her dentist, who was very much alive."[12]

After nearly 50 years combined of studying this question from the point of view of a magician, an educator, and two people deeply interested in spiritual truth, we have to conclude that willful communication with the dead is impossible. That is not to say that all mediums are insincere—some may genuinely believe that they have the power to communicate with the dead.

For example, when André's daughter Robyn was a teenager, a friend's mother became very involved with a spirit medium in Phoenix. Robyn attended one of her seances and was frightened by the experience. When he heard about it, André immediately got angry and wanted to confront the woman and expose her racket. On the way to meet her, however, he realized that his anger at what she was doing was not the right attitude. Instead, he decided to talk gently, showing a genuine concern for the woman.

They ended up talking for several hours, and she began asking questions about reality, the meaning of life, and the Person of Jesus Christ. She had turned to spiritualism while looking for answers and, like many mediums, found that her clients demanded tangible demonstrations of communication with the dead. She had a sincere desire to help people, but felt trapped by her circumstances; she felt forced to cheat and produce spirit forms and other manifestations.

GOD'S WARNING AGAINST MEDIUMS

Generally, people look to mediums for two reasons: Either they have lost loved ones and intensely desire to contact them and establish their existence, or they have a curiosity and interest in the supernatural. However, Christians shouldn't have anything to do with contacting spirits. The Bible makes it very clear that we are to avoid any dealings with mediums. In Deuteronomy, Moses told the Israelites:

> *When you arrive in the Promised Land you must be very careful lest you be corrupted by the horrible customs of the nations now living there.... No Israeli may practice black magic, or call on the evil spirits for aid, or be a fortune teller, or be a serpent charmer, medium, or wizard, or call forth the spirits of the dead. Anyone doing these things is an object of horror and disgust to the Lord, and it is because the nations do these things that the Lord your God will displace them.*[13]

Why doesn't God want His people to attempt to contact the spirits of the dead? First, such activities *distract us from our faith in Him*. They may even prevent us from learning about His plan of salvation. It requires faith to believe in God, and some people will prefer a phony manifestation to the genuine love and concern of the Lord.

Second, most people *will misinterpret what they see and hear*. They so desperately want to believe that they have contacted a loved one that they are easily deceived by fraud. Remember, most people will believe what they see, then exaggerate it when asked to defend it. That's why André used to perform the spirit cabinet, so that people would know what to expect and recognize it as a trick. But I doubt it is ever good for people to put their faith in something that is innately false. Mediums and spiritists will argue that their phone ceremonies merely build people's faith, but to enhance faith in something that we know to be false seems well nigh obscene.

Third, such attempts *put us in a place where we can be deceived by Satan*. We certainly believe in the devil and his wicked schemes. He wants to confuse us, destroy our faith, and lead us astray. He will use anything at his disposal to do so, and particularly enjoys using religious and spiritualistic events to try and mislead us.

Fourth, attempted communication with the dead causes *tremendous emotional and psychological problems*. We have seen several people who were deeply scarred by sitting through a seance. Once a person believes he has contacted a loved one, he longs to continue the conversation, and is open to the suggestions offered him by the medium. God sees the practice as evil, and sooner or later those involved are led into evil.

It is revealing to look at the lives of mediums after many years in their profession. Awareness of their fates is what compelled Lamar Keene to give up his practice of spiritualism:

Looking ahead, if I stayed in mediumship, I saw only deepening gloom. All the mediums I've known or known about have had tragic endings.

The Fox sisters, who started it all, wound up as alcoholic derelicts. William Slade, famed for his slate-writing tricks, died insane in a Michigan sanitarium. Margery the Medium lay on her deathbed a hopeless drunk. The celebrated Arthur Ford fought the battle of the bottle to the very end and lost. And the inimitable Mable Riffle, boss of Camp Chesterfield—well, when she died it was winter and freezing cold, and her body had to be held until a thaw for burial; the service was in the Cathedral at Chesterfield. Very few attended.

Whenever I looked it was the same: mediums, at the end of a tawdry life, dying a tawdry death.[14]

Some people cite the story in 1 Samuel 28, where King Saul visited the medium at Endor and called up the deceased prophet Samuel, as evidence of genuine contact with the dead. As we have noted earlier, that is a dangerous conclusion. For one thing, the witch seemed genuinely shocked by the appearance. In fact, if you study this passage carefully, you will note that Saul himself never actually saw the form. The *medium* described what she saw, and everything "Samuel" spoke she easily could have known, so it is possibly a hoax.

Another possible explanation is that a demon appeared, impersonating Samuel. While we do not believe Satan has the ability to give anyone supernatural powers, he certainly has the ability and desire to try to deceive God's people. We are not convinced that God would go against His specific command and do something He has condemned by bringing the spirit Samuel back from the dead. In any case, this unique example in Scripture should not be used as evidence that contact with the dead is possible.

The Bible explicitly warns us not to attempt to contact the dead. Desire to communicate with a loved one is a real feeling, but comfort doesn't come from a medium. The prophet Isaiah asked, "Why are you trying to find out the future by consulting witches and mediums? Don't listen to their whisperings and mutterings. Can the living find out the future from the dead? Why not ask your God?"[15]

As Christians, we can say with the apostle Paul that to be absent from the body is to be present with the Lord. That is where our focus should be. Our hope is that when our loved ones die, they will be in Christ, and we will join them at the time of our death. But in the meantime, we won't be expecting to talk with them.

CHAPTER EIGHT

Look Into My Eyes

To the sound of mysterious music, André's attractive assistant walks onstage. She is placed into a trance, then as the audience watches in amazement her entire body slowly dematerializes and visibly passes through a large plate of steel.

Later in the show, André puts himself into a trance as he sits in front of a circle of lights. Concentrating intently, he slowly begins to rise into the air. The levitation appears to result from a hypnotic state.

Right now, world famous magician André Kole is going to let you in on one of his secrets: *When you see him hypnotized or hypnotizing someone else on stage, it's all for show.* No one is actually in a trance. This is true for all stage magicians. It's simply good showmanship—something expected of illusionists. (We figure most people recognize this fact, but we wanted to make sure!)

131

WHAT IS HYPNOTISM?

An aura of mystery surrounds hypnotism. Many books have been written on the subject, yet most people still misunderstand it. Most people think it can do more than it actually can, while others think it is a tool of the devil. It has been used effectively in place of drugs for anesthesia in dentistry and minor surgery, and as a tool to help people break habits such as smoking.

The father of modern hypnotism was Anton Mesmer, an eighteenth-century German physician. Through controversial experiments, he tried to prove the existence of magnetic fluids in his patients. Using magnets, Mesmer attempted to cure physical illnesses. He later set aside the magnets and used methods such as waving his hands over a patient until the individual went into a trance. Surprisingly, many of his patients found relief from their symptoms through his unorthodox practices. The term "animal magnetism" and the field of study called "mesmerism" resulted from his work—as did the expression "to be mesmerized."

In the 1800s, British surgeon James Braid coined the term "hypnotism" when he induced his patients into a sleeplike condition before performing minor operations. The word comes from the Greek word *hypnos*, meaning "to sleep." Later Dr. Braid realized that he had misnamed the phenomenon, for a hypnotized person definitely is not sleeping, but it was too late to change the term, since the general public had readily accepted the word.

The simplest way to understand hypnosis is to regard it as a state of mind characterized by increased suggestibility—the acceptance of an idea without being critical of it. It is a method for bypassing the conscious mind. Whatever is presented to the subconscious mind, under certain conditions, may be automatically accepted and acted upon. This does not mean the person under hypnosis is in a "trance" however, since there is no widely accepted definition of trance, and no way to test for that state. In the words of one researcher, "It appears more likely that hypnotism is a mutual agreement of the operator and the subject that the subject will cooperate in following suggestions and in acting out various suggested scenarios."[1]

Unfortunately, that leaves us with a rather vague notion of what hypnotism is and how it works. Psychologist Ray Hyman says that when it comes to clearly defining hypnotism, no one really knows *what* it is. "The only way we have of knowing someone was hypnotized is if that person says he was. There is no external way of measuring the hypnotic state—there is no physiological sign on which everyone can agree."

Hypnotism is used in a number of ways. Some entertainers hypnotize members of the audience and cause them to do unusual, humorous things that they normally would not do. Another widespread use of hypnotism is for medical purposes—to block pain and to help patients break bad habit patterns. Hypnotism is also used for interrogation, although we'll see later that there are serious questions about its effectiveness.

THE POWER OF HYPNOSIS

We have all heard stories about hypnotists wielding tremendous powers over their subjects. Kreskin, Peter Reveen, Ormond McGill, and other stage hypnotists have made a name for themselves by hypnotizing members of the audience and encouraging them to do all sorts of novel activities. Some movies have portrayed hypnotists dominating weaker minds, using the hypnotist's power for evil purposes. This may be true in movies or books, but in real life that cannot happen.

To better understand what hypnotism is, it helps to know what it cannot do. For one thing, *you cannot be hypnotized against your will.* To be hypnotized, the patient must want to be hypnotized, and must trust the hypnotist. Peter Blythe wrote in his book on hypnotism:

> *If someone says, "Go ahead and see if you can hypnotize me," the answer is that you cannot. The person who makes the statement is challenging the hypnotist; and*

*as he intends to resist, any chance of success is aborted
from the outset.*

*When one gentleman first started using hypnosis he
tried out various induction methods on his wife, but without any result. She knew they worked on other people,
because she had seen them being applied, but she resis-
ted because she felt no need to cooperate. Then on a
hot summer's day she fell asleep in the garden while
sunbathing, and as a result was quite badly sunburned.
That same night she tried to sleep, but her skin was so
tender that sleep eluded her.*

*After tossing and turning for more than an hour she
asked her husband, "Could you hypnotize me, and take
the pain away so that I can get some sleep?"*

*At that moment she discovered a need for hypnosis and
quickly allowed her critical censor to be by-passed, and
entered into the hypnotic state.*[2]

Another misconception is that a person under hypnosis can be
forced to do things that violate his moral values. That is not true; a
person under hypnosis remains conscious of what the hypnotist says
and does. The patient willingly submits to the hypnotist, doing what
he instructs and accepting his suggestions, but if the hypnotist inserts
a command or suggestion against the patient's will, the patient will not
respond. *Hypnotism cannot force you to do something you don't want to do.*
Blythe gives an interesting example of this:

*Four people were on the stage in the hypnotic state and
were carrying out the various suggestions of the hypnotist. Then, at a certain point, he suggested they were all
concert pianists and were going to give a piano recital.
Three of the subjects acted out this suggestion, one with*

greater aplomb than the other two; but the only lady on the stage just sat on her chair, deeply relaxed, and did nothing. . . .

I talked to the lady after the demonstration and asked her why she had chosen not to react to that piano-playing suggestion. Her answer was personal, but very logical. She told me that as a small child she had been made to take piano lessons against her will, but as soon as she was old enough to exert some pressure on her parents she stopped playing, and made a promise to herself that nothing would ever induce her to play again.[3]

A third thing to keep in mind is that *information gained through hypnosis may not be any more accurate than other forms of interrogation.* This area is controversial, so allow us to elaborate. Some states allow evidence gained through hypnosis to be used in court. Others do not. Dr. Martin Orne, editor of the *International Journal of Clinical and Experimental Hypnosis,* explains the problem: "You don't ever know whether you have testimony *created by* hypnosis or whether it was in fact *refreshed* by hypnosis. Until we have hard evidence of the differences between these two things, we can't distinguish between helping an eyewitness to remember what he saw versus creating an eyewitness who never was."[4]

The problem has become particularly evident in UFO cases, where evidence gained under hypnosis is displayed as conclusive proof. Orne states that under hypnotism the most accurate information comes from "free narrative recall," but this produces the lowest amount of detail. When a witness to a crime is questioned about details, accuracy decreases. "Hypnotic suggestions to relive a past event, particularly when accompanied by questions about specific details, put pressure on the subject to provide information for which few, if any, actual memories are available. This situation may jog the subject's memory and produce some increased recall, but it will also cause him to fill in details that are plausible but consist of memories or fantasies from other times.... It is extremely difficult to know which aspects of hypnotically aided recall are historically accurate and which aspects have been confabulated."[5]

Further difficulties arise if the hypnotist has specific beliefs about what actually occurred. It is easy for him to inadvertently guide the subject's recall to fit his own beliefs. Ernest R. Hilgard, professor emeritus of psychology at Stanford University and former president of the International Society of Hypnosis, claims that hypnotic recall, as evidence of UFO abduction, is an abuse of hypnosis. He explains how it is possible to fabricate stories:

> *For example, under hypnosis I implanted in a subject a false memory of an experience connected with a bank robbery that never occurred, and the person found the experience so vivid that he was able to select from a series of photographs a picture of the man he thought had robbed the bank.*
>
> *Another time, I deliberately assigned two concurrent—though spatially very different—life experiences to the same person and regressed him at separate times to that date. He gave very accurate accounts of both experiences, so that a believer in reincarnation, reviewing the two accounts, would have suspected that the man had really lived the two assigned lives.*[6]

In one sense, when you submit to hypnosis, *you actually give control of yourself and your mind to another individual.* Therefore you should be extremely cautious about who you submit yourself to.

THE IMPORTANCE OF FAITH

To be effective, hypnotism requires faith. If a person wants to lose weight or stop smoking, he or she can often get similar effects through vitamins, a good doctor, and exercise. Hypnotism is not some magic formula; its effectiveness depends on the patient's faith. "Recent research has shown that weight loss and cessation of smoking, both popularly advertised as curable by hypnotism, *cannot be accomplished without the earnest desire of the sufferer to achieve the desired results.* This leads to the question of whether or not the results might be as easily attained by some other form of approach, such as religious inspiration, the caring of a family member, or the intervention of another mystic-sounding but ineffective therapy. This is an idea that professional hypnotists do not care to hear."[7]

André has seen this demonstrated in primitive cultures. For example, a witch doctor in Liberia put a curse on a man, and the victim took it so seriously that he went out of the village, lay down, and died. That same witch doctor became furious with André for exposing the secret methods used by witch doctors, and put a curse on him. That curse had no effect, because André did not believe in the witch doctor or his powers. Missionaries in Africa have told us that they have had to talk people out of responding to curses they believed were placed on them.

In a sense, this validates some statements that Ray Hyman made in an interview at his home. Dr. Hyman said that the same results obtained through hypnotism can be gained without hypnotism. "There have been studies done on this, and they've found that with the right motivation, a patient *can do the same things without hypnosis that he can with it.* For example, take the area of pain tolerance. They'll take one group of subjects, hypnotize them, stick needles in them, and they won't wince. The second group is offered a sum of money and told that someone will stick needles in them, and they are to act as if nothing is happening. When they bring in trained hypnotists, they can't tell the difference."

There is probably a hypnotic state, but experts have had difficulty defining it. Researchers can measure brain waves and tell when a person is asleep. They also can measure them to determine when a person is dreaming. But there is no comparable measurement of the hypnotic state, leaving some researchers to believe that hypnosis is often a game, in which the subject obeys because he wants to. For example, the quiet woman who is hypnotized in a stage show and suddenly runs around clucking like a chicken is probably not hypnotized so much as given a wonderful excuse to act crazy.

"Some people will play the role," Hyman says. "In given circumstances, they will try to figure out 'what's expected of me' and behave that way. They will even do things they would never do under normal circumstances. Some psychologists argue that this is because they really wanted to do those things, and this just gave them an excuse. Most hypnotists will tell you that a person will not do something under hypnosis that he really doesn't want to do. The subject will resist or come out of the hypnotic state."

HYPNOTISM AS PSYCHIC PHENOMENA

Technically, hypnosis is not in the realm of the paranormal, but people claim to use it in that realm, and many psychic performers also do public hypnotism shows. Mediums and channelers have also relied on hypnotism in order to lend credence to their supposed "wisdom." They allegedly contact the dead, read minds, predict the future, and do other feats while in a hypnotic trance. In fact, the trance is usually a cover-up to justify their activities. Jerry once observed a man claiming to go into a trance so that beings from another planet could communicate through him. It was a hokey, thoroughly unbelievable performance, but sure enough, there were those who came away believing the psychic had connected them with life on other planets.

We have also seen people who have become "hypnosis junkies," routinely going to visit the hypnotist to help them cope with life. In that case, the hypnotist, much like the tarot-card reader, serves in the same capacity as a counselor, offering friendship and "wisdom"— though always for a price. There are those who visit their reader every week, seeking guidance for life, and those who insist on seeing a hypnotist in order to cope with the pressures of the day. People still look for answers from mediums, fortune-tellers, faith healers, and astrologers. They search for something to give them hope and direction, and they think they'll find it in the realm of psychic phenomena. But it is only an illusion. Instead of seeing genuine displays of supernatural power, they are treated to simple magic tricks posing as miracles. These are frauds that prevent us from recognizing the real thing.

Christians are not to be taken in by this sort of spurious activity. In the first place, we are *to know God*, so that the truth resides within us. Over the last few years there have been dozens written on discovering God's will in recent years, but many of them sound as though they were written by diviners. If God is a loving and caring Father, He will not hide His will from us, turning our faith into something akin to "find the penny." All we must do is remain close to Him, and His will becomes clear. Most Christians we know who attend a good church, read their Bibles and pray each day, keep themselves accountable to other believers, seek wise counsel, and develop a heart for God do not struggle with "finding" God's will—it is clear to them!

A second thing to keep in mind is that we are not to be controlled by anything except the Holy Spirit. Paul's advice to "not get drunk on wine…instead, be filled with the Spirit," is not simply a command against drinking. It is a command against anything else controlling us. If a person drinks too much, he is no longer in control of himself—the alcohol has taken over. But Paul's words suggest that believers should be exactly that way with God. We should be "filled with the Holy Spirit," allowing Him to control us. We are not suggesting that a Christian never submit to hypnotism, but that he or she very carefully explore the situation before participating. Besides, we are influenced by the things we see and hear, even when we don't realize they are happening. One of the reasons it is not good for our spiritual lives to watch evil movies or listen to degrading music is that the message of those things can influence us at some level. Our ideas and values and thoughts are shaped by the images we see, the messages we hear, and the activities in which we participate. A man who spends his time watching pornographic movies is sure to be shaped by them, whether he intends that to happen or not. By the same token, why should a person allow himself or herself to be influenced by a hypnotist, particularly one who is faking it? If something is true, it is reasonable to have faith in it. But if something is obviously false, faith is misplaced, and the result is mindlessness.

Finally, Christians should remember that *we belong to God*. The devil has power to try to deceive us, but he cannot control us—unless we choose to surrender control of our lives to him. We don't believe in satanic possession of believers, since we now belong to God. When Christ entered a life in the New Testament, the demons were *gone*, and He promised Christians that "no one can snatch them out of my hand." Therefore, we do not think that a believer can be filled with demons through hypnotism, as some recent writers have suggested. But we do believe that the enemy will try to confuse us, and he will use every method he can to try to ruin our faith. The best thing that we can do is remain close to the Lord, having faith that He will keep us in His hand until the day of His coming.

CHAPTER NINE

The Latest from the X-Files

Everyone likes a good mystery—just look at the popularity of television's *Unsolved Mysteries*, *The X-Files*, and *America's Most Wanted*. Books on such mysterious events as Jack the Ripper and the Bermuda Triangle have enjoyed good sales over the years. In the 1970s everybody was reading Erich Von Daniken's *Chariots of the Gods*, which misused science to propagate the theory that "gods" from space used earth more or less as a laboratory experiment. Despite the fact that Von Daniken's theories were absurd and his lack of scientific and historical knowledge laughable, his writings are still in print—and still brought up as "evidence" by those who believe in alien abductions.

In the 1980s there was a substantial market for tabloids and paperback books with stories concerning alien encounters, unidentified flying objects, the lost civilization of Atlantis, and other mysterious phenomena. And in the 1990s tens of thousands of people picked up books in which Ann Rule got inside the minds of serial killers, Charles Berlitz visited with alien invaders, and Colin Wilson explored the unsolved crimes of the ages.

People love a good mystery. It allows us to examine possibilities and appraise evidence as though we were investigators. It also leads us into an exploration of possible paranormal phenomena. For example, when Jack the Ripper terrorized London in the late 1800s, some writers theorized that the murders were too dastardly to be the work of a human being. They created explanations whereby demons were taking the lives of young prostitutes—a notion that still comes up in print occasionally, though by now most of us have been jaded by news coverage of even more bizarre murders.

Von Daniken's idea about supermen from space starting the human race fits into that same mold, as do Berlitz's beliefs in a lost continent called Atlantis. All of these tales rest on the assumption that supernatural powers connected with mankind in some way, and all of them leave the reader with the notion that man can once again harness such power. As television shows and movies advance the argument that mankind can "contact" the supernatural world through ghosts, mediums, or aliens, the popularity of paranormal theories increases. But if we look carefully at a few of the most popular mysteries, we find that much of their appeal vanishes as the facts become clear.

HELL AND HIGH WATER

Have you heard about the Siberian geologists who drilled a hole nine miles deep into the earth and *accidentally discovered hell?* According to one report, when microphones were lowered into the hole, "they heard human screams...from condemned souls." Unfortunately, no one has yet been able to identify the geologists, the hole, or anything else that could verify this bit of nonsense. But that didn't stop tabloids from reporting it—or Christians from talking about this far-fetched tale as though it were fact.

Atlantis is another myth which continually pops into the minds of those bent on discovering mysteries. Plato first described this so-called "lost continent" as having existed in the middle of the Atlantic Ocean, but said it was destroyed by a volcanic explosion and the resulting tidal wave. The story is doubtless based upon the true incident on the Island of Santorini, which was destroyed exactly that way about 1500 years B.C. Former Minnesota congressman Ignatius Donnelly revived interest in Atlantis when he published a book in 1882 describing its "advanced society." Ever since then spiritists have been adding to the yarn, until now the residents of Atlantis have grown into some sort of superhuman race of men. But now that we can map the bottom of the ocean floor the evidence is clear: Atlantis simply did not exist.[1]

A more recent myth was created by Cleve Backster, a lie-detector expert who worked for the U.S. Navy. Mr. Backster discovered that when he hooked up a polygraph to his houseplants, they "responded" to his moods. This led him to believe that plants can communicate with one another, tell us how they're feeling, and experience emotion. Backster even went so far as to suggest that plants were psychic, since they were able to tell when he was "thinking about fire." He wrote all these absurdities into a bestselling 1973 book, *The Secret Life of Plants,* and suggested that the Navy conduct experiments with seaweed aimed at "training" plants to warn us of danger. So far the U.S. military hasn't taken Backster up on his idea. (It should also be noted that Backster hooked up his polygraph to two quarts of yogurt, and came to the conclusion that they were "communicating" with each other!)[2]

Another recent myth has been the invention of the *crop circle,* a geometric diagram formed by flattening out a grainfield. First appearing in the U.K. in 1979, crop circles have been hailed by UFO fans as an attempt at communication by aliens from outer space. The first were simple circles, but in recent years they have "evolved into Mandlebrot figures and complicated networks, as if extraterrestrial kids were competing with one another in an intergalactic drawing contest."[3] This created a whole new group of believers, who refer to themselves as "cerealogists," convinced that an advanced society in space has decided that the best way to communicate with earthlings is by drawing figures in farmland. However, in 1992 the perpetrators of the crop circles—Dan and Dave, two retired pranksters—admitted that they had started it all, then taught some of the younger set to join in. A newspaper even had them create a crop circle in secret, then called in "experts" who immediately pronounced it a genuine space-alien phenomenon.

These same experts also declared a huge crop circle in Hungary as the real thing in June of 1992, even warning local residents of high radiation levels and exclaiming the whole thing to be "beyond the ability of humans to fabricate." One expert, "time-scientist" Gyorgy Kisfaludy, claimed the drawing was a coded message that he had been able to solve by "exploring the design in six dimensions." Unfortunately, Kisfaludy made these assertions while appearing on a TV show, and the producers next brought onstage Robert Dallos and Gabor Takacs—the two 17-year-olds who had created the crop circle. When the "expert" protested that he didn't believe their story, they showed the videotape they had taken the night of their handiwork.

Of course, this sort of evidence is never enough to dissuade a true believer. UFO fanatics were quick to point out that *those* circles were somehow different from the *real* circles. The fact that crop circles are easily made with boards and ropes by those who understand the importance of rain (which softens the crops) and gentleness (to not leave footprints) leaves this in the realm of a teenage prank rather than an unsolved mystery.

MONSTERS AND MAYHEM

Do you remember hearing about *King Tut's Curse*, which supposedly afflicted the men who entered into the tomb of King Tutankhamen in 1922? The leader of that exploration, Lord Carnavon, died one year later, and word leaked out that an inscription on the tomb placed a death threat on all those who entered. It was later revealed that this legend was instigated by the archaeologists themselves, as a way to keep natives from sacking the tomb. It turns out that Carnavon had been in poor health for years, and the other 22 participants were not affected. In fact, the guard who slept inside the tomb was still alive in 1980, when a reporter for the London *Times* decided to do a follow-up story on the curse!

You might be one who is inclined to believe in the existence of the *Loch Ness Monster,* a mythical creature who some claim exists deep in a lake in Scotland. This creature has not only been able to keep itself from being photographed, but a dead carcass has never washed up on shore, and five separate investigations, using sophisticated sonar equipment, have offered no supportive data for its existence. The very existence of such a huge creature in a small lake is improbable—but not entirely impossible—so belief in "Nessie" continues.

Another popular legend is that of *Bigfoot*—also known as *Yeti, Sasquatch,* and the *Abominable Snowman.* It is said to be seven to ten feet tall, with huge feet and a noticeably bad aroma. Sightings came first in China and Tibet, though the creature has apparently immigrated to Siberia, Canada, and the Pacific Northwest of the United States. Giant footprints in snow have been photographed, but any outdoorsman will tell you that tracks left in snow tend to enlarge when exposed to sunlight, so tracks of bears or mountain lions may have been mistaken for something much larger. Other tracks are the admitted results of hoaxers. A short bit of film made by Roger Patterson at Bluff Creek, California, in 1966 appears to show Bigfoot strolling casually through the woods, but its authenticity has been hotly contested:

> *It is possible that Patterson himself was hoaxed; the figure he saw and filmed might have been a person in costume. In the 1968 film 2001: A Space Odyssey, most viewers were not aware that the apes shown were actors in costume holding real baby chimpanzees. The 1989 film Gorillas in the Mist used actors in costumes that were totally convincing. The Patterson figure is nowhere nearly as good as those representations, though we cannot expect that a genuine Bigfoot must move like an ape, and it may very well move like a human dressed in an uncomfortable costume.[4]*

Experts have pointed out two major problems with the existence of Bigfoot. First, for such a creature to survive there would need to be a considerable number of them to maintain the gene pool and ensure survival of the species. Surely if such a large number existed, somebody would have seen one. Second, when you get past all the claims and speculation, *not one shred of physical evidence from a Bigfoot* has ever been produced. No skeletons, no droppings, no lair, and no hair. But lack of facts seldom interferes with a true believer.

One other popular "monster," at least in the eyes of Christians, is *Bridey Murphy*, a fictional character from the 1800s that Virginia Tighe of Denver claimed to live inside her. In the early 1950s, Tighe received plenty of press for going into a "trance" and telling stories about living in Ireland, complete with Irish brogue and quaint Irish expressions. Believers in the paranormal called it evidence of reincarnation and believers in Christ called it possession, but a series of articles by Melvin Harris in the *Denver Post* showed it to be nothing but a hoax. It turns out that Tighe, a budding actress with a knack for accents, had grown up across the street from an old Irish woman named Bridie Murphey, who had entertained the young lady with stories of her homeland. Rather than being supernatural, it was simply a hoax.

Our rationale for pointing out all these hoaxes is not merely to poke fun at people's gullibility, but to remind Christians that the lure of fakes and frauds has gone on for centuries. We all love a good mystery, but most mysteries are easily explainable when they are researched thoroughly. In our culture, there is a rush to brand mysteries as "supernatural," in an attempt to foster a belief in humans connecting with mysterious inner powers. On at least two recent occasions, André Kole has had the opportunity to investigate these claims.

THE BERMUDA TRIANGLE

A number of years ago, André started getting questions about the supposed mystery of the Bermuda Triangle. Several movies and television shows had helped popularize it, so André decided to research the subject. Unfortunately, it would be difficult for him to gain firsthand experience on this subject, as he had with other phenomena, for he couldn't go out into the middle of the Triangle and wait for something to happen. Instead, André decided to examine reliable sources.

In his bestseller *The Bermuda Triangle,* Charles Berlitz defines the geographical area in question:

> *There is a section of the Western Atlantic, off the south-east coast of the United States, forming what has been termed a triangle, extending from Bermuda in the north to southern Florida, and then east to a point through the Bahamas past Puerto Rico to about 40 west longitude and then back again to Bermuda. This area occupies a disturbing and almost unbelievable place in the world's catalogue of unexplained mysteries. This is usually referred to as the Bermuda Triangle, where more than 100 planes and ships have literally vanished into thin air, most of them since 1945, and where more than 1,000 lives have been lost in the past twenty-six years, without a single body or even a piece of wreckage from the vanishing planes or ships having been found. Disappearances continue to occur with apparently increasing frequency, in spite of the fact that the seaways and airways are today more traveled, searches are more thorough, and records are more carefully kept.*[5]

The author goes on to describe how planes have vanished while in radio contact with control towers, and how others had radioed "the most extraordinary messages, implying that they could not get their instruments to function, that their compasses were spinning, that the sky had turned yellow and hazy (on a clear day), and that the ocean 'didn't look right.'"[6] Boats, large and small, have allegedly vanished without a trace. Others were found drifting, but with no survivors or bodies on board.

There have been numerous attempts to explain the mystery—some of them extremely creative: sudden tidal waves, fireballs, time warps, electromagnetic aberrations, even attacks by UFOs. But the best source of information is neither folktales nor popular fiction—it's fact, based on investigative research. As André began his investigation of this subject, he made an amazing discovery: the man most responsible for researching the facts of the Bermuda Triangle lived less than two miles from André's home in Arizona. André was able to meet with Dr. Larry Kusche, who was on the faculty of Arizona State University and author of *The Bermuda Triangle Mystery—Solved*. From Kusche and others we can learn enough information to draw several conclusions.

First, *15 to 20 percent of the incidents reported about the Bermuda Triangle never happened*. For example, Berlitz reported that in October of 1978 three people on a 40-foot cabin cruiser disappeared in clear weather and calm seas during a short trip between Bimini and Miami. But investigator Michael Dennett did a detailed investigation of this and other recent Triangle incidents, and decided:

> *This case is, as Berlitz might describe it, a classic Bermuda Triangle disappearance. It has all the hallmarks of such an occurrence: namely, an unidentified vessel, with three unnamed people on board, vanishes on an unspecified date. The local newspaper carried no report of this incident and the Coast Guard was unable to confirm that a vessel matching this description had been lost in October of 1978.*[7]

Second, *25 to 30 percent of the mysterious disappearances did not take place within the boundaries of the Bermuda Triangle*. When it suited their purposes, mystery writers included air and sea disasters in the Gulf of Mexico and the far reaches of the Atlantic ocean, hundreds of miles outside the Triangle borders. An American Globemaster that "disappeared north of the triangle in March 1950" actually exploded 600 miles southwest of Ireland—at least 1000 miles outside the Triangle!

Third, *those who describe most of the cases try to convince readers that the disappearances took place on calm, clear days, when in reality nearly all recorded accidents in the area took place in very severe weather*. In the epilogue to his book, Kusche wrote:

*After examining all the evidence I have reached the fol-
lowing conclusion: There is no theory that solves the
mystery. It is no more logical to try to find a common
cause for all the disappearances in the Triangle than, for
example, to try to find one cause for all automobile accidents in Arizona. By abandoning the search for an overall theory and investigating each incident independently,
the mystery began to unravel.*

*The findings of my research were consistent.... Once
sufficient information was found, logical explanations
appeared for most of the incidents.It is difficult, for
example, to consider the Rubicon[a missing ship] a mystery when it is known that a hurricane struck the harbor
where it had been moored. It is similarly difficult to be
baffled by the loss of the Marine Sulphur Queen after
learning of the ship's weakened structure and the
weather conditions as described in the report of the
Coast Guard investigation.*[8]

Fourth, the *number of disappearances within the boundaries of the
Bermuda Triangle is actually no greater than the number of disappearances in
almost any other comparable part of the world.* Accidents happen to ships
and planes the world over. There is no evidence to suggest that things
are worse near Bermuda. In an exclusive interview in the *Globe*, a
national tabloid, Charles Berlitz claimed that 50 planes and more than
100 ships had vanished in two years, and that the government was con-
spiring to keep this information secret. But Michael Dennet found
that only a dozen "unexplained" incidents occurred during the 25-
month period ending in January of 1990. He systematically reviewed
all 12 of the incidents mentioned by Berlitz and found that, with sufficient information, most of the "mysteries" were solved.

It's surprising that Berlitz hasn't tackled another mystery: On an
average of nearly once a month, a small private airplane takes off from
a United States airport and disappears. Despite searches, no debris is

found. Everyone assumes that the lost plane crashed, but no one can find it. Occasionally it is found years later in some rugged mountains— yet no one has proposed the existence of a "U.S. airport triangle."

Bermuda Triangle writers also make a big fuss over the fact that no debris is found. The fact is, when flights are lost over water, debris is rarely found, especially if the crash is at night in rough seas. By the time morning light allows a search to begin, the seas have hidden all traces of the crash.

FLIGHT 19

Perhaps the most famous mystery of the Bermuda Triangle was the disappearance of Flight 19. The legend makes for eerie reading: On December 5, 1945, five Avenger torpedo-bombers took off from Fort Lauderdale Naval Air Station on a routine patrol. An hour-and-a-half later, when they should have been starting their return to base, the flight commander reported that he was lost over the Florida Keys, many miles from where he should have been. For the next few hours, frantic efforts were made to find the planes and guide them back home, but they were never located. A massive air and sea search turned up no evidence of the planes.

Over the years the story became a legend, to the point where it was almost impossible to separate fact from fiction. Larry Kusche meticulously studied all the available information, including the official Naval investigations, and interviewed most of the surviving people involved in the incident in order to reconstruct what actually happened. His book *The Disappearance of Flight 19* is exciting reading, but it is hardly the "Twilight Zone" type of mystery that Berlitz and others would have us believe.

Kusche concluded that the five Avengers almost certainly were over the Bahamas—their intended target—and not the Florida Keys. An accomplished pilot himself, Kusche flew the intended route of Flight 19 and observed several reasons why a pilot could become disoriented. He noticed that a haze, caused by the humid air, can cause the sky and ocean to blend so that there appears to be no horizon. On that fateful day in 1945, visibility was less than ten miles, and a slight error in navigation could cause the pilots to miss expected landmarks. Parts of the Bahamas and the Keys look remarkably alike. Thinking he was over the Keys, the leader, Chuck Taylor, apparently headed north in order to find the Florida mainland. But he never reached land. In the dark, with extremely rough seas, the planes ditched in the ocean approximately 200 miles off the Florida coast. Rather than being a supernatural mystery, the disappearance of Flight 19 was a tragedy brought about by human error.

The popularity of the Bermuda Triangle mystery has spawned similar mysteries, such as the Devil's Sea near Japan and the so-called *Great Lakes Triangle*. But these mysteries exist only in the minds of those who make up and write the stories concerning them. There was no great mystery to the Bermuda Triangle, nor was there one grand conspiracy to silence the facts. Instead, there were a few events that, when jumbled together, created the illusion of mystery. Perhaps we should not be surprised that the individual most responsible for "creating" the Bermuda Triangle myth was a magician—Vincent Gaddis, a man André knew as a magician, but who later turned to writing sensational books and stories. This is further evidence that when anything, no matter how ridiculous, is presented in a serious manner and in an atmosphere where honesty is taken for granted, it can mislead even the most intelligent people—*if they do not investigate the facts.*

ANDRÉ KOLE: GHOSTBUSTER

Through the years, André has been called on by corporations, local police departments, and even the United States Government to help investigate "unexplainable" phenomena. Recently, he was contracted by a private detective, who had been hired to investigate a 24-hour public service company that was allegedly being haunted by ghosts. The situation became so serious that some employees had refused to work, and a few had even quit as a result of their fears of the hauntings. Some of the reported phenomena taking place included:

- chairs rocking on their own
- various objects mysteriously moving from one place to another
- papers scattered everywhere in the morning
- doors opening, toilets flushing, and the alarm going off for no reason
- the elevator going up and down by itself, and occasionally "bouncing"
- television and lights turning on and off by themselves at night
- the door to the dryer suddenly flying open
- footsteps and voices
- "feeling" the presence of someone they could not see.

As talk about these incidents began to spread, more people began suggesting other strange events, until it seemed as though the place was being overrun with reports of the paranormal. Most of the reports lacked specificity and detail. The events nearly always occurred at night, and there were usually the same employees on duty when these things took place. It was purported that the facility was built on an old Indian burial site, and that many residents and a few staff had died on the grounds. As residents and staff began talking about their discomfort with the disturbances, the organization's board decided to act.

They called in a self-proclaimed "expert" in discovering psychic phenomena, who did not even address the possibility that some of these incidents were caused by explainable, natural occurrences. Instead, she immediately announced it was "safe to assume that the phenomenon is caused by a ghost." She also suggested training the staff in how to make the ghost go away, and claimed that, while she had not seen a ghost, she had meditated in a room and "sensed" contact with it. Her assistant spent his time asking about residents and staff who had died recently, and proposed the notion that someone who had a grudge against the organization might be projecting himself into the building by means of an "out-of-body experience."

All of this talk about ghosts and the paranormal created an attitude of acceptance among the employees, to the point that when another investigator suggested the events were naturally occurring phenomena, he was criticized as being "inexperienced in the field." However, he also discovered that, unlike the rumors which had begun to spread, the building was *not* built on an old Indian burial ground, nor had anyone died on the premises. Exaggeration was leading people to all sorts of conclusions, so that soon everyone was "experiencing" psychic goings-on.

It was at that point someone on the board contacted André, to see if he could propose a solution. André believed the only way to solve the mystery was to train a qualified person to observe first hand what was taking place. Arrangements were made for his personal assistant, Michelle, to be hired as a temporary employee with the company, to be his eyes and ears as an undercover observer, and to convey to him the information he needed to know.

Since most of the reported phenomena took place at night, Michelle spent a week as an "undercover" investigator working the graveyard shift. Every night she would go to the facility and spend the night assisting the staff in their various duties, taking notice of anything that might have been considered "paranormal."

Her discussions with staff provided a wealth of information which helped do away with the notion of a ghost haunting the premises. But rather than finding *one* solution to all the mysteries, she found a number of elements that all worked together to create the illusion of a ghost.

The physical phenomena were the easiest to dispel. Many of the lights were fluorescent, and as the bulbs got old they would flicker, giving the appearance of being turned on and off. This was not something that would be noticeable during the daytime, but scared many people at night. The problems of elevators bouncing was no mystery: It was simply a bouncy elevator. When Michelle would suddenly put all her weight on one foot, the elevator would begin to bounce.

Discussions with the janitorial staff turned up explanations for some of the other problems. The person who mopped liked to turn the television on at night, which is why some people had heard it after hours. And that janitor was the one who revealed the secret of the dryer door: When someone was drying tennis shoes, the shoes would occasionally bang against the door, knocking it open.

People were occasionally the problem. One young man was troubled with depression and thoughts of suicide, and he would occasionally cause problems by acting up. It turns out he was the one who had thrown papers around the office, and it is quite possible he was the cause behind some of the other activities. "Pranks" is a more appropriate word than "phenomena," since many of the events were nothing more than schoolboy pranks. It appears that two of the young men on staff had heard about the fears of the young women, so they would occasionally knock on windows, slam doors, or walk on the roof in order to throw a scare into them.

Apparently the women who worked at night had reason to be scared, for the neighborhood had seen some decay, so that occasionally a derelict or troublemaker would find his way into a building. On several occasions the police had been called to escort intruders from the site—further heightening the fears of staffers. An alarm had been installed, but everyone conceded it was a very sensitive device, and any sort of jiggling was known to set it off—therefore the mystery of the nighttime alarms was also solved. A security firm had also installed surveillance cameras, and had never caught on film anything close to a ghostlike activity.

In André's investigation, the most important element he uncovered was the attitude of some nighttime staffers. They had begun to believe in the ghost, and that fostered belief in all sorts of mysteries. Once, as he leaned against a filing cabinet, it tilted and accidentally knocked over a whiteboard and markers. "Do you see that?" one of the women exclaimed. "That sort of thing is *always* happening here!"

That same woman had claimed to once see a ghost sitting in a rocker late at night. When asked to describe the ghost, she said that it looked exactly like a red-haired woman. It was pointed out to her that there were several redheads on site, but she stuck to her story, saying, "It may have *looked* like a red-haired woman, but it wasn't real. It *had* to be a ghost!" Pressed, she couldn't offer any reason for that conclusion other than the fact that she "felt funny" about seeing the redhead.

She also admitted she enjoyed watching scary movies and mystery programs, and she believed in supernatural happenings.

After a week of research, André wrote his report. His conclusion: The organization didn't have a ghost, but they did have a couple staff members with overactive imaginations. He presented a logical answer for every situation, along with explanations from several of the staff involved. The board accepted it gratefully, happy to put to rest any rumors of a haunting. They even gave André a note of thanks for moving from magician to "ghostbuster!"[9]

This case is just another illustration of one of the most significant lessons André has learned in his lifetime of investigating claims of the supernatural: *The unexplained is usually nothing more than the unexamined.*

IT'S FUN TO BE FOOLED

When the great magician Harry Blackstone traveled the country doing his magic show, his posters always carried the words "It's Fun to Be Fooled!" And it is fun—that's why magic has been so popular, and why mysteries remain in the public eye. But it's important to remember that, given the proper circumstances, *we can all be fooled.* King Solomon offered valuable insight into this matter when he wrote, "The first to present his case seems right, till another comes forward and questions him."[10] In other words, be careful not to believe everything you hear, for the story may change when someone asks the right questions.

This advice proved valuable to André while he was doing research on levitation. On several occasions, while explaining the lack of solid documentation for this supposed psychic manifestation, he was encouraged to speak to a university professor. Many people told André that this man, who teaches at a well-college in the United States, had seen a demon-possessed woman levitate ten feet into the air.

In February of 1990, André met firsthand with the professor to question him about the levitation story. But the professor admitted he had never seen a levitation, and that the story had actually come from a colleague at *another* seminary. In proper investigative fashion, André called this other professor, who was apparently the source of the story, and asked for details. When told about the levitation, the professor laughed and said, "My, that story has been greatly levitated!" What he had witnessed was a terrified woman thrash about on the floor, but she had never levitated. This is just one more example of how sincere individuals can be accomplice to turning a simple story into a tale of legendary proportions.[11]

While most people think themselves critical thinkers, their superstitious worldview belies that idea. Dr. Paul Bauer, in his book *Horoscope and Talisman*, suggests that finite man is always going to be interested in the infinite. In hopes of gaining control over the infinite, the superstitious man tries various rites and ceremonies to outwit fate and become lord of his own life.

At the same time, he seems never to be convinced by logical proof. He does not want to be enlightened, even when there is a rational argument in place, because he is in search of some sort of "deeper" knowledge. "The fact that many superstitious ideas are not pure nonsense gives them substance and leads to their persistence. They contain a grain of truth derived from some obscure piece of knowledge from ancient times or from some real event which, because of its puzzling nature, gave rise to a false interpretation."[12]

In 1917, two little girls created a myth that fooled the greatest sleuth of the century. Elsie and Francis Wright, cousins who lived in Cottingley Glen, England, said they had met some fairies in the woods. They even produced five photographs of themselves with the tiny fairies dancing around them. The father of one of the girls had the good sense to toss the photographs in a drawer, but the girls pulled them out and sent them to a local newspaper. It was there that Sir Arthur Conan Doyle, creator of supersleuth Sherlock Holmes, first read about them. Reasoning that two girls "from the artisan class" would not dare try to deceive someone as important as himself, Conan Doyle declared them genuine.

Looking back, the whole story is hard to believe. The photos are obvious fakes—amateurish productions featuring fairies cut from illustrations in a children's book. They are supposed to be flitting around in the photographs, but those were the days of extremely slow shutter speeds, so all movement would appear fuzzy and ghostlike.(Curiously, the waterfall in the background is fuzzy, but the fairies are crystal clear.) Nevertheless, the brilliant detective mind of Conan Doyle pronounced the Cottingley Fairies real, believed that such creatures were flitting through the English countryside, and even went on a lecture tour in America using slides of the fairies as his "evidence." Occasionally the pictures still turn up in tabloids as proof of sprites and fairies.

Spiritists trumpeted the news, and years later Elsie Wright, when shown a photograph of the huge church the spiritists had built with money they had made selling copies of the photos, grumbled that she had never made a dime off the affair. "Elsie was amazed that people accepted their hoax. She wrote, 'Surely you know that there cannot be more than one grown-up person in every five million who would take our fairies seriously.' Elsie's dad, she wrote, was dismayed by it all. He asked his wife, 'How could a brilliant man like Conan Doyle believe such a thing?'"[13] The answer, of course, is that we all love a mystery. After all, *it's fun to be fooled!*

CHAPTER TEN

Beam Me Up, Scotty!

On June 24, 1947, civilian pilot Kenneth Arnold was flying his single-engine plane over the Cascade Mountains of Washington State when he noticed bright objects that appeared to be flying in and out of the mountain peaks. They did not look like aircraft, and Arnold calculated that they were not just moving faster than any craft of that time, but they were jetting up and down more fluidly than any craft he had ever seen. Arnold was quoted in the paper as saying, "They flew like a saucer would if you skipped it across the water"—and with that quotation the popular notion of "flying saucers" was born.

Suddenly everybody was seeing flying saucers. Up to that point in time there had been very few historical sightings of *unidentified flying objects* (UFOs), but since that time there have been hundreds. The idea of space travel and intelligent life on other planets has evolved into a mystical belief in time warps, alien abductions, and guidance from

159

higher life forms in space. This acceptance can best be tracked through popular culture: Whereas the early decades of motion pictures offered merely a handful of science-fiction films, after the invention of flying saucers we have been inundated with movies about extraterrestrials and their contact with earthlings. Those films began as horror movies, changed to adventures, and now are largely "friendly" movies about mankind getting in touch with "the force" and being guided by our astral friends.

At the same time, there has been a growing notion that UFOs are genuine, and that the government knows about them. Conspiracy theorists have concocted all sorts of hypotheses regarding government cover-ups, "investigative" books and television shows have made wild surmises in hopes of attracting an audience, and public pressure has even forced the United States Air Force to examine the possibility of flying saucers and alien life. Those who believe in UFOs have even given themselves a name, *UFOlogists*, and have created a library of books to support their cause. In the midst of the hoopla, a careful summary of the facts is in order.

THE FACTS ABOUT UFOS

With all this flying saucer hysteria, it is almost comical to see how badly people want to believe in extraterrestrials. There are no explanations you can offer which will satisfy them other than the idea that there must be intelligent life on other planets. But there is simply no evidence to support such a conclusion. Take, for example, Kenneth Arnold's initial sighting of a flying saucer. In the years since then, researchers have carefully examined Arnold's description. The size and distance of the objects in his report were nothing more than wild guesses, and the speed at which he claimed the objects were flying would have been extremely difficult to gauge. However, what is no longer hard to gauge is Arnold's drawing of the craft: It is remarkably similar to an F-84 Thunderjet, which at that time was a military secret, and which was being used for training in that area of the country.[1] Kenneth Arnold saw a group of jets being tested, not a UFO.

Another story given prominence in early UFO books took place over Goldman Air Force Base in Kentucky on January 7, 1948. Air Force Captain Thomas Mantell flew up to investigate "an ice cream cone topped with red." He radioed back to say that it looked "metallic and of tremendous size," and that it was moving upward quickly. "I'm going up to 20,000 feet," Mantell said, "and if I'm no closer, I'll abandon chase." Nothing more was heard from the captain, and his crashed plane was located later that day. Those fearing flying saucers were terrified at the story—but it turns out the captain was chasing a Skyhook weather balloon, another military secret being tested in the area. It was further determined that the pilot blacked out from lack of oxygen, causing his plane to crash.[2] Thomas Mantell saw a metallic weather balloon, not a UFO.

Six months later, the pilot and copilot of a DC-3 told of seeing a dull red glow streaking through the sky. At 2:45 A.M., Clarence Chiles and John Whitted watched something 30 feet in diameter pass them about one-half mile distant. It glowed blue and had a red tail or exhaust, and one of them thought he could make out a cockpit. It turned out to be a meteor.[3] Two months after that, George Gorman was in an F-51 fighter, chasing something unknown over the skies of North Dakota. He claimed it had been blinking, and that it seemed to keep moving away from him as he flew. Suddenly it disappeared. A careful investigation turns out that Gorman first saw a lighted weather balloon, then found himself chasing a mirage of the planet Jupiter, which commonly happens in certain temperatures. Notably, Jupiter sank below the horizon at the exact time the UFO "disappeared."[4] Rather than UFOs, these pilots saw natural phenomena.

These descriptions have launched an avalanche of UFO sightings, as though our planet has suddenly been invaded by hundreds of spacecraft from other worlds. The response reminds us of what happened to the *Audi 5000*. That automobile, introduced in 1978, was doing moderately well until November of 1986, when *Sixty Minutes* did a story claiming that 13 drivers had complained of a mysterious sudden acceleration in the cars, sometimes causing accidents. Within a month, 1400 people had complained about sudden acceleration in their Audis.

Subsequent investigations by the National Transportation and Safety Board revealed that the problem had occurred very few times, and was the result of driver error—it seems a few people had stepped on the accelerator when intending to step on the brake. There was no trouble with the Audi at all, but the herd mentality of people gave the impression that there was a major problem.[5]

A similar incident occurred in 1992, when a man claimed he found a hypodermic needle in a can of Pepsi. He appeared on national television and became an overnight celebrity, and suddenly there were more than a hundred people around the country claiming that they too had found hypodermics inside cans of Pepsi. Investigation showed that *every report was a lie*—but that didn't stop people from thinking something was wrong with Pepsi manufacturing. In the same way, we have been told that UFOs are real. Fake news shows like *Unsolved Mysteries* and *Sightings* have primed the pump, and recently we have seen more respected programs like *48 Hours* and *Larry King* take the same approach. Philip J. Klass, a respected researcher, has estimated that 95 percent of UFO information on television is pro-UFO.[6] With that sort of publicity, it's easy to assume there is something to the myth of UFOs.

There have been thousands of sightings in the last 40 years, but the huge majority of them can be attributed to aircraft, balloons, satellites, hoaxes, hallucinations, or naturally occurring phenomena like ball lightning. We'll consider the few exceptions, but first it is important that we think through the idea of a UFO.

DETERMINING THE TRUTH

The single greatest hurdle any UFO researcher faces is the problem of evidence. Many of the stories about UFOs are secondhand, and there have been so many exaggerations and hoaxes that one must dig deep to separate fact from fiction. Therefore determining the truth is a tough task. In order to make our job easier, we propose that every researcher be guided by four principles.

First, *we must insist on hard evidence*. In the words of skeptic Alan Hale, "Extraordinary claims require extraordinary evidence." UFOlogists want us to believe that there are intelligent beings on other planets, that they have somehow located Earth in the vast reaches of space, and that they are regularly visiting us in spacecraft that defy the laws of physics. All three of these hypotheses are incredible—indeed, if a scientist could prove any one of them, he would be hailed as one of the greatest researchers in history. But for us to believe in these as truth, there has to be some credible evidence offered.

For example, if someone could hand over a spacecraft or an alien for competent scientists to study, there would finally be hard evidence. If someone could produce some star charts to see where aliens came from, so that scientists could compare their planet to ours, it would be possible to reach a firm conclusion. As one astronomer puts it, "I want the aliens visible front and center, where there can be *no reasonable doubt* as to their existence. Stories about 'lights' or 'things' in the sky do not impress me, especially when such reports come from people who have no idea of the vast array of natural and man-made phenomena that are visible in the sky if one would only take the time to look."[7]

Second, *if it is true, there has to be proof*. UFOlogists are quick to point out that "several hundred million people now believe that UFOs are real,"[8] and that "40 percent of Americans believe that UFOs are real."[9] But that is all intellectual claptrap. It doesn't matter *how many* people believe it to be true—what matters is that *there is incontrovertible proof that it is true*. At one point in time 90 percent of Europeans thought the world was flat, but their mistaken belief didn't change the facts. And the facts when it comes to UFOs are in awfully short supply.

Have you ever wondered why radar has never recorded a UFO actually entering into our atmosphere?[10] Or why nobody ever quite gets a clear look at one? Or why, with all the shots that have been fired at them from Russian and America fighter jets, none has ever been hit?[11] Have you ever paused to reflect on the fact that no two UFOs are ever exactly the same, leading to the conclusion that supposedly advanced aliens must be building single-use vehicles? Or how such crafts would be able to fly such incredibly long distances? Even more important, with all the vastness of space, how were they able to find us? And how can beings from another ecosystem survive on earth? And for goodness sake, if these beings really exist and are so advanced, why don't they make some clear connection with us? Could they really believe that playing cat-and-mouse with airplanes and drawing designs in fields are the best way to communicate? If they are so far ahead of us technologically, they surely don't need to fear us.

The onus is on the believers in UFOs to prove their point, not on us to disprove it. Furthermore, they must prove their case beyond a reasonable doubt, using direct evidence. "You can't prove it by eliminating a few token explanations and then crying, 'Well, what else can it be?'"[12] It might seem likely to some people that life evolved on other planets, that it created advanced technology far beyond our own, and that this life has discovered a way to transport itself from one corner of the universe to another, but before we believe in something quite so far-fetched, we need some proof.

Third, *the evidence ought to be firsthand and relatively recent.* One of the recurring difficulties we faced writing this chapter is that a researcher can rarely talk with someone who sighted a UFO firsthand. Conversations usually begin this way: "Well, I didn't actually see it...but if you talk with this other guy, you'll get the truth." Eventually this leads the researcher to conclude that many of the UFO stories are simply legend—on a par with the story of children being kidnapped in grocery stores and found in the bathroom, their clothes and hair already altered. It makes a great tale, but it isn't true.

Bookstore shelves are packed with people claiming to have seen UFOs, but the claimants are usually hard to pin down. For example, we have found in print several stories of commercial airliners having close calls with UFOs, and can identify at least three stories where someone claims their jet was actually scraped by the UFO while in midair, but none of these can be tracked down and verified.[13] Many books tell stories of the ancients seeing lights in the sky, or early Americans writing about cigar-shaped spacecraft, but it is impossible to accept that as hard evidence. The modern interpretation of a confusing historical event hardly qualifies as "proof."

Fourth, *the evidence needs to be reasonable to a researcher.* Until some-body comes up with an alternative to the laws of physics, we will have to insist that evidence for UFOs exist within some sort of logical framework. The explanation that "flying saucers come through a worm-hole in the time/space continuum" might seem a reasonable explanation of space travel for a true believer, but a researcher is going to require something a bit more logical than this.

Once again this is the principle of Occam's razor: When confronted with a series of explanations, choose the simplest one that fits all the known facts. While it is true that many people claim to have seen objects in the sky for which they have no explanation, it is also true that people routinely make mistaken observations. And a person's preconceived notions can affect his or her observations. For instance, on April 22, 1987, when a British Airways flight from London to Bangkok was passed by a bright object displaying a line of lights, the five witnesses described it five different ways. Some thought it gave off a red light, oth-ers thought it was green. Some thought it stopped to "follow" them, oth-ers thought it simply streaked past. One saw blinking lights, the others thought the lights were steady. Most of them were convinced they had seen a UFO—even after it was revealed that they had observed a satel-lite reentering earth's atmosphere, as confirmed by radar.[14]

When weighing the evidence in total, the simplest explanation is that most sightings are explainable. Encounters with UFOs have gen-erally proven to be either a mistake or a hoax.

CHARIOTS OF THE FRAUDS

There have been hundreds of hoaxes perpetrated upon UFO believ-ers. In 1995, several ultralight flyers got together in New Mexico, attached red lights to their vehicles, and flew in a triangular formation. Their flight, which was illegal because of the proximity of the aircraft, was captured on videotape and proclaimed "proof" of UFOs. This sort of thing has dogged UFOlogists for years. Whitley Streiber made a fortune when *Communion*, his story about being abducted by aliens, hit the best-seller list. But most of his claims have been challenged or proven false.

Those who believe in UFOs are quick to point to the photographic evidence as one of the strongest evidences of intergalactic spaceships, but most researchers consider that the weakest evidence. Even believers have had to admit that "photographs of UFOs prove nothing, because virtually any UFO photograph could be faked by a skilled photographer."[15] Occasionally people have snapped pictures of unexplainable objects, but that is no evidence of spacecraft. For example, one lucky tourist took a picture of a mountain, only to discover a strange cylindrical object in the background. It was trumpeted as a UFO, though it turned out to be a dummy missile, launched from a Navy ship doing some testing. It is good to remember this sort of thing when faced with photographic "evidence" of UFOs.

One photo after another has been proved a trick—but the true believers are always quick to point to some other picture as offering "proof." When Almiro Barauna claimed to have watched a UFO rise up and down between the rocks on the Brazilian coast in January of 1958, the press hailed it as incorruptible evidence—but then it was pointed out that Barauna had published fake UFO photographs earlier in his career.[16] The same thing happened in the late 1980s, when a young man created miniature UFOs from paper plates and strung them in the sky. "Experts" pronounced them genuine, until the boy showed his best friend the UFO he had sitting in his closet!

Another common problem with UFO photographs is that they are nearly always blurry, sometimes to the point of appearing as balls of light. While UFOlogists consider this significant evidence, all it really proves is that there are pictures with balls of light—not proof of flying saucers. Hoaxers have used images, double exposures, and models tossed into the air to create phony pictures of spacecraft. One photograph which received quite a bit of publicity turned out to be nothing more than a garbage can lid hurled into the air!

Perhaps that means we ought to be asking ourselves, "Does this make sense?" Does the notion of a higher life form someplace else in the universe fit what we know to be true about God and man? While it may be reasonable to assume that life could exist in some form someplace else, is it reasonable to think they would "evolve" into something greater than mankind? As Christians, we believe that God *created* life, and that man is the highest aspect of His creation. Therefore there are some theological problems with the existence of intelligent beings on other planets.

First, there is no clear indication anywhere in Scripture that God created life in another part of the universe. Mankind was created on earth as a demonstration of His greatness; would He need to prove this twice?

Second, if God created life on another planet, He would no doubt have made these beings agents of choice. (If not, they would be automatons, unable to choose God, and thus not on a plane with mankind.) The problem with this idea is that it makes no sense: If life was created on earth to act out the grand play of good versus evil, there is no logical reason for doing so in another location.

Third, if God did indeed create agents of moral choice, they would be in a fallen state. That is, life on another planet would be incapable of sinlessness, for the Bible makes it clear that no one can save himself. If an individual could live a sinless life, Christ would not have had to come and die. So if there is intelligent life somewhere else, that would mean Christ would have to go there and die for those people all over again—a heretical notion, since Christ has already lived and died, and exists in heaven with wounds in His hands and side to prove it. He is coming back to earth one day to declare His triumph over sin and death, and at that point all created things will be made new. Since the Bible makes it clear that this is the end of time, apparently those other planets would have to end their histories at the same moment.

While the existence of some type of life elsewhere in the galaxy is a possibility, the notion of advanced life on other planets seems to be in opposition with theology. Those who believe in higher life forms from space always seem to tie those beliefs into their theology, but that all falls apart when one takes into consideration the words of Scripture and the character of the Lord Jesus. UFOlogists may claim to be riding the chariots of the gods, but they're actually aboard the chariots of the frauds.

WHO ARE THE EXPERTS?

A former president of the International Brotherhood of Magicians, Bill Pitts, is one of the leading investigators of UFOs. He has told us that there are really no authorities on the subject: "There are only authorities on *reported sightings* of UFOs. There are no authorities on the UFOs themselves because we have not had, to my knowledge, one UFO that we could take pictures of, and examine every nut and bolt, and interview the beings on the craft. I have been an investigator for many of the serious research organizations as well as for several government agencies. I periodically receive calls from law enforcement personnel and from radar control tower operators who are trying to explain unusual things. No one has yet provided any hard evidence of a UFO."

Pitts takes each case and tries to provide an explanation—to turn a UFO into an IFO, an *identified* flying object. "We can't do that in every case, but I try to find out what it could have been. I don't say this is definitely what they saw, because once it's gone, I don't know. But I have ways of finding out what it could have been. I carry with me phone numbers from the FAA, control towers, various police departments, Norad, etc."[17]

The United States Air Force has conducted two exhaustive investigations and concluded that "there is no evidence for the existence of UFOs with supernatural, extraterrestrial, or military origin."[18] A thorough reexamination of the military documents concerning UFOs was completed in 1997, again reaching the conclusion that there is no hard evidence in favor of UFOs, and that in fact the evidence generally is *against* interplanetary spacecraft, noting that more than 90 percent of all UFO sightings can be attributed to purely natural causes. Yet UFOs have become increasingly popular with movies such as *Close Encounters of the Third Kind* and *ET, The Extraterrestrial.* The number of UFO sightings increases markedly when movies like these are shown or when the media report about a person who had a spectacular "encounter."

Philip J. Klass has done extensive research in this area. In his book *UFO's Explained* he gives some very sensible explanations for the UFO phenomenon. The following is a sample of his "UFOlogical principles":

- Basically honest and intelligent persons who are suddenly exposed to a brief, unexpected event, especially one that involves an unfamiliar object, may be grossly inaccurate in trying to describe what they have seen.
- The problem facing the UFO investigator is to try to distinguish between those details that are accurate and those that are grossly inaccurate. This may be impossible until the true identity of the UFO can be determined, so that in some cases this poses an insoluble problem.
- News media that give great prominence to a UFO report when it is first received subsequently devote little if any space or time to reporting a prosaic explanation for the case when all the facts are uncovered.
- Once news media coverage leads the public to believe that UFO's may be in the vicinity, there are numerous natural and man-made objects which, especially when seen at night, can take on unusual characteristics in the minds of hopeful viewers. . . .This situation feeds upon itself until such time as the news media lose interest in the subject....
- The inability of even experienced investigators to fully and positively explain a UFO report for lack of sufficient information, even after a rigorous effort, does not really provide evidence to support the hypothesis that spaceships from other worlds are visiting the Earth.
- Many UFO cases seem puzzling and unexplainable simply because case investigators have failed to devote a sufficiently rigorous effort to the investigation.[19]

THE ROSWELL CASE

A perfect example of the lack of expertise is the infamous Roswell case. On the Fourth of July weekend in 1947, something crashed in the desert around Roswell, New Mexico, that many people believe to have been a UFO. During the fiftieth anniversary of that incident, all sorts of media stories retold the memory-enhanced stories of people claiming to have seen a spacecraft, alien bodies, and other such evidence. But the facts of the Roswell case have been known for years.

Rancher Mac Brazel reported to the local sheriff, George Wilcox, that he might have recovered the remains of "one of them flying saucers." Wilcox informed military authorities at Roswell Army Air Field, and Major Jesse Marcel was assigned to investigate. The first accounts were that the military had discovered a "flying disc," but the next afternoon the excitement came to an end when General Roger Ramey displayed the pieces and announced they were debris from a Project Mogul device—a radar-reflecting weather balloon shaped in a geometric pattern. Those same devices had been the source of several UFO sightings in the American Southwest. The entire affair was forgotten about until 1978, when UFO believer Stanton Friedman dredged it up and claimed not only that a UFO had crashed, but that the United States government had covered it up.

The writings of Friedman and his friends are a classic case of deception. For example, in *The Truth About the UFO Crash at Roswell*, they claim to have interviewed 90 witnesses to the events. That may generally be true, but a closer look reveals that only five were firsthand witnesses to the actual crash site, and some of them are adamant that it was *not* an extraterrestrial spacecraft. Friedman's writings[20] were embraced by conspiracy theorists, who believe the government is in contact with alien life forms and is somehow withholding that information from its citizens. This idea seems downright laughable to most of us, but is held by those who don't have any actual evidence in order to support their belief that something is "out there."

The star witness for Roswell is Marcel, who is criticized in his military record for exaggerating events. Marcel claims to have been an ace pilot who shot down five enemy aircraft, and who "personally" flew the debris from Roswell to the airfield—but Marcel was never a pilot, a fact that kept him from rising in the Air Force. He also claims to have a degree in physics (investigators proved this to be untrue), that he saw alien bodies (later proved to be dummies from a crash test), and that the "genuine" debris was switched for the weather balloon debris. Unfortunately for Marcel, the officer in charge of the debris, Colonel Thomas DuBose, is on record of having been in possession of the material the entire time, and has sworn it was never switched, as have the other two officers accompanying him.[21]

Like most mysteries, the entire story falls apart when you investigate the details. The military has opened all the files and concluded there is nothing to it. Kal Korff, in his thoroughly researched *The Roswell UFO Crash*, even interviewed Dr. Charles Moore, who launched the very balloon recovered at Roswell, and came to the conclusion that "the time has come for the UFO community to take an honest look at itself in the mirror concerning Roswell. If and when they ever decide to do this, they will see for the first time that they have two black eyes and a huge hole in their head. All of which have been self-inflicted."[22] So while UFOlogists *want* to believe something happened at Roswell, to this point they have no proof.

ALIEN ABDUCTIONS AND AUTOPSIES

The sensational publicity garnered from cases such as the alleged abduction of Travis Walton in November of 1975 in Arizona results in further interest and in further distortion of the truth. Jeff Wells, a reporter for the *National Enquirer*, was sent to Phoenix to interview Walton shortly after he claimed to have spent five days aboard an alien spacecraft. Wells reported that the most experienced polygraph examiner in Arizona gave Walton a lie detector test, but the results were not revealed in his article. "The kid had failed the test miserably," wrote Wells later. "The polygraph man said it was the plainest case of lying he'd seen in 20 years."[23]

Much of Walton's story developed during hypnosis sessions. "It seemed that the kid's father, who had deserted him as a child, had been a spaceship fanatic, and all his life the kid had wanted to ride in a spacecraft. He had seen something out there in the woods, some kind of an eerie light that had triggered a powerful hallucination…. There was no question of any kidnap by mushroom men. The kid needed medical help."[24]

The idea of alien "abductions" has become all the rage among UFOlogists, so that a researcher can barely keep up with the number of first-person books being published by those who claim to have met an alien. Yet *in no case has anyone proven beyond a reasonable doubt that they have been abducted.* All we have are their stories, sometimes wildly imaginative, but never accompanied by any proof. No one has come back with a book, tool, or gift from an alien. No one has had his or her picture taken with one. Often the claimants cannot even remember what happened unless they are in some subconscious state. So while there may be a mass of people claiming to have had encounters, the physical evidence of such meetings is entirely nonexistent.

Another popular story has been the "alien autopsy" film, shown on Fox TV in 1996. Purported to be from the late 1940s, the film claims to show doctors dissecting an alien body. But every surgeon who examined the film found it laughable—the "doctors" are hacking away with no plan, no skill in instrument handling, and no idea how to perform an autopsy.[25] Special-effects artists have also pronounced it a fake, noting that the alien's body was obviously a cast, since the muscles sag toward the toes and not the table, and pointing out small details such as the occupational health and safety signs on the wall of the room—something that came into existence in the late 1960s, and did not exist in the 1940s.[26] In July of 1997, Timothy Carr, the son of the man who produced the "alien autopsy," revealed that his father had a vivid imagination, often was unable to distinguish between fantasy and reality, and enjoyed telling alien tales to "make himself seem more interesting."[27] The autopsy, like nearly everything else associated with UFOs, is a hoax.

A SOURCE OF DECEIT

There seems to be widespread belief among UFOlogists that contact with space aliens will be a good thing, and lead mankind toward a brighter future. Yet many researchers, have noticed the exact opposite. Dr. Jacque Vallee, a world-renowned researcher and the model for "Lacombe" in Steven Spielberg's *Close Encounters of the Third Kind*, has put forth the notion that UFOs are engaging in a "worldwide enterprise of subliminal seduction." The various contacts that people claim to have had with aliens are nearly always negative, placing "human beings under the control of a strange force that is bending them in absurd ways, forcing them to play a role in a bizarre game of deception." Vallee goes on to note that UFOs are helping to create a new form of belief, an expectation of actual contact among large parts of the public. In turn this expectation makes millions of people hope for the imminent realization of that age-old dream: salvation from above, surrender to the greater power of some wise navigators of the cosmos."[28]

That theory goes right along with what other researchers have found: UFOs are often linked to occultic phenomena. Dr. David Swift, a sociologist at the University of Hawaii, has noted that the underlying message behind alien encounters are that they have some incredible knowledge and power. "This is an alluring message," Swift notes, "and it will become more attractive with each failure of conventional attempts to solve our complex problems. The thought of salvation from the sky is likely to grow in appeal."[29] Many observers have noted the dangers of this type of thinking, particularly when there are such scary parallels between "alien" philosophy and demonic thought.

John Ankerberg and John Weldon, in their book *The Facts on UFO's and Other Supernatural Phenomena*, note that the lessons offered by scores of abduction books can be summarized by five principles: 1) Biblical religion is false; 2) man must develop his psychic ability; 3) we are on the threshold of a New Age; 4) God and man are the same; and 5) the aliens are here to help us leave our old ways and adjust to this new truth.[30]

These ideas are clearly the same old lies that Satan has been prop-agating since the creation of the world, and it leads us to believe that he is using man's belief in UFO's for his own purposes of deception. One U.S. Air Force report, *UFO's and Related Subjects*, seems to come to that same conclusion, noting:

> *A large part of the available UFO literature is closely linked with mysticism and the metaphysical. It deals with subjects like mental telepathy, automatic writing and invisible entities as well as phenomena like poltergeist manifestations and "possession." Many of the UFO reports now being published in the popular press recount alleged incidents that are strikingly similar to demonic possession and psychic phenomena.[31]*

John Keel, considered by many researchers to be the world's fore-most expert on UFOs, has reached a similar conclusion. His firsthand research with those who have claimed a close encounter have led him to conclude that their experiences are "similar if not entirely identical to" those who have claimed contact with demons.[32] His collaborator, Trevor James, has observed that "a working knowledge of occult sci-ence...is indispensable to UFO investigation."[33]

This is a difficult issue, but if indeed people think aliens have come to "change our belief system,"[34] and if many participants experi-ence the same terror and troubles as those involved in Satanism,[35] then we must be extremely careful in how we handle the topic. Some Christian writers, including Ankerberg and Weldon, have theorized that UFOs are demonic manifestations, citing Whitley Streiber's story of alleged abduction,[36] and conclude that his tales of alien beings who enjoy inflicting pain on innocent victims, in addition to Streiber's ref-erence to them as "Lord and master of the air," constitute evidence for their spiritual source. That is an interesting theory, since most UFOlogists are involved in the occult, and the publishing trend has definitely been toward trances, spiritual contacts, and connections that smack of Satan's trickery. The writers of UFO books have moved toward accepting extraterrestrials as wiser than earthlings, so we suppose it's possible that someone is setting us up to listen to some sort of fake "space master." However, our basic premise is that most UFOs are completely explainable phenomena, and Satan is trying to use them to trick people into believing a lie.

UFOS AND SCIENCE

Taking all the evidence into consideration, we are willing to admit that there have been some sightings that are truly UFOs—that is, there were objects in the sky that were *unidentified*. But to date there is no evidence to suggest that they were spacecraft housing men from Mars. The fact that something is unidentified proves nothing, since the incidents in question might very well have been a rocket, satellite, or natural phenomena of some kind. Science requires credible evidence, and to this point, believers in UFOs have been unable to provide any such evidence.

Robert Sheaffer is a student of UFOs. He has spoken at conferences such as the National UFO Conference and the Smithsonian Institution UFO Symposium. Sheaffer wrote a book, *The UFO Verdict: Examining the Evidence*, in which he applied rigid scientific methods to the UFO question. The following was his conclusion.

I maintain that we have found the answer to the question "What are UFOs?" through a rigorous application of the scientific method. As an unexpected dividend, we find that we have also obtained the answer to the same question that might be raised about ESP, Bigfoot, the Loch Ness monster, "psychic" spoon-bending, and other dubious...phenomena. Our answer must be that UFOs do not exist.

This answer is certain to disappoint many people who are eager to find that our galaxy...is populated by all manner of exotic and exciting creatures. No one would be happier than I should it actually be discovered that our earth is paying host to strange creatures from some unknown planet or universe. But wishing will not make it so. And so long as we wish to adhere to the scientific method (that is, to make factual statements about the real world, as opposed to seeking subjective mystical insight), we are forced to face up to the conclusion that UFOs as real and distinct entities simply do not exist. Those who continue to insist otherwise are openly proclaiming their allegiance to a different worldview, one which, although popular, is incompatible with the worldview of science.[37]

One thing our investigations have taught us is that sensational stories of mysterious events usually lose their mystery under careful investigation. The absence of a possible explanation most often indicates the lack of sufficient information. It should not lead to rash conclusions about time warps, strange electromagnetic fields, and invasions from outer space.

Larry Kusche put it this way: "The withholding of information and the failure to use reliable sources are standard procedures among sensationalists, since full disclosure of information destroys the false mystery they are trying to build."[38] So be wary of jumping to conclusions when you read some incredible "real-life" mystery. If a story seems too unbelievable to be true, it probably isn't true.

CHAPTER ELEVEN

Stargazing

"Make sure you don't spend too much on pleasure and later regret it."

"Be careful on the highways today—there may be danger."

"You may not like what a fellow worker is doing."

"One who has problems expects your aid."

We've all seen this type of advice printed on the horoscope page of our daily newspapers. Researcher Lawrence Jerome has estimated that more than a billion people around the world "believe in and follow astrology to some extent."[1] There are more than a hundred magazines devoted to astrology full-time, thousands of books in print on the topic, and 175,000 people who earn at least a portion of their income as stargazers.[2] More than 500 newspapers in this country carry daily horoscopes, and a Gallup poll revealed that over 32 million Americans believe that "the stars influence their lives."[3] Another poll revealed that 10 percent of evangelical Christians give credence to the concept of stars determining our fate.[4]

Courses in astrology are offered on some high school and college campuses, many high-profile Hollywood stars have expressed a belief in it, and a 1988 CNN report claimed that at least 300 of the Fortune 500 companies "use astrologers in one way or another."[5] Prince Charles, heir to the throne of England, had his birth sign incorporated into the design of his crown. John West and Jan Toonder, in their best-selling book *The Case for Astrology*, claim that astrology now "enjoys a popularity unmatched since the decline of Rome."[6]

In 1988, former White House Chief of Staff Donald Regan shocked the Christian world by talking openly about the influence of astrology in the Reagan White House. While newspapers had reported that first lady Nancy Reagan had consulted an astrologer after her husband's assassination attempt, it was Regan who revealed the extent of her interest in stargazing, noting that the astrologer's advice was extended to "every major move and decision."[7]

Following his performances, André Kole is frequently asked his opinion of astrology. The questions come from Christians and non-Christians, old and young, educated and ignorant. There has been so much written on the subject that the average person thinks, "There *must* be something to it!" But even a cursory examination of the evidence will reveal the total lack of support for our lives being guided by the celestial bodies.

WHAT IS ASTROLOGY?

Astrology is the divination of the supposed influences which the stars and planets have on human affairs and earthly events. As far back as 2000 B.C. the Chinese were mapping the stars and planets as a means of divining the future, in order to determine the appropriate actions for each day. In 1800 B.C. the Babylonians believed the celestial bodies were gods who influenced all facets of life, and they attempted to correlate such things as famine, war, and death with the positions of the planets. Around 400 B.C. a Chaldean priest by the name of Berosus introduced astrology to Greece, where it flourished into the legitimate science of *astronomy*, which studies the motion and composition of celestial bodies without suggesting any connection between the stars and mankind.

When astrology was introduced to the Romans, it became an integral part of their political system. Naming the planets after their gods, stargazing "became such a political and psychological weapon that astrologers decided the fate of several emperors simply by convincing their opponents that the 'stars were with them' and that their conspiracies were 'fated' to succeed."[8] Astrology began as a genuine search for knowledge—an attempt to find some sort of overall plan of God hidden in the universe, to be ascertained by humans in order to determine the future. Each of the planets were assigned a god, and it was that relationship between planet and god that caused the ancients to examine the night skies.

"Such a notion is seductive because it seems to make life simpler. It attributes everything from interpersonal relationships to the destiny of nations to the stars. It appears to eliminate the understandable confusion offered by life, confusion created by the advances of new technology and by highly specialized knowledge that are beyond comprehension of the average person, and it seems to remove the need for personal responsibility, handing it all over to fate but allowing a glimpse into the future that might provide some advantage."[9]

The rise of modern sciences began to push astrology aside as an archaic bit of nonsense. Isidore, Archbishop of Seville around 620 A.D., made a point of distinguishing between "superstitious astrology" and the physical science of astronomy. The fatalistic perspective of astrology proved at odds with the theology of the Middle Ages. During the Renaissance, interest was revived due to the rediscovery of ancient Greek and Roman authors, but in 1490 Mirandola published his *Dispute of Astrology's Divinity*, which would be the standard work disputing astrology for more than 200 years. When the works of

Copernicus and Galileo proved the sun to be the center of the universe, the significance of astrology nearly died out.

It wasn't until Robert Smith published his *Manual of Astrology* in 1825, followed by Aleister Crowley's *Astrology* early in this century, that interest was revived. During the spiritualism craze of the 1920s, channeler Alice Bailey authored the three-volume *Treatise on Seven Rays*, which became wildly popular with those seeking a divine connection between life and the stars. When the famous psychologist Carl Jung announced that he was using astrology in his counseling work, it became not only popular but mainstream. The New Age movement has embraced astrology as truth, attempting to reconcile the spiritualistic aspects of it with modern science.

A PSEUDOSCIENCE

Take a walk through any bookstore today and you're sure to notice our culture's infatuation with astrology. People have become convinced that their lives are ordered by the stars, and that by studying them we can become better prepared for our futures. While understanding all the various ingredients of astrology would take volumes, Christians should at least understand some of the basic claims of astrology.

First, stargazers believe that *astrology is a science.* The principal tool an astrologer uses is a *horoscope,* or map of the heavens. This chart supposedly calculates the exact position of the heavenly bodies at an individual's moment of birth. There are 12 "houses" or sections, and each of these is represented by a constellation—Leo the lion, Pisces the fish, Taurus the bull, and so on. These 12 sections form what is called the "zodiac," and depending upon the time of year you were born, the earth would have been in a particular section of the zodiac. To further complicate the process, the planets in each section influence the various signs, sometimes for good and sometimes for bad. The way the planets line up with each other is also supposed to produce good or bad influences, and the days when the earth moves from one section to another can create a good or bad day, depending upon the signs.

Astrologists believe there are hidden, mysterious relationships between the celestial bodies and terrestrial life, and that these relationships influence our lives. You were "stamped" with your sign the moment you drew your first breath, and these signs are largely responsible for your personality and destiny.

If all this sounds confusing, it is. Though astrologists claim their "science" represents a well-ordered system of calculation, in reality it has no basis in science at all. Its foundation is rather antiquated, since it is based upon the mistaken notion that the earth is the center of the universe. The fact that the earth's axis has shifted so that the constellations are no longer in their former positions further diminishes any pretension of science. And the very idea that one-twelfth of the world's population share the same inherited characteristics is ludicrous. A horoscope may suggest that "today is a good day to make dietary changes," but those words would have to apply to an English lord, a New Guinea tribesman, and a Bolivian businessman.

Astrology is based upon the superstition that nature manifests personal characteristics in the lives of disparate people. For example, all those individuals born under the influence of Venus will manifest love and sensitivity. But the world doesn't work like that, and astrology cannot account for the fact that an airplane disaster kills people with all sorts of astrological signs, not just those sharing the same sign.

French researchers Michel and Francoise Gauquelin conducted statistical experiments in order to research the astrological claim that the signs of the zodiac exercise influence on people. After examining 52,188 personality traits taken from 2000 subjects, the Gauquelins concluded that "there is no correlation between character traits of the subjects and the signs under which they were born."[10] A 12-year follow up study of French sports champions, exploring the possibility of "warriors" being born under the planet of Mars, concluded that there was no evidence at all to support any astrological claim to sporting achievement.[11]

John McGervey's study of 16,634 scientists and 6475 politicians came to the same conclusion: There was no correlation between the individual's career success and his or her "sign."[12] A landmark study of

2978 couples proved that the supposed compatibility or incompatibility of astrological signs had no correlation to those couples who experienced good marriages and those who divorced.[13] And more than three dozen scientific studies have failed to indicate any causal relationship between the movement of the moon or planets and human behavior.[14]

Physicist Shawn Carlson conducted a double-blind test of astrology for *Nature* magazine in order to give some of the best astrologers in the country an opportunity to prove their "science." The astrologers were provided three personality profiles for each of 116 subjects—one was genuine, the other two were false. They were then told the birth date of each subject, and asked to choose the profile that best matched each individual based upon his or her horoscope. With a one-in-three chance of selecting the correct profile, the astrologers were confident they could pass the test. Their score: 33 1/3 percent—*exactly what they would have scored if they had made their choices by chance!* Carlson concluded that "the experiment clearly refutes the astrological hypothesis."[15] Sir John Maddox, editor of *Nature,* had this to say:

> *It turned out that the people couldn't recognize their own charts any more accurately than by chance...and that seems to me to be a perfectly convincing and lasting demonstration of how well this thing works in practice. My regret is that there [are] so many intelligent, able people wasting their time and, might I say, taking other people's money, in this hopeless cause.*[16]

THE "ART" OF ASTROLOGY

The most glaring problem with astrology is that no two astrologers will interpret their charts the same way. Stargazers like to claim that is because *astrology is an art,* which must rely upon intuitive skill as well as objective knowledge. This second claim creates a beautiful "out" for anyone interpreting signs and planets, for it allows the interpreter to make almost any claim imaginable. One famous astrologer puts it this way:

"[Doing a reading] involves interpretation and art, too, in terms of what meaning is assigned to the data. These meanings are constantly evolving and changing—they are tested and revised."[17]

In researching this book, we asked three professional astrologers to give us a reading for the day, and we received three distinctly different responses. Though each of them offered basically general information, one suggested it would be "a bad day to make major decisions" while another offered almost exactly the opposite advice. You would think that, with 4000 years of development, if there were any truth to astrology there would be some sort of coherent system of interpreting events. Yet one of the readers spent most of her time talking to us about making fashion decisions, while another talked at length about travel. It left us thinking that these "experts" were being awfully subjective, trying to find something that we liked.

So doing an astrological reading may be an art, or it may simply be a stab in the dark. For example, is you were to ask five different astrologers what different areas (called "houses") of the zodiac represent, you'll more than likely get five different answers. One will claim that the first "house" represents money, but another says that it represents personality—and of course, the logic upon which any of them make a claim is nonsensical. If astrological readings were really based upon years of human observation, one would think the various proponents would at least agree with one another.

The scientific evidence against astrology is extremely conclusive: It simply isn't true. Yet the response of stargazers is to ignore the facts. When one researcher analyzed more than a hundred books on astrological readings, he found 2375 specific adjectives to apply to the various sun-signs. Yet they overlapped one another badly, and in trying to get astrologers to create clear categories, he found that the various readers sorted them at random. In the words of the researcher, "I often get the feeling, after talking to astrologers, that they live in a mental fantasy world, a kind of astrological universe where no explanations outside of astrological ones are permitted, and that if the events of the real world do not accord with astrological notions or predictions, then yet another astrological technique will have to be invented to explain it!"[18]

In recent years, stargazers have begun talking quite a bit about numerology, claiming that the interpretation of the zodiac is mathematically based. Yet the subjectivity of the entire system argues against astrology being founded on any sort of genuine science—and even if it were, this would still offer no valid reason for believing that the movement of planets affects our lives. So this "art" is nothing but hokum, masquerading as science.

To truly appreciate the "art" of astrology, check out the following titles we found at a New Age bookstore: *Your Dog's Astrological Horoscope; The Cat Horoscope Book; Astro-Power at the Racetrack; Cooking with Astrology; The Astrologer's Guide to Counseling; Find Your Mate Through Astrology; An Introduction to Political Astrology; Homosexuality in the Horoscope; Sex and the Outer Planets; Financial Astrology; Hindu Astrology; Asteroid Goddesses; Astrology in the Bible; A Guide to Cabalistic Astrology; Astrology and Past Lives;* and *Astrology, Alchemy, and the Tarot.* Apparently there is no area of expertise to which astrology doesn't speak!

LIVING BY THE STARS

The third claim astrologers make is that *astrology can guide lives.* Not only does your "sign" determine your mental and physical attributes, but supposedly the movement of the celestial bodies influences your life and can offer you direction for the future. Thus astrologers look to the stars to protect them, predict their future, and bring them success. As John Ankerberg puts it:

> *Astrology offers people the belief that they can "control" their own destinies, and it also provides them a ready-made justification for failure or sin. Astrology offers the false hope that through the "knowledge" of the stars, one can manipulate people or events for his own welfare or selfish desires. Astrology specializes in answering almost all the questions people ask concerning the future. In fact, it claims to offer power over life and*

death, love, sex and relationships, money and finances, personal health, and happiness.... Above all, astrology sells hope—and today people need hope desperately! In every age of social breakdown, the masses of people have turned to the occult and superstition for solace and counsel.... Astrology is popular because it claims to offer people hope through the knowledge of the manipulation of the influences of the planets and stars. With this secret knowledge, people believe they have greater control over themselves as well as present and future circumstances. [19]

Of course, this puts astrology in the same camp as reading tea leaves, examining palms, and feeling the bumps on one's head. Astrology is an attempt at divination, plain and simple—and that links it to all the other phony schemes that Satan has developed to keep people from turning to God.

Yet in offering "guidance" to people, astrologers are often guilty of manipulating people. Science writer Lawrence Jerome concluded his study, entitled *Astrology Disproved,* by saying that astrology is "nothing more than a magical system for controlling others."[20] Sociologist Edward Moody went even farther, referring to those involved with astrology as "pre-Satanists," since they are really seeking a way to gain power over others. "Those who eventually become Satanists usually have begun with astrology."[21]

Since the premise behind astrology is to somehow secure supernatural knowledge and power, it should be viewed as an occultic practice. Webster's dictionary actually defines it as such, because it employs secret practices and relies on divination. Any astrologer will tell you that his or her practice seems to work best when he is psychically sensitive to spiritual forces—a blatant connection to the occult.

However, astrology wants to be seen as a science, and several spokesmen for astrology have insisted it has nothing to do with the occult or alleged psychic power. For example, Carroll Righter, who creates some of the horoscopes that appear in the nation's newspapers, "feels strongly that astrology should not be considered [part of] the occult."[22] Righter insists he is "a scientist." Another influential astrologer, Charles Carter, claims that "astrology does not involve any form of psychism."[23]

Yet from its very beginnings, astrology has been linked to spiritism and paganism. As a matter of fact, astrology is often the introduction to a wide variety of spiritistic influences. Edgar Cayce, the medium who claimed to channel spirits, was a huge proponent of astrology. Helena Blavatsky, psychic fraud and mystic, also promoted astrology. In *The Case for Astrology*, West and Toonder go so far as to state that astrology "owes its revival" to Ms. Blavatsky and her Theosophical Movement. Many famous astrologers of our own day, including Daniel Logan, Marcus Allen, and Sybil Leek, are deeply tied into witchcraft and other occultic practices. In *A Manual of Occultism*, Sepharial states: "The astrologic art is held to be the key to all the occult sciences."[24]

In every case we have investigated, the astrologer considered himself or herself "psychic." Some claimed to get information from spirit guides, while others spoke of "impressions" that "led" to conclusions. In talking about horoscopes, several astrologers mentioned their "intuitive" powers, and some even advocated going into mediumistic trances to garner special knowledge. This all points to the fact that astrology, even in the simple horoscopes printed in the paper, is nothing more than a form of divination.

GOD AND ASTROLOGY

The Bible warns Christians to stay away from astrology, since it is a form of divination and *leads people into contact with Satan* : "Let no one be found among you who...practices divination or sorcery, interprets omens, engages in witchcraft, or casts spells, or who is a medium or spiritist or who consults the dead," the Lord warned the Jews in Deuteronomy 18:10,11. God's people are to know and trust Him, and when they searched the skies for some sort of "sign," it proved they were trusting in something else.

*"Keep on, then, with your magic spells and with
your many sorceries,
which you have labored at since childhood.
Perhaps you will succeed, perhaps you will cause
terror.
All the counsel you have received has only worn
you out!
Let your astrologers come forward, those stargazers
who make predictions month by month,
let them save you from what is coming upon you.
Surely they are like stubble;
the fire will burn them up.
They cannot even save themselves from the power
of the flame....
Each of them goes on in his error;
there is not one that can save you (Isaiah 47:12-15).*

The word of God sees astrology as being a waste of time—something utterly futile and useless that pulls people away from the truth. It leads people toward worshiping the stars and planets, so that men and women are worshiping the *created* rather than the *Creator*. That is why Moses warned us by saying, "When you look up to the sky and see the sun, the moon and the stars—all the heavenly array—do not be enticed into bowing down to them and worshiping things the Lord your God has apportioned to all the nations under heaven."[25]

To do so is to worship demons, according to 1 Corinthians 10:20, and it will result in separation from God. The New Testament prophet Stephen said that when the nation of Israel got involved with idols, "God turned away and gave them over to the worship of the heavenly bodies."[26] Those involved in astrology do not recognize the heavenly Father for who He is, but instead substitute some sort of secretive power in hopes of tapping into it. In essence they are worshiping *nature*—the stars and planets, rather than the One who flung the stars into space and set the planets spinning in their orbits.

By the same token, astrologers reject the biblical portrait of Jesus in order to worship him as nothing more than an enlightened man. Marcus Allen, in his *Astrology for the New Age*, talks about Christ having "all seven ancient planets" in just the right houses, so that He "initiated the Age of Pisces, which is now coming to an end with the dawning of the Age of Aquarius, which is initiated by the second coming of the Christ Life within *all* of us.... In the Age of Aquarius, everyone is the Avatar, everyone is tuned into their higher self."[26]Of course, this is all utter rot, but it is interesting to see how astrologers begin to combine their supposed "science" with their religious views.

In a similar way, it is easy to see how the problems of sin and salvation are re-shaped within the boundaries of astrology. Rather than man being lost in sin, in need of a personal Savior, astrology teaches that man is simply out of harmony with the divine forces of the universe. It argues that salvation is not found in forgiveness, but in enlightenment to the patterns of the universe. The Bible, on the other hand, teaches that mankind has chosen to reject God and commit sin. Salvation is a gift of God, offered through His Son, Jesus Christ, who died on the cross to pay the penalty for our sins. When men and women believe on the Lord and surrender to Him, their sins are forgiven and they gain eternal life.

DID DANIEL READ THE STARS?

Perhaps the most common misapplication of Scripture in astrological circles is the claim that the prophet Daniel was involved with astrology. That argument, which has been propagated by nearly every major astrological writer, is based upon two facts. First, that Daniel was able to interpret the king's dreams in the Book of Daniel, chapters 2 and 4. Second, that Daniel was in charge of the "wise men" of Babylon, which the text clearly says included astrologers. Based on these two facts, New Age writers have concluded that Daniel was involved with stargazing.

The problem is that *any* coherent reading of the text reveals just the opposite. Daniel pointed out the utter failure of the Babylonian astrologers to interpret the king's dream, instead relying on the *one true God* to supply him with the information he needed. Indeed, Daniel was at odds with many of those wise men, for they were the ones who arranged for him to be thrown into the lion's den a few years later. The story of Daniel is not one of astrology, but of the *failure of astrology and the victory of God.*

In fact, astrology has nothing at all to do with traditional Christianity, though many astrologers claim otherwise. They argue that they are "believers," but they reject biblical claims of Christianity in order to espouse a "New Age Christianity" that is closer to the occult than it is to the historical faith. Famed psychic Jeane Dixon, a lifelong Catholic, even said: "I have never experienced any conflict between my faith and the guidance I receive from my church on the one hand, and the knowledge I find in the stars on the other...actually, much of what I know about astrology I learned from a Jesuit priest."[27]

Dixon went on to link each of the 12 apostles with the 12 signs of the zodiac, and noted that "astrology fits into God's plan for mankind by helping us understand both our talents and our shortcomings.... We will be much better equipped to turn everything we are to the service of the Lord."[28] But God specifically called the practice of stargazing evil. The thought that it can somehow be turned into something good by clearing away the occultic influences is wrong. The Lord didn't say to clean it up; He said to *stay away from it.* Christians are to stay away from *all* forms of divination, and astrology in particular because it opens us up to idol worship and other forms of evil.

Christian researcher John Ankerberg has explored the issue of astrology and concluded that it is a door through which Satan draws people into other psychic snares. It encourages Christians who participate to worship idols—something we are warned about repeatedly.

Worship is more than simply bowing down to something. It involves that which we serve and grant our *devotion* to, that which we praise and hold in awe, that which we acknowledge as directing our lives, and that which we reverence. Christian astrologers may not literally bow down to the stars, but neither do other astrologers. Both the heavenly objects and astrology itself fit the characteristics of worship in the lives of astrologers, Christian or not.

The bottom line is this: Astrology doesn't work, isn't scientific, is tied to the occult, and is prohibited in Scripture. It can lead to all sorts of spiritual and psychological damage, and it is the most common door through which people enter and explore other psychic phenomena. If there were any merit to astrology, God would not have barred His people from participating. As it is, God has spoken: Christians should stay away from the practice of astrology.

CHAPTER TWELVE

Amazing Operations

The first reports were of wonderment: People in the Philippines were going to certain "doctors," having major surgery without anesthesia, then walking out of the clinic in a matter of minutes without so much as a scar. It was a known fact that many people had experienced healing—*and the surgeons were using the Bible and urging their patients to pray and trust God.*

"What should we make of this?" asked a prominent Christian leader in that country. "What these men are doing seems so good, yet we aren't sure if they're really gifted by God, or if they are tools of Satan meant to deceive us." He went on to tell how these surgeons could make a small incision in the body using only their fingers, then reach through it to remove diseased tissue and organs. When they removed their hands, the skin closed, leaving no scar. André could not give the man an explanation, but it sounded like some similar "operations" he had observed in Africa and Latin America, so he promised to attempt an investigation when he visited the Philippines later that year.

The area of faith healing is one that has intrigued people for years. In the course of André's travels around the world, he has observed a wide variety of healers from various cultures and religions. His desire has been to try to determine *which* healings are truly miraculous, and which, if any, of the healers have genuine supernatural powers. André's research has yielded some interesting insights into the methods of various faith healers, as well as the innate healing properties of the human body. In this chapter we will concentrate on his research of psychic surgery, and later in the book we will deal more specifically with the subject of faith healing in general.

THE MIRACLE SURGEONS

In almost every part of the world there are stories of miraculous healers. One of the most unusual was Jose Pedro de Freitas, a Brazilian peasant known throughout the world as "Arigo," the surgeon with the rusty knife. For more than 20 years he saw 300 patients a day, five days a week. Each patient received a diagnosis, a therapy, and a written prescription. His normal method of treatment was to take a pocketknife, jab it into the body of the patient, twist it around, then reach in and pull out a growth or diseased tissue. Patients walked away without a scratch, and many of them claimed to be healed.

Johanna Michaelsen tells much the same story in *The Beautiful Side of Evil*. She spent 14 months as the assistant to "Pachita," a psychic surgeon practicing in Mexico. During that time Michaelsen claims to have witnessed tumors being pulled from bodies, eyes yanked out and plugged back in, and even damaged vertebrae pulled out and reinserted—all without incisions or painkillers.

André Kole's first contact with psychic surgery was in Liberia, in 1968. Since then he has witnessed more than 300 operations in Asia and Latin America, and has even performed his own demonstrations of psychic surgery on television. The best demonstrations he has ever seen were in the Philippines.

One summer, a few months after a friend had asked him about the alleged healings in the Philippines, David Aikman, a foreign correspondent for *Time* magazine, asked André to help him investigate several psychic surgeons in Baguio and Manila. During a tour of the island, the two men took some time between shows to observe seven different healers, five of whom were among those most frequently mentioned in magazine and newspaper articles about spiritual healers. During this time André witnessed more than 50 operations performed by the seven healers. These men, thinking he was a newspaper reporter, were very open and cooperative. They even asked him to *assist* in some operations, which gave André the best possible vantage point for studying their actions.

We first visited a plain, white, one-story building. Some 200 people were lined up from the door and down the street, waiting to see the surgeon. The photographer from *Time* magazine and I were invited into the operating room. I felt anxious, not knowing what to expect, but the doctor, dressed in a colorful native shirt, immediately put me at ease and asked me to assist him. He was operating on a woman's back, removing a small cyst just below her shoulders.

The doctor began by holding my right index finger in the air and moving it in a short line about 12 inches above the cyst. As he did, what looked like a small incision, about an inch long, appeared. A numb feeling came over me when I saw that cut and realized it was genuine. I knew that if the incision closed and the woman walked out of the clinic without any scar, I truly would have witnessed something supernatural.

Quickly the doctor reached into the cut and removed a small mass of material that looked like gristle. Then he took a piece of cotton on a stick, dipped it in coconut oil, *lit it, and cauterized the cut; he did not heal the incision supernaturally. The whole operation took about three minutes.*[1]

It didn't take long for a world-class magician to discover that the doctor used a very clever form of sleight-of-hand. The cut that André's finger seemed to make actually was done with a small razorblade hidden in the healer's fingers. He concealed in his other hand the supposed diseased tissue, before apparently pulling it from the patient's body.

Strictly from the magician's point of view, apart from the moral and ethical issues, watching these healers was fascinating. They performed their fake operations using some of the most clever sleight-of-hand André had ever seen. Their incredible dexterity was similar to the ability of Ben Chavez, a Philippine magician with nimble fingers and a quality of manual dexterity almost unequaled in the magic world. Before his death, Chavez trained some of the world's best-known magic performers, and he taught André Kole almost everything he knows about sleight of hand. It quickly became clear that these miracle healers were not surgeons at all but rather a group of men who had learned a few magical illusions that eventually deceived millions.

HOW THEY DID IT

Most of the operations were performed on the abdominal area. Sometimes the surgeon made the operation more dramatic by making a small cut and covering it with a coin. Then he would take a cotton ball soaked in coconut oil, lay it on the coin, and light it. Next he would cover it with a small glass, creating a suction that drew blood into the glass. While the people watched the procedure, the "healer" secretly secured a piece of animal tissue in his fingers. When he removed the glass and coin, he rubbed his fingers in the blood and made it appear the tissue was being removed from the incision. It would be very difficult for most people to detect the clever slight-of-hand techniques these men were using, and even harder when their hands were covered in dark blood.

Most of the time the doctor did not actually cut the patient, yet his fingers appeared to mysteriously reach through the skin and into the body—usually the stomach area. As André watched carefully, he could see that there was no opening in the skin—just a recessed area where the surgeon pushed down, forming a small cup or depression. By bending his fingers, the surgeon *appeared* to push his hand in much deeper than he actually did.

That left a mystery: When there was no incision, where did the blood come from? A little investigation revealed that the healers had put animal blood in a refrigerator to coagulate. They then took some animal tissue, added a little of the blood, and wrapped cotton around it until it formed a ball. When it dried, the ball could be handled without getting messy. A bowl of water was always near the operating table. By quickly dipping this cotton in the water and gently massaging with it in the stomach area, blood "appeared," and the animal tissue was available for quick removal as a "tumor." André later learned that some surgeons used a red dye made from betel nuts, rather than real blood, because it was less messy.

It was interesting to see the doctors' various procedures. Two of the doctors hid their loads (that is, the tissue which would appear to be removed from the patient) underneath the table. Two others put their loads in the open side of the pillowcase on which the patient was lying. By simply stroking the pillow, the doctor could steal away his secret ingredient for making blood and tissue appear. One doctor got his load in the cotton when his nurse handed it to him, and another wore a loose shirt and hid his loads under the bottom hem.

A popular operation involved removing an individual's eye. The healer began by poking around the patient's eye, causing it to bulge from its socket. As he covered it with cotton, he appeared to take out the eye, but actually produced a cow or goat's eye. After washing it off and examining it, he supposedly replaced it. This procedure would fool those taking a quick glance, but anyone who saw repeated performances would start to catch on. One doctor had used his animal eye so much that it had turned green!

MIRACLES OR MAGIC?

While viewing all these operations, plus a couple hundred more in various parts of the world and on film, André never witnessed any evidence of supernatural healing ability. In every case the surgeon used sleight-of-hand. Never was anyone cut open, nor did the surgeon actually insert his hands into them. Regardless of how genuine it appeared, it was all a trick.

Some people have said that the operations *must* be real because they have seen movies of them and could not see any tricks. André's reply: Of *course* they could not see any tricks! If an average person—that is, one not trained in sleight-of-hand techniques—could discover how the operations were done by watching them on film, the healers would never have allowed the cameras into the operating rooms in the first place. Several of André's performances are on film, and hundreds of copies are used around the world. People can slow the projector, or even examine the film frame by frame, yet still not be able to discern how he performs his illusions. As André has pointed out, "I would not have put my effects on film if they could!"

In fact, what people are seeing when they watch a psychic surgeon is an experienced magician at work. He or she cannot perform miracles. He has no supernatural power. What he has is showmanship, some sleight-of-hand skill, and a heart so cold that he is willing to steal money from people with serious illnesses.

We've heard people claim that the accuracy of these doctors' diagnoses is evidence of their powers. Indeed they often do make correct diagnoses, which usually are educated guesses resulting from years of experience. A good psychic surgeon can "read" a person and size up a problem very quickly. When he isn't sure, he will couch his guesses with general statements that sound impressive but have little substance. If you kept a record of their diagnoses, you would find that they *miss* at least as many as they hit.

Soon after his experience in the Philippines, André was asked to be an expert witness for the Federal Trade Commission in a case against several travel agencies in the Pacific Northwest. The agencies were promoting special tours to visit these healers in the Philippines. Unfortunately, some people never made it home, and others died soon after they returned, experiencing no benefits from their treatments.

Jerry MacGregor's grandmother was one of the patients. She had cancer, and her American doctors had tried everything. In a last-ditch effort for a cure, she spent her life savings on a trip to the Philippines. The psychic surgeon she visited performed the operation exactly as André described, pulling out small chunks of tissue he explained were "tumors." He then told her to read her Bible every day and pronounced her cured. She died in the hospital a few months later from the cancer, her money wasted.

That is what disturbed André the most about these "doctors." He saw people who needed genuine medical attention come to the psychic surgeons, and leave without receiving the treatment they required. One young boy had burned his nose, and it was swollen to the size of a tennis ball. The psychic healer claimed to take care of it, but the swelling never went down. Another patient had his appendix "removed" three times before a regular doctor finally removed it surgically. The bottom line is that these surgeons were deceiving people, and they knew it.

Many of these healers appeared to be very sincere. Some felt they were helping people believe in God, and they prayed over their patients and read from the Bible. But they also told people that if they didn't have enough faith, they wouldn't be healed. The impression was given that there would have been healing if only the patient had more faith. That gave the doctor a good excuse when a person wasn't healed: *it wasn't his fault, but the patient's.* The impression was given that there would have been healing if only the patient had more faith.

THOSE WHO ARE HEALED

After viewing the operations, André interviewed a number of the patients, asking them if they were helped. Many answered "I think so" or "I hope so." Yet as he went down the line of people waiting to see the healer, he noticed many returning with the same problems they had brought during previous weeks. Some had the same operation per-formed on them week after week, continually hoping to generate enough faith for a cure.

To be fair, a few people were genuinely helped or even cured by these surgeries. The percentage of people cured, however, is much lower than an average doctor would cure, regardless of what the glow-ing articles written in the tabloids would lead one to believe. And the healings did not result from the operations, which were fake, but from the *operations' psychological effect on people who believe they are real*. In other words, some people believed in the healing properties of the psy-chic surgeons, so they were healed. It might be because the initial problem was psychosomatic, or it might be due to the remarkable cur-ative powers of the mind. "Visualization treatment" programs have sprung up around the world in recent years, using nothing more than good thoughts and the patients' belief to help themselves get better. The truth is that often it doesn't work. But there are certainly times when it does work, depending on the nature of the illness.

Before we explore healing, it is important to differentiate between *functional* illness and *organic* illness. As Dr. Eric Chico has said,

> A *functional* disease is one associated with a change in function of a bodily organ or tissue without any tissue damage. An *organic* disease is one associated with a demonstrable change in a bodily organ or tissue.

> Therefore, in dealing with functional diseases such as high blood pressure, addictions, low back pain syn-drome, or most headaches there is no demonstrable tis-sue damage, yet the organ or tissue is certainly not functioning as it should. By contrast, organic diseases such as broken bones, paralysis from severed nerves, congenital malformations, or coronary artery disease evidence a very clear change in the tissue. Medical sci-ence can demonstrate these changes through the use of X-ray evaluation, nerve condition studies....

Symptoms are indeed present in both. The difference is whether there is demonstrable tissue damage or not. It is the difference between a painful arm being caused by sprain/strain or caused by a broken bone.

One additional point we need to understand is that in all diseases, both functional and organic, there exists an emotional component. It is this emotional component that elicits a true physiologic response such as seen in the placebo effect. This response, along with the fact that many symptoms are very much subjective, is responsible for patients experiencing decreased pain with a broken bone, decreased insulin requirements in diabetes, decreased frequency of chest pain or pressure episodes in coronary artery disease, etc.[2]

Therefore, a sore back or a breathing problem are susceptible to healing suggestions, because a person who has been told he is healed can suddenly feel somewhat better. Even serious illnesses can sometimes respond to this sort of psychological healing, particularly if the disease is one of degree. For instance, we have seen patients with multiple sclerosis claim to be somewhat better after visiting a faith healer. They are not cured, but the placebo effect allows them to "feel" better for a while. Organic illnesses, on the other hand, will not respond to suggestions. Broken bones will not respond to a mental suggestion, nor will a brain hemorrhage be healed.

"In the highly festive and emotionally charged atmosphere of a faith-healing service, the brain can be stimulated to release endorphins into the nervous system which science says are pain suppressants 200 times more potent than morphine. This is why people can honestly say 'the pain is gone' and sincerely believe they are healed—until the effect wears off hours or days later."[3] The pain might be lessened momentarily, but true healing will not take place unless the patient receives proper medical treatment.

HOW ARE THEY HEALED?

One of the best studies on this phenomenon was done by William A. Nolen, M.D. In his book *Healing: A Doctor in Search of a Miracle*, Nolen examined hundreds of volumes and visited several of the best-known faith healers, including several Filipino psychic surgeons, looking for "adequately documented examples of cures that could not reasonably be explained except in terms of miraculous powers."[4] He could not find one such case.

In the final chapters of his book, Nolen describes the healing process, which he concludes is a mystery: "We doctors don't do the healing; the *body* does. And even though, by examining specimens of tissue in various stages of healing, we know something of how healing occurs, we don't as yet have any idea how to control it. We put things back together; the body—God, if you prefer—heals."[5]

So how are these people healed? Nolen writes: "It is possible that 'healers,' by their machinations, their rituals, their sheer charisma, stimulate patients so that they heal more rapidly than they otherwise might; charismatic doctors do the same. In all probability, this is why doctors who have warm rapport with their patients seem to get better results than doctors who treat their patients briskly and impersonally."[6]

The whole point of Nolen's book is that certain illnesses successfully lend themselves to treatment of this type. Others will naturally, over the course of time, heal without any outside help. And the doctor explains that at least *half of all illnesses* fall into these two categories—so any psychic healer automatically should have a success rate of at least 50 percent!

In his book, Dr. Nolen explains that the real problem people face is with *organic* diseases, such as heart attacks, infections, gallstones, hernias, slipped discs, broken bones, congenital deformities, and cancers of all kinds. He writes:

> **These are the diseases that faith healers, even the most charismatic, cannot cure. When they attempt to do so— and they all fall into this trap, since they know and care**

nothing of the differences between functional and organic diseases—they tread on very dangerous ground. When healers treat serious organic diseases they are responsible for untold anguish and unhappiness; this happens because they keep patients away from possibly effective and lifesaving help. The healers become killers.

Search the literature, as I have, and you will find no documented cures by healers of gallstones, heart disease, cancer, or any other serious organic disease. Certainly, you'll find patients temporarily relieved of their upset stomachs, their chest pains, their breathing problems; and you will find healers, and believers, who will interpret this interruption of symptoms as evidence that the disease is cured. But when you track the patient down and find out what happened later, you always find the "cure" to have been purely symptomatic and transient. The underlying disease remains.[7]

Several doctors actually have endorsed certain psychic healers, while recognizing the absurdity of the operations. They are taken in because they are not trained in the field of deception. It would take too much time and space to describe all the variations and techniques these healers use, but the average person could never detect their trickery. It takes a magician to spot a magician.

Many people are deceived because they try to explain the operations in terms of science, psychology, theology, or medicine. But that actually *assists* the healers by further drawing attention away from their sleight-of-hand.

The late Tony Agpaoa, probably the best-known Filipino surgeon, sometimes stretched a thin piece of goat intestine over the patient before making an incision. Cutting through it created the illusion of cutting the skin and caused a snapping sound. Then he reached down into the incision and pulled out what he claimed was a diseased organ, such as an appendix, tumor, or damaged vertebra. He disposed of the extra piece of skin in a bucket below the table, and left no trace of an incision on the patient, since no cut was made. It was a remarkable sleight-of-hand performance—but it was a trick, aimed at fooling someone who needed genuine medical treatment. Some people were cured after seeing Agpaoa, but it wasn't because of his manipulations.

THE QUESTION OF FAITH

Over the years, a number of quack remedies have gained popularity, usually because somebody made unsubstantiated claims about a new "wonder treatment." For example, in the 1890s Dr. Wilhelm Fliess proposed that there are three cycles to each person's life—physical, emotional, and intellectual—and claimed that each cycle had a different length. He further argued that these three cycles go up and down according to the day you were born, and that you ought to make choices with your three cycles in mind. So a "down" day on your intellectual chart is a bad day for taking a test. Fliess even went so far as to predict that the most critical day of a person's life will occur at the age of 58 years and 68 days. He created complicated graphs and charts to buttress his claims, gave it the scientific-sounding name *"biorhythms,"* and it has been defended by pseudoscientists ever since. Studies have shown there is absolutely no value to the theory. It's an ancient form of divination, dressed up in modern-day clothes.

Applied kinesiology is another diagnostic myth that has endured into our modern era. AK, as it is usually called, consists of having a patient stick the fingers of one hand into a substance, while holding the other arm out straight. The doctor then presses down on the straight arm. Adherents claim that when the patient sticks fingers into a harmful substance, the other arm will easily depress, but when the fingers are poked into a harmless substance, the outstretched arm will be stronger because the body is not weakened by the vibrations of the negative substance. "In the United States, in response to our increasing demand for nonsense, expensive courses are now being offered to doctors and dentists in which AK is taught to them as a diagnostic tool, and many otherwise sensible medical professionals have taken these courses and have accepted the effect as genuine."[8] But all tests have shown it to be utter nonsense. The effect is due entirely to the expectations of the doctor, which has been proven in blind studies. Yet AK has thrived, particularly among dieters and the health-conscious.

Chiropractic medicine can be very beneficial to those with back problems, and has proven to help relieve muscle spasms, but many exaggerated claims have been made in recent years about chiropractic treatment curing everything from asthma to AIDS. The founders, David Palmer and his son B.J., claimed that misalignments of the spine cause most illnesses. In recent years we have seen a huge increase in the claims of chiropractors, with the attendant references to applied kinesiology, biorhythms, and every other form of quackery. On top of that, what used to be advertised as a cure is now generally regarded as long-term therapy, in which patients return time after time for the same problem. The American Medical Association has weighed in by labeling chiropractic "an irrational, unscientific approach to disease causation."

Homeopathy has a similar history. Begun in the early 1800s by a man who believed all diseases sprung from sexual sources, it claims that a medicine which produces certain symptoms will cure like symptoms. In other words, it you've got a stomachache, take a medicine that makes your stomach ache and you'll get better. Of course, the "medicine" doled out is usually watered down so much that it offers nothing more powerful than a glass of drinking water, which is supposed to bring about vibrations that heal the body. The Royal Family of England maintains a homeopathist, and in recent years those purporting to be doing homeopathic research have made claims about the healing powers of magnets and copper wire. Like all such nonscientific healing, it might offer a placebo effect, but it does nothing organic to an individual.

More than anything else, these are a form of magic, requiring the faith of the patient to work. In recent years the medical community has been inundated with crackpot ideas, many of them with their roots in occultic beliefs. People practicing the *healing touch*, in which a healer straightens out a patient's "energy waves," and *acupuncture*, in which needles interrupt the flow of the patient's *qi gong*, are examples of occultic-based healing. They rely on a nonbiblical (and nonscientific) philosophy, which claims that eternal energy flows through the universe and into our bodies. Some psychics, such as Edgar Cayce, have relied on this same sort of twaddle, pretending to make diagnoses based on his divine connections. He was generally wrong, though he always claimed he was right, and he figured that the patients' faith in his words would heal most of them.

André writes,

> "Because of my experience, I am very skeptical of reports about miraculous healing. People describe all sorts of spectacular feats that the healers could not possibly have done. Most operations are relatively minor, and exaggerated reports about cancer being cured, ruptured disks being repaired, and gallstones disappearing simply can't be substantiated.

> "For years during my show I cut my wife in half, then apparently divided the two parts of her body and walked through the center. I would have her move her head on one side of the stage, and move her feet on the other side. People were baffled by the effect. They didn't know how I did it, but they knew that it must be a trick because I called myself a magician and performed it on a stage.

> "But suppose I called myself a *surgeon* and performed the same procedure in an operating room, smearing some blood and using medical terms in a serious manner. If I claimed to correct an internal problem while she was divided, and even produced some tissue for effect, many people would think they were witnessing something supernatural. It certainly would be far more dramatic than anything these psychic healers produce—but it would be just as fraudulent."

Don't waste your time and money on somebody claiming to heal through miraculous powers. A successful appendectomy depends on the surgeon's skill, not the patient's faith. Jesus warned of the consequences of falsely claiming supernatural power: "Not all who sound religious are really godly people. They may refer to me as 'Lord,' but they still won't get to heaven. For the decisive question is whether they obey my Father in heaven. At the Judgment many will tell me, 'Lord, Lord, we told others about you and used your name to cast out demons and to do many other great miracles.' But I will reply, 'You have never been mine. Go away, for your deeds are evil.'"[9]

CHAPTER THIRTEEN

Deception in the Name of God

The service was underway as André slipped into the back of the packed auditorium and glanced around, looking for a seat. Finding none, he moved toward a group of people in wheelchairs and stood among them to observe the unfolding events.

The audience eagerly listened to the 200-voice choir, accompanied by a five-piece band. Some patients tried to keep time with their feet or hands. One child was attached to an intravenous tube that hung from a pole on his chair. A quadriplegic had a motor-driven chair he controlled with a lever in the palm of his right hand. Another patient, in the advanced stages of multiple sclerosis, leaned over far to one side. All of them had a look of expectation that this night would mark their return to health.

After enthusiastic singing by the congregation, an offertory, and a rousing solo by a young gospel singer, the faith healer came on stage.

"God wants to do a miracle in *your* life tonight!" he exclaimed. The more than 3000 people present applauded. "God is in the miracle-working business! If you're here tonight and you have problems with your finances, God wants to heal your finances. If you're here because of problems in your marriage, God wants to heal your marriage. And if you're here tonight because you are sick physically, I am here to tell you that *God wants to heal you.*"

The crowd was ecstatic with those words. Some raised their hands and shouted "Praise God!" and "Hallelujah!" while others leaned forward in their seats to catch every word. The speaker held a well-worn Bible in his hands and spoke confidently about the miracles it recorded. He claimed that across the country today, wherever he spoke, he saw God perform miracles just as He had in the time of Christ. He proclaimed that tonight some people with cancer were going to be healed. Others who suffered chronic back pain were going to be cured. And some who had debilitating illnesses were going to experience healing. "I do not heal anyone," he emphasized. "It is the Holy Spirit who heals."

When he finished preaching, the wonder-worker invited all who desired healing to go into the aisles surrounding the auditorium, so that workers could pray for them and anoint them with oil. For nearly an hour the auditorium hummed with prayer and counseling. Finally the crowd began to thin. Many left rejoicing in the great work that God had done in their lives. Others left with tears in their eyes as they pushed away their crippled children. Not one of those with a visible deformity had been healed. The faces that only an hour ago had shone with anticipation now betrayed a deep and bitter dejection. They had come hoping for a miracle, but left bewildered, wondering why God had not healed them after the preacher's assurance that they could expect to be healed.

A SUPERNATURAL WORK?

Why can some people give dramatic testimonies about God's healing, while others are left wondering if God has even heard their prayers? Why does He allow some people to experience pain and tragedy, while others face no such difficulty? Many friends fervently prayed that André's first wife would be healed, yet despite their faith she died. Is God playing a lottery game in which only those with the lucky combinations win?

We have purposely saved this subject for now because we wanted to critically examine the supposed claims of men before contrasting them with the supernatural work of God. The service just described illustrates the conflict which many Christians feel concerning the subject of healing. We hear much about the exciting testimonies of God's healing, but there are also many silent tragedies—people who are hurting because God chose not to heal them physically. Many suffer deep guilt because they believe they did not have enough faith to be healed.

The fact is that the preacher in the service we described was probably sincere. He didn't intend for anyone in attendance to leave depressed and disheartened. But that isn't true of all the preachers. Today there are a number of popular evangelists and faith healers who prey on the hopes of the suffering. They have developed theatrical shows complete with detailed "revelations from God" about individuals in the audience and "miraculous cures" on stage for a wide variety of ailments.

Kathryn Kuhlman, the flamboyant faith healer who claimed to have healed thousands of followers throughout the sixties and seventies, apparently believed in what she was doing. But one of her closest associates, who is now one of André Kole's best friends, admits that even though he had great admiration for Kathryn, during the years he assisted her he never saw an undeniable, organic healing take place at one of her crusades. Similarly, the Reverend Earnest Angley achieved notoriety in the early 1980s by holding "miracle crusades," but one of the people working with him revealed to us that he never observed a genuine organic healing take place.

In Russia, Kashpirovsky and Chumak became psychic superstars by encouraging people to place jars of cold cream on their television sets during their programs, then rubbing the "energized" cream all over their bodies to receive healing. In Blackburn, England, people have traveled from around the globe to meet Edison the healing cat—that's right, a tubby tabby whose owner claims heals people through her miraculous paws!

In recent years, Benny Hinn has become hugely popular through his own "miracle crusades," claiming hundreds of people are healed in each of his citywide campaigns. Although we won't question Benny's motives, we believe his demonstrations to be unbiblical and deceptive. André has had the opportunity to meet with Benny Hinn for several hours. During that time André asked Benny for verification of some alleged miracles, but to this point in time, Benny has yet to produce any hard evidence of an instantaneous organic healing. His long-awaited book, which we hoped would offer some sort of documentation, instead presented a mere ten cases of alleged healing, none of which could be verified as an organic healing.

The fact is that Benny Hinn and André Kole have both created illusion acts which inspire awe and wonder. The difference is that André makes it clear to his audiences that what they are seeing is a trick—crafted for entertainment only. Benny claims his illusions are "miracles of God." When André confronted him with the truth, Benny said, "André, I see you as a friend, and I believe God has called me to a healing ministry. I believe the miracles are genuine. Yes, some are psychosomatic, but I don't ask people if their disease is psychosomatic. I just ask God to heal them anyway." In private, Mr. Hinn admitted that at least some of his "miracles" were not supernatural. Unfortunately, immediately after making those remarks to André privately, Benny said on his national television broadcast, "The skeptics are surfacing and saying these miracles are psychosomatic. Can you believe that? We all know that these miracles are real." He then asked for people to send in their stories of healing. Again, none of the stories we have investigated have checked out.[1]

We can't begin to deal with all of the theological questions involved in this issue. There are many good books devoted to what the Bible has to say about the gifts of the Spirit. Suffice is to say that we do believe in God's healing power and that He provides various spiritual gifts to individuals in the church. However, we are deeply concerned with the overwhelming evidence that many of these so-called "healers" and evangelists are not demonstrating God's power. Rather, they have used trickery and deception to produce cheap imitations of the supernatural. They have created a religious theatrical production, using God as a placebo to create the illusion that every kind of disease is being healed—when in reality only those with illnesses responsive to psychological drama are being helped. As a result they have attracted thousands of followers and millions of dollars. But they have also left many people confused about how God works.

It is likely that many of the followers of these healers have benefited from their ministry despite the deception. Unfortunately, there are many more who have been hurt and disillusioned because God didn't operate in the way the preacher promised He would. Still others have a false impression of Christianity because of these men and women and they are hindered from seeing the truth. That's why we believe it is necessary to openly examine the claims and actions of those who claim supernatural healing power, to see how they measure up to the standards of Scripture.

A GIFT OF KNOWLEDGE

The man who has most thoroughly researched this area is a professional colleague, James Randi. Although we disagree with Randi about the Christian faith, his investigations confirmed some damaging facts regarding the nature of theatrical healers. Randi's investigation focused on three popular preachers—W.V. Grant, Peter Popoff, and David Paul. Each of them conducted rallies and healing services around the United States, and each taped his services for viewing on television stations across the country. (Grant alone was appearing on almost 100 TV stations.) The investigation centered on two areas: the practice of "calling out" members of the audience to demonstrate the preacher's gift of knowledge, and the methods and results of healing.

First, consider the alleged "gift of knowledge" as practiced by these three men. Each of these preachers either wanders through the audience and talks to individuals or calls people to the stage, supposedly led by the Spirit of God. The evangelist usually identifies the person by name, proceeds to identify that person's street address and other information, then offers an account of the individual's affliction and the doctor who is treating it. Usually the preacher makes it a point to assure his audience that he has never spoken to or questioned this person before. Of course, people find this amazing, and it gives credibility to subsequent pronouncements that God wants to heal the individual.

Has the Holy Spirit actually given these preachers inside information about certain people in the audience? If He has, it is purely through natural means, for the three alleged "healers" that Randi investigated all gained their information by thorough research. Randi and his team of observers always arrived for the services at least two hours early, at the moment the doors of the auditorium opened. They found that all three of the evangelists had their wives or other "front men" walk through the auditorium and strike up casual conversations, during which they gather names, addresses, and other information, including a brief description of the person interviewed and the location of his or her seat. In addition, cards were often passed out so people could write out prayer requests, along with their names and addresses. This proved to be another rich source of information.

Each of the evangelists used a different method for recalling that information. For a long time David Paul had his information on small slips of paper inserted into his Bible (apparently as bookmarks to mark passages he would refer to during the service). On the slips were first and last name, a disease, a doctor's name, and sometimes an address. Former employees of Paul said that he would burn those slips following each service.

Randi showed how such information can be used by the preacher:

> Suppose you have on the slip "William Parsons," "Dr. Brown" and "heart attack." Those six words can be expanded into a minor melodrama. To wit (the following is taken from an actual recording of David Paul in

action): "*I have an impression of you clutching at your
chest. The pain is more than you can bear. It's enough to
make you cry out in agony. You fall to your knees. 'Dear
God!' you are saying, 'Take this burden from me! Let this
travail pass!' The doctors are working over you, doing
what they can for you. But they can't do anything except
get you to bed, and Dr. Brown tells you, 'Take it easy,
Bill. You're a sick man.' But doctors are only human.
Only Dr. Jesus can do what you need, Bill. I want you to
go home—because I see an angel of the Lord standing
at your front gate right now, Bill—and tell all the folks
there that Dr. Jesus has put a whole new heart into your
body! It's done! Hallelujah!*"[2]

TECHNOLOGY OVER TRUE FAITH

Peter Popoff made use of modern technology to gain his information during a service. One of Randi's associates noticed a small radio
receiver in Popoff's left ear. At a service in San Francisco, he arranged
for an expert to set up a radio scanner to intercept the transmissions.
They discovered that Popoff's wife was feeding him information about
individuals in the audience. A recording of the service plus the transmissions revealed that *every single one of Popoff's miraculous revelations
was fed to him by his wife* from a sealed-off section of their mobile television studio trailer. She and an assistant had gathered the information
before the service, and added gleaned information from some of the
more spectacular prayer cards.

Initially, after Randi played an excerpt from the recordings on *The
Tonight Show,* representatives from Popoff's evangelistic organization
denied the charge, claiming that the electronic receiver in Popoff's ear
was used only to stay in touch with the television crew. Later, Popoff
said his wife supplied him with about half of the names and said he
intended to start putting a disclaimer at the beginning of his television
shows. His "disclaimer" consisted of an attack against magicians who
he claimed were "tools of Satan" bent on destroying his ministry.

As far as the explanations by Popoff and his staff, Randi says, "In all the hours we have of Mrs. Popoff speaking to him, *not once* is the television operation referred to. As for the 'occasional' name given…we found that *all* of the people he 'called out' were given to him by the secret transmitter, and that *no* names were given to him that he did not call out."[3] Incidentally, after the revelations on *The Tonight Show* and a subsequent report on the television news program *West 57th Street*, Randi received several threats on his life. However, Popoff's ministry quickly died away after the publicity demonstrated he was a fraud.

It is the gullibility of Christians which plays a large part in continuing this sort of nonsense. It is hard for most people to believe that deception and illusions could play a part in religious services, because most Christians can't believe anyone would stoop so low as to use trickery in something presented as a sacred activity. For example, when André met with the editor of *Charisma* magazine to ask for help in providing documented cases that would meet the biblical criteria of an organic divine healing taking place in their performances, the editor of that Christian publication became very upset. When he learned that we would dare to question the integrity of some faith healers promoted in his magazine, and that we doubted the genuineness of faith healing in our modern day, the editor flew into a rage. He shouted at André, called him a "tool of Satan," and made accusations about Campus Crusade for Christ, the organization with whom André has worked for over 30 years. A few years later, when some of the faith healers were exposed on national television, that same editor wrote an excellent editorial entitled "A Question of Integrity," in which he wondered if "manufacturing miracles" was "trifling with the things of God" and tantamount to "blaspheming the Holy Spirit."

RISE AND WALK!

Now consider the healing ministry of these men. Despite the obvious *natural* means being used to gain information from the audience, some people continue to believe God is still working *supernaturally* through them to heal people. Rather than stating that God never works through these types of healers, we will simply state that the evidence is overwhelming that most, if not all, of the "healing" isn't miraculous.

For example, one of the most popular tools which several of the best-known faith healers use is the borrowed wheelchair gimmick. People who are slightly unsteady in their walk as they enter the arena are invited by an usher to sit in a wheelchair and are pushed to the front of the auditorium. They are the ones usually invited onto the stage, where they are dramatically ordered, in the name of Jesus, to "stand up and walk." Sometimes the evangelist will dramatically declare, "You don't need that wheelchair anymore, do you?" Of course the person says no—he didn't need it in the first place! W.V. Grant occasionally made the display even more dramatic by having the former wheelchair victim push him across the stage or up the aisle. That always brought a rousing ovation from the crowd. But it was a deceptive bit of theatrics, created specifically to lead people into a belief in the evangelist supposedly being God's channel of divine power. The tragedy of this deception is portrayed by Randi in this description of a revival meeting by W.V. Grant in St. Louis:

> *Before we entered the auditorium...we encountered many invalids in wheelchairs. They included children in advanced stages of cerebral palsy. Two chair-bound children, suffering from conditions I would not presume to diagnose, were strapped into their chairs. They made loud noises from time to time and thrashed about uncontrollably while their parents attempted to quiet them.... It was a depressing sight and I wondered what Grant would do when confronted with these cases....*
>
> *People in wheelchairs lined the front and sides of the seating area. Several of these people were subsequently commanded by Grant to get up and walk. But not one of those I'd seen earlier was even approached for healing. They were all placed at the back of the auditorium, and when one of the noisy chair-bound children approached*

> *the stage, Grant turned to an aide and told him, out of the range of the microphone, to "get him to the back." Later the child cried out from the side of the auditorium, where he'd again been placed by his parents. Grant, busy with a miracle on the other side, was forced to acknowledge the shriek and said, "I'm gonna git to that in just a minute." But he never did.*[4]

In the previous chapter, we talked about the difference between functional versus organic diseases. Functional illnesses often respond to suggestion, and in this area we would expect a faith healer to have success. But it is in the area of organic diseases that we struggle with most faith healers. If these men and women were truly God's representatives in His healing business, it would be reasonable to expect that we would see some successful healing of the organic as well as the functional diseases. For example, in a story found in the Gospel of John chapter 5, Jesus healed a lame man by telling him to rise and walk. There was no waiting around, no recovery period, and no reoccurrence of the problem. In chapter 9, He healed a man born blind. It was an instantaneous, total healing, without the aid of medical treatment. In chapter 18, the Lord reattached an ear that had been severed. Miraculously, through His supernatural power, Jesus could cause a person's organic medical problem to immediately disappear. Modern faith healers ought to offer the same strong evidence.

Unfortunately, it's hard to verify the results that these preachers claim. In our own research *we could not find a single verifiable case of someone being healed of an organic disease after attending a healing service*—though André offered $10,000 to anyone who could provide documented evidence of such a case.[5] James Randi decided to follow up on several of the people supposedly healed at some of Grant's services. From a tape of a service in Atlanta, Randi gained the name of a patient who was planning to have a coronary operation on a certain date in a specific hospital, and even heard Grant give the names of the patient's six doctors. Grant had proclaimed that "Dr. Jesus" had put a new heart in the man's body, and that he therefore didn't need the operation. Because of the number of specific facts, this seemed like an ideal case to check out.

Four weeks after that service, Randi visited Atlanta and discovered that not one of the six doctors was listed under the Medical Association of Georgia, which keeps a directory of all of the state's more than 8000 physicians, whether members of the association or not. Neither were the doctors listed as chiropractors. The hospital mentioned had no record of the patient and no such operation planned for the date given. In fact, cardiac surgery had never been performed at that particular hospital. "We had apparently discovered an absolute 'ringer,'" Randi concluded. "The man, for one reason or another, had fabricated the whole story. And he made W.V. Grant and *Dr. Jesus* look pretty good in that videotape."[6]

From the St. Louis revival, Randi was able to follow up several participants. One was a "Mr. Clark," who was blind in one eye. Grant had led the audience to believe that Mr. Clark's vision was restored. But after the service, Mr. Clark was *still* blind in one eye—and very angry that he could still not see.

Randi also followed up some of the testimonies of healing written up in Grant's publication *New Day*. One man from Erie, Pennsylvania, claimed he was healed of diabetes. A phone conversation with the man revealed that, although his doctor still said he had the disease, he believed he was healed because he was taking smaller doses of insulin.

Following Randi's public accusations, Peter Popoff broadcast an appeal to television viewers to send him healing testimonials. He claims he received 200,000 replies. Randi immediately wrote to Popoff and suggested that he choose any five of those testimonials and submit them to an independent, neutral board for evaluation. Popoff ignored the invitation.

FRAUD IN THE NAME OF GOD

All of this is just a small taste of the incredible findings of the various investigations. Even when we first began examining the results, we wanted to believe that these faith healers were sincere but misguided

Christians. After exploring the situation, we can no longer think that. Most of them recognize that what they are doing is a sham, but they continue doing it, covering it over with a veneer of spirituality by claiming "the Lord will somehow use it in people's lives." But we can't imagine God is interested in His representative using deception. If He exists, He must be a God of *truth*, and doubtless expects His people to speak the truth. In our discussions with faith healers, we have found very little willingness to confront the truth.

W.V. Grant once encouraged people to write letters expressing their prayer needs. "I will take each letter and anoint it with this holy oil from Israel, and I will pray over your letters back in my church in Dallas," he promised.

> *But the most callous fact we uncovered was that some letters, some several pages long and filled with heart-rending pleas for the minister's prayers and intercession of God, had been torn up, crumbled, and tossed into the garbage. They never even reached Grant's hands. Only by piecing together the scraps of the congregation's hopes, bit by bit, were we able to finally see the true attitude of this pastor toward his flock.*
>
> *Grant says in no uncertain terms that it is as a result of his anointed status that he possesses the Gifts of the Spirit and that he is thus able to call out members of his audience…. Grant even has the gall to tell them—in several different ways—that he is not doing an "ESP act" or a "magic show." He attributes it all to divine gifts.[7]*

Benny Hinn is famous for repeating this quote from Smith Wigglesworth, a well-known faith healer from the past: "The day will come when a man without legs will be carried down the aisle and we will see legs grow right before our eyes. People without eyes will have eyeballs instantly pop into their sockets." Unfortunately, that day has not yet arrived for Mr. Hinn and the other faith healers. When this type of organic healing finally occurs, there will be no question as to the reality of miraculous cures at the hands of faith healers. Until then, we'll assume it's just theater.

FAITH HEALING

What are we to make of this information? How do we evaluate *what is of God* and *what is of man*? We are convinced that much of the confusion about healing stems from a misunderstanding of faith healing.

Remember, *faith healing means that a person is relieved of symptoms or healed because of his faith.* The object of a person's faith may be God, a doctor, a faith healer, a psychic surgeon, or even a witch doctor. Claims of miraculous cures certainly are not confined to Christianity—they occur in various cultural and religious settings throughout the world. Putting faith in someone and believing in your own healing can have positive effects on certain diseases because that is how God has created us. The bodies and minds we have been given by God have tremendous recuperative abilities. But even the most charismatic healers can never cure some injuries and diseases. Dr. William Nolen explains:

> *Patients that go to a...service, paralyzed from the waist down as the result of injury to the spinal cord, never have been and never will be cured through the ministrations of [the faith-healer/evangelist].... The patient who suddenly discovers...that he can now move an arm or a leg that was previously paralyzed had that paralysis as a result of an emotional, not a physical disturbance. Neurotics and hysterics will frequently be relieved of their symptoms by the suggestions and ministrations of charismatic healers. It is in treating patients of this sort that healers claim their most dramatic triumphs.*
>
> *There is nothing miraculous about these cures. Psychiatrists, internists, G.P.s, any M.D. who does psychiatric therapy, relieve thousands of such patients of*

their symptoms every year. Psychotherapy, in which sug-
gestion plays a significant role, is just one of the many
tools with which physicians work.[8]

A doctor sometimes uses the principles of faith to his advantage. He may prescribe sugar pills to help a patient believe he is getting helpful medicine. He may use suggestions like saying "You should start feeling better in two days." Sometimes this actually helps a person recover.

Dr. Nolen states that half of the patients who go to a general practitioner will improve *even if the doctor does nothing.* Another 20 percent can often be helped through suggestion. This means a cure rate of 70 percent of all patients he sees, which helps explain the successes of faith healing. After his investigation, Nolen also arrived at an explanation for its popularity:

> *I've gotten a better understanding of why intelligent, rational people go to faith healers. They go to healers because, for one reason or another, the medical profession has let them down.*
>
> *Sometimes we doctors let our patients down because, quite simply, we have nothing curative to offer. For example, we don't as yet know how to cure multiple sclerosis, widespread cancer, or congenital brain disorders. We explain to patients with these diseases that we are truly sorry but we can't help them. No matter how nicely we do this, no matter how logically we explain that no one else, to our knowledge, can help them either, patients sometimes refuse to accept this bad news.*
>
> *A second reason people go to healers...is that some healers offer patients more warmth and compassion than physicians do. Sure, we pass our pills and perform operations, but do we really care about the people we treat?...*

MIND GAMES

A third reason why patients go to healers is that healers do, in fact, help them.... We doctors have in the past made the mistake of "putting down" the healers as though they, and those who patronized them, were idiots beneath our contempt. This has been a serious error.[9]

The danger is that most faith healers don't know when to stop. They cannot recognize those disorders that have no psychosomatic cause and will not respond without proper medical attention. For these people a visit to a faith healer can be tragic.

DIVINE HEALING

That which is truly miraculous, divine healing differs from faith healing. *Divine healing is God supernaturally reaching down and healing a person.* His healing is timely and complete. An example of divine healing comes from a Midwestern pastor who told us about being severely burned in an accident when he was a boy. As he was rushed to the hospital, his parents prayed for him. When nurses unwrapped him at the hospital, the burns were gone. As a result of that miracle, he received Christ and later entered full-time ministry. Many others have experienced this type of divine healing, but as far as we can determine, this probably represents less than 5 percent of what people claim are healings.

How can we distinguish God's hand in healing? Confusion in this area causes many people to doubt the reality of God, so it is important to understand a few principles. First, *God is not required to perform in a theatrical setting.* He will work in His own manner, for His own purposes, free from anyone's manipulations.

One respected leader of a charismatic denomination told us that the greatest problem in his churches is "the temptations of pastors to manipulate the emotions of the crowd. People want to see sensational things, so pastors feel they have to cause sensational things to happen in each service."

Often faith or positive thinking can relieve some symptoms for a few days, but them the problems recur. God's healing, however, is total

221

and complete, and He can touch a person anytime. The Lord doesn't require the psychology of a healing service to do His work. Faith healers like to use the excuse "You lack faith!" when a person is not healed. That takes the healer off the hook. But God doesn't need excuses. Our lack of faith never negates His power. He can heal us even if we do not believe. That doesn't mean we don't need faith, for the Bible clearly teaches that we ought to exercise our faith. But our faith or our lack of it doesn't change God's power.

Second, we need to recognize that *God rarely supersedes His laws of nature.* Many people get sick because they ignore God's laws of good health, then run to Him for healing. If two people, one a Christian and the other not, jump out of an airplane and fail to open their parachutes, no matter how much the Christian prays one the way down, both will be flattened when they hit the ground. Likewise, we cannot violate God's laws of good health and expect God to keep healing us.

Third, *we need to be cautious of dramatic testimonies.* People are often eager to claim miraculous healings, but their experiences do not necessarily prove that God was at work. Often the problem is the selection of facts, and this is especially true when hearing about a healing through a newsletter or a secondhand source. Our experience has shown that the teller might exaggerate his story or leave out essential information. When people share dramatic testimonies, they often imply that they were healed because they had exceptional faith. This can cause those who aren't healed to doubt God.

Joni Ereckson Tada graphically illustrates this struggle. After being left a quadriplegic due to a swimming accident, she worked up her faith to believe that God would allow her to walk again. At a special prayer meeting, church elders, pastors, and family laid hands on her, anointed her with oil, prayed for her. She described what happened in the following days:

> *A week went by...then another...then another. My body still hadn't gotten the message that I was healed. Fingers and toes still didn't respond to the mental command, "Move!" Perhaps it's going to be a gradual thing,*

I reasoned, a slow process of steady recovery. I contin-
ued to wait. But three weeks became a month, and one
month became two,,,

Then came to my mind the ten-thousand dollar question,
the question that is in the mind of so many I've met over
the years who have not been healed in response to their
prayers: Did I have enough faith?

What a flood of guilt that question brings. It constantly
leaves the door open for the despairing thought: God
didn't heal me because there is something wrong with
me. I must not have believed hard enough.[10]

After reviewing her doubts, Joni concluded that her problem was not a lack of faith. She came to understand that God sometimes chooses to allow suffering in order to shape us into the kind of people He wants us to become. He does heal people in miraculous ways, but sometimes He elects to *not* heal them. It is God's decision—His sovereign choice. We may not always like His choice, but, like Job, we can accept the fact that God knows what He is doing in determining our lives.

WHEN HEALING DOESN'T HAPPEN

This leads to a final principle: We need to understand that God sometimes chooses not to heal. When André's former wife Aljeana was diagnosed with an incurable brain tumor, he naturally desired to see her healed. Friends prayed for that healing. As they waited, André began to understand why people look to unusual techniques outside the medical profession in hope of finding relief. Looking back, he now believes that divine healing would not have been nearly as great a demonstration of God's power as her demonstration of faith and peace in the midst of the suffering she endured. The Lord used Aljeana's victory over pain, suffering, and eventually death as a testimony to thousands of people.

Certainly God can and does heal, but He does not heal everyone who comes to Him, even when they come in faith. Jesus Christ, when He lived on this earth, healed many people, but *He did not heal everyone.* Many wanted to be healed but never had the chance. God still loved them, and He loves us too. We may never understand His workings, but we can rest assured that His individual plan for each one of us is best. Joni explains it well:

I sometimes shudder to think where I would be today if I had not broken my neck. I couldn't see at first why God would possibly allow it, but I sure do now. He has gotten so much more glory through my paralysis than through my health! And believe me, you'll never know how rich that makes me feel. If God chooses to heal you in answer to your prayers, that's great. Thank Him for it. But if He chooses not to, thank Him anyway. You can be sure He has His reasons.

Charles Swindoll states that there is a consistent pattern when God chooses to perform a miracle. First, God alone is glorified. Second, there is no human showmanship involved, Third, the unsaved are impressed and brought to the Lord, Fourth, biblical principles and statements are upheld, not contradicted. That's the pattern we need to consider when reviewing the possibility of faith healers today. God does not serve at our bidding. Just because a faith healer commands one of his followers to be healed is not proof that he is imbued with the power of God.

Many people are being misled by dynamic personalities who claim to have a gift from the Lord. These preachers may have a gift, but it definitely is not the gift of healing. They simply have learned, accidentally or intentionally, some good psychological principles and theatrics. We need to remember that fact when we next attend a healing service. If you believe God has healed you, rejoice and thank Him. Give Him glory for His miraculous power. But don't attribute supernatural powers to someone using merely natural ability.

CHAPTER FOURTEEN

The Vision of
the Anointed

A few years ago, Dr. Thomas Sowell of Stanford University wrote a book about a group of people he dubbed "the anointed." This group included liberal scholars and politicians who believe they are smarter than the average American, and who create public policy based upon their personal vision rather than upon history, commonly known fact, or public opinion. These self-anointed leaders arrogantly expect the American public to trust them simply because they "know better."

In a similar way, American culture has seen a transformation of its spiritual life during the last 20 years due in large part to some people who consider themselves "anointed," and who promoted spiritual mind games to the masses. A society that used to believe in the importance of church, morality, and the existence of God has been inundated with messages claiming that church is bad, morality is subjective, and God is not a person but a force that exists inside each of us. Those who have been promoting these ideas see themselves as somehow smarter than the rest of us, having rejected historical faith in favor of some New Age paradigm. Once they realized they had this new "truth" that they believed came from God, they felt it necessary to promote it to the rest of us.

In the broadest terms, the vision of these self-anointed spiritual leaders is that man can become God, and they feel it is their responsibility to make sure everybody accepts this idea and rejects Christianity. You can see the growing popularity of their thinking everywhere: The television talk shows routinely discuss counseling issues, replacing the problem of sin with the problem of self-esteem. Public schools endorse yoga and practices of the Eastern mystics, while working to strip history of all Christian references. Mainstream news shows do reports on the latest spiritual crazes, but almost never have anything positive to say about the millions of churchgoing Americans. Newspapers lavish praise on channelers and mystics but criticize Christians who legitimately want to be involved in the political process.

To look at the mainstream media and entertainment industries, one would think that historical Christianity plays almost no part in our culture. Christians have been marginalized and their messages replaced with the unbiblical message of those from the Human Potential movement—the "anointed," if you will. But their message, and the direction they are leading our country, is both dangerous and damaging. In this chapter we will explore the mind games these people have been foisting upon us, including those of us in the church.

THE MIND SCIENCES

To understand the vision of these self-appointed spiritual leaders, we must first explore what has been called *the mind sciences*. This term refers not to any particular groups, but to a basic philosophy that pervades all of those involved in the new spirituality of America. In short, they believe that the mind has special powers that are available to anyone who will put them to use. Further, they believe that the mind of mankind is divine because man is one essence with God. "Therefore, the true mind of man is literally the mind of God expressed on an individual level."[1]

Of course, their vision of God is entirely different from that presented in Scripture. To those in the mind sciences, God is an impersonal consciousness that we are all part of. This teaching, called *monoism*, claims that everything is reducible to one substance, it is all perfect, and it is all divine. Anything bad which happens—like war or crime or disease—isn't real, but is the result of some mental error on our part. "The purpose of the mind sciences is to correct these mental aberrations so that people can see and live the divine perfection that is their spiritual birthright."[2]

Therefore the mind sciences emphasize human potential—the power you have in your mind to correct false perceptions about yourself and your world. One writer suggests we think of it like a thirsty bushman holding a hose. He needs water, but in his ignorance he squeezes the hose too tight, blocking the release of life-giving fluid. He needs someone smarter than himself to help him learn how to receive the water through the hose. If you are unhappy or facing difficulties, the mind sciences would argue that you are living in unreality and ignorance, and that you require someone to help you see your true goodness and correct your thinking through psychic development, visualization, positive affirmation, and altered states of consciousness.

The teaching that man is divine and can control creation strictly through mental power is perhaps the basis of all occultic thinking, but it is an idea that has spread throughout our society. Rather than just being popular in cults like the Christian Science church, it has been taught to tens of thousands of people through seminars like *est* and *Lifespring*, and preached to millions more through the writings of Norman Vincent Peale. Out of this theology has sprung the Church of Religious Science, Divine Science, Unity School of Christianity, Silva Mind Control, Self-Actualization Fellowship, and numerous other groups. However, they all have the same root: *gnosticism*.

Gnostics were an early heretical group who denied that Jesus Christ existed physically on earth and argued that, since He was God,

He must have existed only as spirit. They got their name from the Greek word *gnosis*, which means "to know," for they believed they knew a deeper truth than the average Christian. Gnostics began preaching this unbiblical message in churches, and it led to a two-tiered system of followers—those who had the deeper knowledge, and those who did not. The apostles Paul and John both preached against these heretics, arguing that the Christian church is not based upon secrets, but upon what is plain. John even began one of his letters with a pointed rebuke for the gnostics, stating, "That which was from the beginning, *which we have heard, which we have seen with our eyes, which we have looked at and our hands have touched*—this we proclaim concerning the Word of life."[3] In other words, Jesus wasn't just a phantom, for John had seen and touched Him.

The gnostics also taught that spirit is good and flesh is bad, and since they claimed to be perfect in their spirits, they could choose to do anything they wanted in the flesh. This belief led to all sorts of immorality, which is why the apostle continued his letter with the words, "If we claim to have fellowship with him yet walk in darkness, we lie and do not live by the truth...If we claim to be without sin, we deceive ourselves and the truth is not in us."[4] John understood that any denial of Christ's physical reality, and any separation of our actions from our beliefs, would lead directly to hedonism and sexual sin, so he warned against the teaching of the gnostics. *Yet those same ideas are the very concepts being foisted upon us by the mind sciences.* The vision of the anointed includes getting people to deny Christ's divinity in order to claim it for themselves.

The theological problems of the mind sciences abound. They reject God as a personal being and turn Him into some sort of pantheistic "force." They deny that Jesus Christ was God incarnate, relegating Him to the place of a "self-actualized human." They also reject the principle of sin, diminishing it to a flaw in thinking and describe salvation as a higher state of consciousness, rather than a gracious act of God on man's behalf. Orthodox Christian belief is the ultimate evil, for it keeps people in bondage to old ways of thinking. To those who claim to have been anointed, the Bible is flawed, death is nothing more than reincarnation, and spiritual growth occurs as people are put in touch with the spiritual world.

LED BY SPIRIT GUIDES

One of the most common elements of the various mind science groups is the presence of *spirit guides*. Most of the "anointed" claim to have received messages from the spirit world, and many claim to have had their own personal guides to help them in their quest for knowledge. For example, psychologist Carl Rogers claimed to have had a spirit guide who revealed to him the elements of therapy. Emanuel Swedenborg is another who believed that spirit guides had led him to discover new truth, as did Jose Silva, Werner Erhard, and most other cult leaders.

These men claim to have put themselves into an altered state of consciousness, then opened themselves to teachings from the spirits. The spirit guides usually claim to be the human dead, and are ready to reveal information to people that will hasten their spiritual growth. Further, "the spirits claim they are more evolved than we are because they have lived through many lifetimes and discovered the secrets of life and death. The spirits claim that if enough people will listen to them, they can even help to bring a worldwide spiritual awakening. This will produce a new age of peace and harmony."[5]

Generally, the message of the spirit guides is that man is God, and that man needs to overcome his ignorance if he is to solve his problems. The spirits nearly always deny the existence of evil and hell, and encourage people to not fear the "transition" of death. People will be reincarnated, according to the spirit guides, until they reach perfection. In addition, these spirits universally deny that Jesus is the Savior of the world.

Take, for example, the words of "Jesus," the spirit guide supposedly working through medium Helen Schucman. In her book *A Course of Miracles*, she quotes the spirit as saying things like "God's name is holy, but no holier than yours.... You are the Holy Son of God Himself.... Sin does not exist...no one is punished for sins [and you] are not sinners.... Salvation is nothing more than right-mindedness.... It is so essential that all such thinking be dispelled that we must be sure that nothing of this kind remains in your mind. I was not 'punished' because you were bad.... Do not make the pathetic error of 'clinging to the old rugged cross.'"[6]

"Seth," a spirit guide used by Jane Roberts, offered similar drivel, saying such things as "Jesus will not come to reward the righteous and send evildoers to eternal doom" and "the devil is a projection of your own psyche..."[7] "Lilly," the spirit guide of medium Ruth Montgomery, claimed that "there is no such thing as death" and that "God wishes [psychic ability] be utilized and developed to the fullest potential."[8]

There are two significant problems with all of this talk about spirit guides. First, the teachings of the spirits is almost always in direct opposition to God's revealed Word. Second, there is never any way to verify the messages of the spirits; we are simply told to accept their teaching. As believers in Scripture, we have a very difficult time accepting teaching that runs contrary to the Bible. And as researchers into psychic hoaxes, we have an even harder time accepting teaching from people we know to be frauds.

Many of those who claim to have spoken to spirit guides are the same people who have been involved with fake seances and spiritism. At least two people we talked with admitted the teachings come from their "creative unconscious" rather than from any particular entity. And the writings of those involved with spirit guides all sound awfully similar—as though they were copying one another rather than receiving any "new truth." The danger of demonic possession, or at least demonic confusion, is very real. Most of the teaching of spirit guides reads like Satan's plan for denying the truth and expanding demonic activity in our world. This is even more true of those who invite the spirit to speak directly through them.

CHANNELING THE SPIRITS

We want to clearly state that we believe most channelers are total frauds. They don't speak any new truth, they cannot predict the future, and they have never shown any genuine insight or special knowledge.

One performance we observed, of a woman claiming to channel a 500-year-old man, was so pathetically bad that she had us howling in laughter. When asked by someone how he was able to speak through this woman, she hesitated before replying, "It's a...*glandular* thing." Apparently this 500-year-old character knew all about glands! However, we do not want to trivialize channeling. Anytime an individual knowingly opens himself up to a spirit, he is in grave danger from Satan.

Channeling occurs when a man or woman willingly gives up his mind and body to a spirit being, and the spirit supposedly speaks through him. In the Christian faith we have always referred to that as *demonic possession.* Unfortunately, there are tens of thousands of people willing to pay money to hear what the spirit has to say, so mixed in with those who have been possessed by demons are some outright phonies bent on bilking big bucks from people. An article in *The Los Angeles Times Magazine* reported that channeling is a hundred-million-dollar-a-year-enterprise, due to seminars, tape and book sales, and individual appointments and readings.[9]

Some channelers, like Lamar Keene, have admitted that what they do is completely false—a trick played on the unsuspecting in order to make money. But some channelers really believe that they are allowing another source to speak through them, in order to glean alleged wisdom from the spirit world. As researcher and writer John Weldon notes,

People today have a great need to find meaning in life. They have discovered, often painfully, that it cannot be found in a material view of reality alone. Even skeptics desire to know the answers to questions like, "Who am I?" "Why am I here?" and "What happens when I die?" Whether or not they admit it, the thought of life being no more than a few years of pain and pleasure replaced by eternal nonexistence is frightening to people. Men know they are more than the end product of hydrogen atoms and blind chance. And they are clearly searching for answers. Modern man sees channeling as the proof of the deeper answers to life.[10]

Most people know in their hearts that there is a spirit world, and nearly every culture in history has believed in spirit contact. Every major world religion teaches the reality of spirits, so it is natural that people the world over have turned to the spirit world when seeking answers to life's most difficult questions.

Channeling seems to answer some of those questions by allowing something from "the other side" talk about the nature of reality, death, and human potential. The spirits claim that they have the answers to life's toughest questions, and they speak with certainty about things like reincarnation and the nature of God. But people are deceived into thinking that contacting spirits somehow gives meaning to life. They are fooled into thinking there is no such thing as "wrong" or "sin" or "evil," but only an unending potential for growth. History would suggest otherwise.

KNIGHT, RAMTHA, AND DEMONS

To understand the broader picture of channeling, consider one example: J.Z. Knight channels Ramtha, who claims he is a 35,000-year-old warrior from the lost continent of Atlantis. Perhaps the world's most famous channeler, it is hard for a Christian researcher to know if Knight is simply a fraud (she has done an excellent "imitation" of Ramtha on occasion),[11] or is actually allowing a demon to speak through her (her teachings are almost all antibiblical). On the one hand, it is easy to accuse Knight of faking it all, since she has become a multimillionaire through her channeling, and her ex-husband has claimed it is all a hoax. Knight has never been able to accurately predict the future, know what is going on in other parts of the world, or levitate, though her followers have claimed all those things. On the other hand, Knight openly asks for the spirit of this supposed warrior to enter her, so she may very well believe she is "possessed" by a demon.

A quick examination of Ramtha's teaching speaks volumes about the spirit's theology. Ramtha teaches that the Christian God is an "idiotic deity," that man is God, that "everyone is what you call a psychic," that "there is no such thing as evil," "there is no hell or devil," "the world doesn't need saving," and "the devil is not really evil…because he's really God," etc. etc.[12] Much of Ramtha's talks are rambling discourses that speak generally of believing in yourself, connecting with the spirit world, and acknowledging yourself as god. Though channeled spirits variously claim to be God, extraterrestrials, the dead, and the "universal mind," the teaching of channelers is clearly coming from the same source, for it is all an attempt to insulate people against the truth of Jesus Christ. The Bible teaches the exact opposite of the channelers, insisting that man is sinful, and must personally come before a holy God through the expiatory death of Jesus. Man can no more become a god than he can evolve into an automobile, since man and God are of a different essence. Yet channelers want to blur the line, and convince men and women that they are already God.

Having said that, we do not necessarily believe that all channelers are demon-possessed. In fact, we believe that most are deliberate frauds. Channelers rarely display the actions of the demon-possessed. Scripture presents demoniacs as raving antisocial people, often with physical maladies. Channelers are nearly always reserved and quiet, leading us to believe they are deliberate imposters. While we do not deny the reality of demons, nor the fact that most channelers are telling lies from the pit of hell, this does not mean that everyone telling a lie is demon-possessed.

For example, in posing a question to Kevin Ryerson, channeler to actress Shirley MacLain, Christian author F. LaGard Smith purposefully misrepresented the idea that his mother was no longer living. "The response to the question I had posed wrongly assumed the truth of misrepresentation," Smith wrote, leading him to conclude, "His supposed spiritual sources of cosmic information are best characterized as speculative and imagined. Kevin's act is simply one of the nest road shows in America."[13]

While some people refuse to believe in the existence of demons, the consensus of history is that demons exist, and the testimony of the Scripture is that they are bent on destroying mankind. The phenomenon of spirit-possession is well-documented and interesting, even by unbelieving psychologists, and one of the most overlooked aspects of channeling has been the admission by some mediums that the forces with which they are dealing are evil. Swedenborg himself declared, "When spirits begin to speak with a man, he ought to beware that he believes nothing whatever from them; for they say almost anything.... They would tell so many lies and indeed with solemn affirmation that a man would be astonished."[14]

Edgar Cayce and J.Z. Knight, among others, are channelers who have questioned whether they were being tricked by demons. If channeling is having contact with spirits, and if some of those spirits are evil, it could lead to all sorts of other evils. The Bible speaks of demons bringing physical and psychological ailments, making people violent, and turning them away from God. The teachings of channelers universally oppose the Scriptures, leaving us with two logical options: Either the Bible is false and the spirits are true, or the Bible is true and the channeled spirits are evil demons bent on the destruction of man.

Many lives have been destroyed because they got involved with channeling. In one well-documented case, a professor named Carl became so consumed by the forces of evil that he ended up an incoherent vegetable, requiring exorcism and 11 months of hospitalization. When he told his story, he concluded, "I wish to acknowledge that knowingly and freely I entered into possession by an evil spirit. And, although that spirit came to me under the guise of saving me, perfecting me, helping me to help others, I knew all along it was evil."[15] Be wary of listening to any of the anointed who promise you new truth through a channeled spirit.

PSYCHOLOGY OR SALVATION?

In churches today, Christian counselors are trying to plumb the mysteries of human potential in order to develop "the power of imagination." Jerry MacGregor sat in an evangelical church worship service recently and listened to a Christian counselor encourage the congregation to close their eyes and "watch for the guide to come lead you." An advertisement for a popular Christian counseling center mentions therapies like "relaxation, inner dialogue, gestalt, and dream work," without any mention of the wisdom of God in Scripture being applied to the lives of those in crisis.

Christian schools and seminaries are filled with psychology classes trying to reconcile two irreconcilable ideas. Last year, "psychology" was the most popular major, even on Christian liberal arts college campuses. Yet many of the leading spokesmen for psychology in our world today are involved in occultism, selfism, and shamanism.

Pastors have become "counselors," churches have become "recovery centers," and the worship of God has been replaced with "the healing of damaged emotions." That has moved the church away from a focus on the Lord and towards a focus on self. Far too many people in Christendom seem to be chasing after acceptance by the world of psychology in hopes of finding an integration of psychotherapy with faith.

We're not convinced that biblical theology can *ever* be integrated with psychology. Much of the modern teaching in psychology is based upon the teachings of Carl Jung, who claimed to have gained his insights from a spirit guide, and Sigmund Freud, who believed that all behaviors are based upon unconscious forces generally developed during childhood. Freud's ideas mean that man cannot be held personally responsible for his actions—a notion that has helped turn our culture toward an Eastern worldview focused on the self. And his emphasis on childhood development has led us into "rebirthing," focusing on past memories, and the whole idea of needing to resolve the past before moving into the future.

Although Freudian thinking is endemic to our culture, we would argue that the whole notion is an unbiblical mind game. "Paul, whose legalistic upbringing would seem to make him a primary candidate for healing of the memories, was not only free from any bad effects but declared, 'Forgetting what lies behind and reaching forward to what lies ahead. I press on toward the goal for the prize of the upward call of God in Christ Jesus' (Philippians 3:13,14 NASB)."[16] While past events may certainly influence our present perspectives, that doesn't mean we have to re-experience them in order to change our behavior. The Bible says that Christ has set us *free* from the past. Being born again is a better option than seeking some fuzzy notion of "inner healing."

IS PSYCHOLOGY THE SOLUTION?

During the last 20 years the church has adopted so many counseling strategies from psychology that they have become part and parcel of modern-day Christianity. But if the therapies are drawn from non-biblical theories, and are put into practice by those who completely reject the concept of God, perhaps it is time for the church to rethink its involvement with them. Many of the Christian counseling books are based upon pagan concepts of self-talk, visualization, spirit guides, and personal power. In the words of one psychologist, "The irony is that many people who are not fooled by astrology for one minute subject themselves to therapy for years, where the same errors of logic and interpretation often occur."[17]

Man has been trying to save himself for centuries. He has built monuments, created ceremonies, and suppressed his inner desires as a way to make peace with God. He has thrown himself into projects, dived headlong into pleasure, and surrounded himself with possessions as a way to deaden his pain and forget he faces an uncertain eternity. No amount of psychology can negate that truth.

It is time for the culture to examine itself and see if psychology is really the answer for which we have been searching. While counselors are attempting to find tricks to "awaken the giant within," "become your own best friend," and "pull your own strings," the fact is that all their therapies fail to touch on the heart of the problem with man: *sin*. The Bible says that "all have sinned."[18] Everybody recognizes that fact, whether people want to acknowledge it or not. And sin has consequences, something that Christians are to remember and non-Christians fear to talk about. "The wages of sin is death," according to the Bible.[19] That means eternal death—a separation apart from God that will last forever. It is *sin* that causes the uncertainty in a person's soul, not a lack of self-esteem. Until psychologists admin that *sin* is the basic problem of people, their discipline will always be futile.

To be fair, in recent years some Christian counseling programs have rejected the rantings of Freud and Jung, attempting to find a solidly biblical alternative model. But others, following the lead of non-Christian counselors, have embraced the humanist philosophy of Carl Rogers, who rejected God and the Bible as sources of truth.

Man is depraved. He is born in sin, his nature is to sin, and he will choose to live in sin unless he is introduced to the method for making peace with God. This is a hard fact, and one that many people in the church don't want to readily admit. But if we fail to acknowledge our sin, we will never recognize our need for a Savior. Man has been trying to save himself for centuries. He has built monuments, created ceremonies, and suppressed his inner desires as a way to make peace with God. Man has thrown himself into projects, dived headlong into pleasure, and surrounded himself with possessions as a way to deaden his pain and forget he faces an uncertain eternity. No amount of psychology can negate that truth.

The only solution for sin is salvation through Jesus Christ. According to Scripture, the wages of sin is death, "but the gift of God is eternal life in Christ Jesus our Lord."[20] Man can find peace with God only when he bows before the Lord, acknowledges his sin, and asks God's forgiveness. The heavenly Father sent His Son, Jesus to die on the cross and pay the penalty for our sins. Anyone who believes this fact and surrenders his or her lie to Him will find the forgiveness and the peace they so desperately desire.

But in making that decision, we put ourselves at odds with this world. As Christians we will never "find ourselves" in this world, no matter how many psychological mind games we try. We are not citizens of this world; our citizenship is in heaven. In this world *we will have troubles*, the Lord told us in John 16:33. But we can take courage in the fact that He has also promised us that He has overcome the world. Therefore, even though "death is at work in us," and "outwardly we are wasting away,"[21] we can find peace by putting our faith in God.

The fundamental problem with mankind is *sin*, not lack of self-esteem or unhealed memories from the past. The solution is found in the forgiveness of God, not in visualizing ourselves into wholeness. Yet psychotherapy routinely dismisses faith in God as something evil or neurotic. Freud hated the church, and Albert Ellis, founder of the popular "rational-emotive" system of therapy, was convinced that all believers in religious orthodoxy were "distinctly disturbed."

When all is said and done, the vision of the anointed is that mankind should reject biblical Christianity and embrace the mind games of shamans and spiritists. But that path leads directly away from God and toward Satan. It is his trickery and deception that has allowed many people in the church to accept—and at times *endorse*—these sorts of ideas. Surely Christians should be turning toward *the Word of God* for wisdom in counseling others rather than toward the recommendations of atheistic pagans.

VISUALIZING OUR WAY TOWARD GOD

"No matter how much we like to pussyfoot around it, all of us who postulate a loving God and really think about it eventually come to a single terrifying idea: God wants us to become Himself (or Herself or Itself). We are growing toward godhood. God is the goal of evolution."

Had Christians heard these words a few years ago, they would doubtless have dismissed them for what they are: occultic heresy. But those words have been read and enjoyed by countless believers. They are from the Christian bestseller *The Road Less Traveled*, a book considered by evangelicals to be one of the most influential books of the past 20 years. It's author, M. Scott Peck, is a psychiatrist who wanted to merge his psychologically based worldview with his Christian faith. The fact that so many believers have embraced it is scary.

Psychology, visualization, success, and self-improvement techniques are all mind games that have begun to undermine biblical theology. They all preach the message that we are to enjoy life, become successful, and "be the person you want to be." And they all propagate Satan's fundamental message that *you can be like God.*

Nearly every mind game has an inherently selfish perspective, since they all are aimed at helping the individual accomplish something for himself or herself. Thus, contemporary theologians such as the late Dr. Norman Vincent Peale try to put a positive spin on God and do away with any negative messages so that Christians can feel good about themselves. Dennis Waitley and Og Mandino preach a message of success, using the occultic practices of visualization and possibility thinking in order for Christians to feel personally successful. The so-called "faith" preachers encourage Christians to embrace a theology of God-as-genie, where our words can bring us anything we want, so that each of us can own for ourselves anything we imagine. The selfish focus of these preachers is appalling.

These mind games are also heretical. They sound good at first, for they appear to promote good feelings and achievement. But the focus is on ourselves rather than God. And He has no interest in sharing His position of authority with us. Perhaps all of this is appealing in the same way it appealed to Eve, as she stood in the Garden and envisioned being "like God." We all want that—the power and authority that comes from being like Him. But the Lord has made clear that we are *not* like God, and that to take steps to try and become God is sinful. So when Christ for the Nations Publishing promotes the writings of John G. Lake, who said, "God intends us to be gods,"[22] they are promoting a mind game that draws believers away from the truth.

SELF-TALK AND SHAMANISM

How would you respond to somebody who claimed we need to make Christianity in our culture more "positive?" Would you agree with a pastor who encouraged his people to stay away from talking about sin and punishment, because those messages turn off non-Christians? What would you say to somebody who called for the advent of a "positive Christianity" in our modern day?

If you agree with these ideas, you might be surprised at their originators: Adolph Hitler and Joseph Goebbels. In the 1930s they encouraged the notion of a "positive Christianity" in German churches, leading the body of Christ into a position of compromise and eventual decay. Lest you think that a poor analogy to what is occurring today, compare it to the theology of some of today's "positive thinkers," whose axioms include such remarks as "Believe and you will achieve." Such teachings tend to make mankind master of his fate, claiming that we can change reality merely by thinking about it.

That is a pagan notion, based on the Hindu philosophy that this life is not objective reality. A person cannot alter reality with his mind; if he could, he would have godlike power. For example, if you were lying beside the road with a broken leg, you could not stand up and make it healed by putting on a happy face. We do not change our situations by changing our thinking, though we can sometimes change *ourselves*. But the positive thinkers have tried to discount reality, selling Christians the lie that we can create new realities.

"Your unconscious mind [can] turn wishes into realities when the wishes are strong enough,"[23] according to Norman Vincent Peale. "Vividly imagine, sincerely believe, ardently desire, enthusiastically act, and it must inevitably come to pass," echoes Paul Meyer.[24] This concept, which they refer to as "positive imaging" or "re-imaging," is nothing more than paganism dressed up in a baptismal robe so as to appear Christian. It has no basis in Scripture. If Peale is correct, everything a believer wishes for should come true—a ridiculous thought, if not a horrible one. God shapes the path of our lives. He sometimes allows bad things to happen, because that is how we grow.

We are in no way suggesting that we believe in any sort of determinism. Christians ought to be people who are filled with joy and hope, for we are the only people on earth who can have assurance of what will take place after we die. It is possible to maintain a good attitude without buying into this pagan nonsense about "re-imaging" our world. Pastor Chuck Swindoll has written several excellent books in which he reminds us to trust God and keep our chin up, without ever suggesting that by keeping a good attitude we can somehow recreate reality. While we are certain that those who pastors who are proponents of visualization techniques love the Lord, and they have moved many people toward a better relationship with Him, we have grave doubts about the theology behind all this talk of visualization and positivism.

HARD THINGS ARE GOOD FOR US

The fact is that God *wants* hard things to come our way occasionally. If tough times never occurred, we would remain immature forever. The apostle Paul went through some incredibly difficult and depressing times:

> *I have worked much harder, been in prison more frequently, been flogged more severely, and been exposed to death again and again. Five times I received from the Jews forty lashes minus one. Three times I was beaten with rods, once I was stoned, three times I was shipwrecked, I spent a night and a day in the open sea, I have been constantly on the move. I have been in danger from my own countrymen, in danger from Gentiles; in danger in the city; in danger in the country; in danger at sea; and in danger from false brothers. I have laboured and toiled and have often gone without sleep; I have known hunger and thirst and have often gone without food; I have been cold and naked. Besides everything else, I face daily the pressures of my concern for all the churches. Who is weak, and I do not feel weak? Who is led into sin, and I do not inwardly burn?*[25]

Would the "positive thinkers" suggest that the apostle Paul could have avoided all this if he had only had a better attitude? Taken to its logical end, no Christian should ever get sick or injured, should never experience failure, and probably should never die. We ought to just disappear in a blinding flash of faith, moving next to the Lord for eternity without going through the trouble of death. But that won't happen, because no matter how good my attitude is, I've still got to face the reality of this world.

Consider what all this positive thinking has at its aim: It seeks to take power out of the hands of God and slip it into the hands of man. For a Hindu, that is the natural way of thinking. For a Christian, it turns God into some sort of cosmic genie. If we believe in something, God ought to make it happen. Whatever we demand He has to do. We become like Aladdin, rubbing the magic lamp of our Bibles and waiting for God to show up and grant us our wishes.

This philosophy has moved the church away from its theological basis. Not surprisingly, it has forced those involved to water down the gospel so as to not offend the world.

Have we forgotten that the world is at war with God? The world rejected and crucified Christ when He came to earth, and the Lord explained that they would do the same to His followers. The world *hates* God, and if you are His representative, they will hate you, too. Jesus said, "If they persecuted me, they will persecute you also.... They will treat you this way because of my name, for they do not know the One who sent me."[26]

The truth of God is not all about good feelings. Preachers of old used to talk about the "offense" of the gospel, for they knew that becoming a Christian meant bending down and acknowledging someone greater than ourselves. To admit our sinfulness and our powerlessness to do anything about our condition is humbling, and the very idea is an offense to someone who refuses to acknowledge his predicament. But that's what happens when truth is preached: Some people will be offended. We cannot expect the world to embrace God by making the gospel somehow more palatable. And we cannot expect God to honor those who distort His truth in order to gain favor with men.

VISUALIZING OUR WAY TO HELL

According to the possibility thinkers, all that an individual must do to achieve success is to "visualize" it. Adelaide Bry, one of the leading spokespersons for creative visualization, describes it as "the deliberate use of the power of your mind to create your own reality. You can use visualization to have whatever you want."[27]

All of the popular New Age methodologies rely on visualization and self-talk. Most cultural experts agree that "the use of the imagination is one of the most rapidly spreading new trends in psychology and education."[28] Thus everybody from Amway salesmen to members of the American Medical Association are keen on the idea of visualization. Of course, not all visualization is bad. Baseball players are encouraged to use it to help them "see" themselves hitting home runs. Dieters are encouraged to visualize themselves getting thinner. Management gurus have been encouraged to use visualization in order to expand their creative thinking abilities. Even André Kole "visualizes" what his next illusion will look like. But when taken to an extreme, this type of thinking can lead to the pagan notion that we can change the material world simply by thinking about it. That sort of philosophy has begun showing up in the church, with pastors exhorting Christians to let their imaginations run wild: "Through visualizing and dreaming you can incubate your future and hatch results."[29]

All the popular ideas about visualization and self-talk have created a belief that we can change our world simply by changing our thinking. For example, those promoting a one-world government issue bumper stickers that read "Visualize World Peace," as though by thinking about it we can somehow cause it to occur. Norman Vincent Peale has spoken about self-talk being a method for tapping into the eternal power of God. *But if we can recreate reality, we have become like God*—and who is to say we are to play God? "If visualization taps into some power inherent within the universe and available to anyone, it would be the ultimate weapon to hand over to human egos; and the result would not be paradise, but hell on earth."[30]

In a similar way, many Christians involved in multilevel marketing schemes have preached the importance of self-talk and visualization. They like to talk about Napolean Hill's famous tome, *Think and Grow Rich*, not realizing that Hill claimed he was given the success principles in the book by the Ascended Masters while in a state of astral projection. But that sort of thinking is common among the success gurus. "We create reality by what we visualize," according to one Amway speaker. "If you start visualizing what you desire, you shall have it!"[31]

Pastor and psychologist David Stoop has said that the "renewed emphasis on the power of the mind reflects a swing back to ancient ideas concerning the interrelationship of the body and the mind."[32]

Thus fantasies are more helpful than truth, and psychology replaces sanctification as the means of renewing our minds. This same thinking encourages people to visualize God. Pastor C.S. Lovett tells his followers to "develop the art of visualizing the Lord Jesus Christ in order to enjoy Him better.[33] Christian novelist Calvin Miller has urged believers to "create in our minds the Christ"[34] in order to build faith. Yet we can find no passage of Scripture to support this type of practice, and it appears to come dangerously close to a kind of idol worship.

The use of creative visualization is an ancient occultic practice, used by shamans to get people in touch with the spirit world. The basic premise of visualization is that *you can become like God and reshape reality*. That is exactly the same argument Satan used in the Garden of Eden to entice Eve into sinning. The notion that thought controls everything relegates God to an impersonal force and elevates man to deity. Christians should stay away from this sort of mind game, for it directs us toward occultic practices and leads us into the heresy that we can develop godlike powers.

English author C.S. Lewis warned believers of the inherent danger involved with self-talk and visualization. In *The Screwtape Letters*, a top-level demon instructs his underling to "turn [believers'] gaze away from Him toward themselves. Keep them watching their own minds and trying to produce *feelings* there by the action of their own wills.... Keep him praying to *it*, not to the Person who has made him. You may even encourage him to attach great importance to the correction and improvement of his composite object. Suggest that he keep it steadily before his imagination during the whole prayer."[35] The result: The Christian focuses on a *self-created* God rather than the genuine God of Scripture. The mind game moves him away from God.

CHAPTER FIFTEEN

Witchcraft Repackaged

He exudes a sense of complete confidence, and when he speaks—in a fast-paced banter that promotes a sense of authority among those seated semi-circle around the otherwise sterile hotel meeting room—it's in soft tones tinged with a New York accent. Dressed in the sort of clothes a friend would wear if he were coming over for Sunday dinner, John Edward has won his audience over even before he gets a single "hit."

A "hit" is what he and others in his field—the realm of psychics and parapsychologists—call it when one of these barrages of words connects with a target. Sort of like a cosmic bulls-eye. The woman who raised her hand when asked, "Is there anyone here whose name begins with P?" could be considered such a "hit." And from there, Edward steps up the pace, "cold reading" her until she has supplied enough information to his questions so that he can move from "cold" to "warm."

In a previous chapter, we discussed a classic mindreading technique commonly used by performing magicians, known as "cold reading." Edward, one of the hottest psychics on the scene today, often uses the technique, in his syndicated television series called "Crossing Over." Claiming to converse with the dead, he calmly builds a level of expectation in the members of his audience, most of whom have lost a loved one recently. These individuals are still grieving and trying to come to terms with that great loss, admit they believe in life after death and that it is indeed possible to contact the dead, and want desperately to believe that Edward will spot them in the audience, single them out, and channel their "Aunt Sue" before the night is over.

But those who know the ropes, so to speak, can spot Edward when he moves into "cold reading" his audience. He doesn't do the reading: His subjects do. When he fires out a lot of questions, he uses the information coming back from his subjects to gather more data so that he can move from "cold" to "warm."

The tactic known as "warm reading"[1] utilizes the same principles that apply in psychology—principles that apply to practically everyone. For instance, the psychologically savvy individual may understand more than you think about the process of grief, and thereby easily detect that a certain piece of jewelry, worn conspicuously around the neck, in open view, by a mourner may have been the ring once worn by a deceased spouse. Take, for example, NBC "Today Show" host Katie Couric, who lost her husband to cancer. When she returned to the show after his death, she wore his ring on a gold chain around her neck. Edward knows the way people mourn, and uses every bit of data coming in to help him in his display of "discourse" with the dead. So it is not uncommon, once he moves into "warm reading" his audience, to ask, "Do you have a ring or a piece of jewelry on you, please?" When the subject, who cannot believe his or her ears, complies by producing such a sentimental item, Edward utters a quick "thank you" and moves on to the next item on his agenda, all the while implanting the idea that he "divined" the significant jewelry from information gathered from another spiritual plane.

Similarly, he seems to "divine" the cause of a loved one's death—when, in actuality, he knows there are simply only about a half-dozen common causes of death, and that while "warm reading" it's fairly easy to get a "hit" here. He may clutch his chest and mutter, "I'm feeling a lot of pain in the chest." If the subject he is zeroing in on gives a "nod," he moves on to the next level: "Did he have cancer?"

If the response this time is "No," he merely shifts gears: "Heart attack?"

"Yes."

And what did not begin as a "hit" has ended appearing to be one after all.

SO WHAT'S WRONG WITH A LITTLE COMFORTING SCHMOOZE?

One might argue that all Edward is doing is trying to help the grieving find relief. Who cares whether he really "sees" and "hears" Aunt Sue from the other side, as he so adamantly claims is true? If his readings help people start to move past their pain, why not just let him do what he does—charge $250 a session for a private reading and entertain curious audiences five nights a week on the Sci-Fi Channel?

"Crossing Over with John Edward"—with its nightly audience estimated at more than 600,000 American households—is far more than your stereotypical "séance" program. Edwards, who now enjoys "superstar" status, suddenly has what seems to be "the Midas Touch." His autobiography became an instant best-seller. His live appearances are sell-outs, and there is a two-year waiting-list for personal consultations.

As spiritualism surges to the fore for the first time since the mid-1800s, when parlor games often included a good round of "Ouija" or the occasional séance, Edward and others who call themselves mediums are doing what amounts to a land-office business while simply using standard tricks of a magician's trade.

As the cameras roll, Edward appears to get a number of "hits" as he not only employs "cold reading" and "warm reading" tactics, but another tactic known as "hot reading."[2] Rolled together, it all seems plausible and many of those who receive their so-called "messages from beyond" from their dead relatives go away without ever realizing that they themselves supplied most of the data needed to make it all so unbelievably real.

"Hot reading" has to do with ferreting out more detailed information—not in front of the cameras, but before they ever start to roll. Edward has been caught in the act, deliberately gathering details about an individual before a reading is actually done. For example, prior to "reading" an NBC "Dateline" producer on-camera, during an investigative segment by John Hockenberry, Edward discovered—during filming of a related segment in which he was shown, ballroom dancing just for fun—that the producer had recently lost his beloved father, for whom he was still grieving. Later, on camera, Edward singled out the producer for a reading, and of course, his dead father came into the picture. When queried about the incident by Hockenberry, Edward admitted the topic may have come up during the filming of his footwork on the dance-floor. . .but then just shrugged his shoulders and again, shifted gears, moving onto a fresh topic without really ever taking responsibility for using information gathered in a discussion with the producer prior to his so-called "reading" as the "Dateline" cameras rolled.

Michael Shermer, publisher of *Skeptic* Magazine, writes, "The reason John Edward, James Van Praagh, and the other so-called mediums are unethical and dangerous is that they are not helping anyone in what they are doing. They are simply preying on the emotions of grieving people. As all loss, death, and grief counselors know, the best way to deal with death is to face it head on. Death is a part of life, and pretending that the dead are gathering in a television studio in New York to talk twaddle with a former ballroom-dance instructor is an insult to the intelligence and humanity of the living."[3]

According to Shermer, most of the time mediums don't need to "cheat." The reason? It has to do with the psychology of belief. "This stuff works because the people who go to mediums want it to work (remember—*they* do the readings, not the mediums). The simplest explanation for how mediums can get away with such an outrageous claim as the ability to talk to the dead is that they are dealing with a subject the likes of which would be hard to top for tragedy and finality—death. Sooner or later we will face this inevitability, starting, in the normal course of events, with the loss of our parents, then siblings and friends, and eventually ourselves. It is a grim outcome under the best of circumstances, made all the worse when death comes early or accidentally to those whose 'time was not up.' As those who traffic in the business of loss, death, and grief know all too well, we are often at our most vulnerable at such times. Giving deep thought to this reality can cause the most controlled and rational among us to succumb to our emotions."[4]

Charles Colson, best-selling Christian apologist whose radio program "BreakPoint" is syndicated throughout the world, comments: "Rejecting the biblical God doesn't change the fact that, as humans, we are incorrigibly religious and need to believe in something. Nor does it mean that questions such as 'Is there life after death?' cease being important. It simply means we've been cut off from the real answers to these questions. And that makes us vulnerable to superstition and irrationality. Paul says, professing to be wise, we become fools instead. C.S. Lewis and G.K. Chesterton, who lived during the earlier age of mediums, understood this well. Our age is, if anything, even more credulous and needy than theirs. So we need to help people understand that the answers they seek are not to be found in cable television mediums. Instead, they're to be found through faith in the One who really did cross over—from death back to life."[5]

Interestingly, all Edward's otherworldly spirit-contacts seem to be nice, ordinary people, not mad at anybody, and maybe even a little bit boring. They like to talk about their favorite fuzzy bathrobes, nicknames for their loved ones, the pets they left behind, and such. All very general, non-specific stuff. . .important only to the loved one who so desperately wants to be contacted by their dearly departed. However, not very solid factual evidence for life beyond the grave.

"Everyone wants to be reassured about loved ones who have passed. Just once I want to find a spiritualist who says, 'Oh, well, sorry. She went to hell and I can't reach her!'" says James Randi, in an interview for a news story about Edward and his fellow psychics that was carried by Gannett News Service.[6]

Meantime, Edward charges big bucks to keep on channeling the dead and delivering incipient messages about insignificant topics. And how does he justify that hefty $250-an-hour fee for a private reading? Pretty expensive "mind games," it turns out.

According to Edward, everybody has to make a living—even television psychics.

OPENING DANGEROUS DOORS

What Christians are most agitated over, concerning Edward and other so-called mediums, is that their claims to talk to the dead are in direct violation of God's warning in the Book of Deuteronomy against involvement with anything having to do with witchcraft, the occult, or necromancy—the biblical term for communication with the dead. "There shall not be found among you any one that maketh his son or his daughter to pass through the fire, or that useth divination, or an observer of times, or an enchanter, or a witch, or a charmer, or a consulter with familiar spirits, or a wizard, or a necromancer. For all that do these things are an abomination unto the Lord: and because of these abominations the Lord thy God doth drive them out from before thee" (Deuteronomy 18:10-12).

Yet Amazingly, when an on-line poll asked respondents—"Do you believe it is possible to communicate with the dead?"—76 percent answered "Yes." When asked another question—"Have you personally experienced communication with a dead loved one?"—53 percent answered "Yes." So it seems that never before in the history of our planet has interest been so high in these forbidden subjects. And never before have so many sought extra-biblical sources to support their belief in an afterlife.

When one sits idly by as Edward claims to "channel" Aunt Sue, a dangerous door is opened, a door that may lead further into the dangerous and dark realm of the occult.

These practices are nothing new; they date back to biblical times, and carry serious consequences to those engaging in them. For instance, the demise of King Saul occurred only after he consulted the Witch at Endor for a "reading" from the deceased prophet Samuel.

After that, it was all downhill for poor King Saul. He wound up going mad and dying a violent death.

Programs such as "Crossing Over," rather than performing a valuable service to those who are grieving, instead promote a dangerous curiosity into the occult in an age when it is all-too-easy to explore deep into the occult from the comfort of one's own home computer. Hundreds of web-sites offer up everything from induction into Wicca to advice on casting spells and curses to get what you want out of life while avoiding having to work for it. At least 1850 books on witchcraft are available by simply logging onto Amazon.com. And from the fruit of the disaster at Columbine, Colorado, when two seemingly innocent high-school students killed scores of their fellow classmates and teachers because they felt ostracized and rejected, we see that so-called innocent wanderings into the realm of the occult can cause consequences that go on forever. The boys who committed these heinous acts admit they had a penchant for violent video games, books on witchcraft, and web-sites on the net that had to do with occult practices. In their quest for power and personal vengeance, they destroyed many lives—their own included. No matter how it's "packaged," witchcraft is witchcraft, and vigilant Christian parents should easily realize they have cause to worry when the kids come home wearing black trenchcoats, black nail polish, and spiked-and-gelled hair.

Messages like those are pretty overt, and should easily signal a parent that there may be some storm clouds gathering. It would take no rocket-scientist to realize that clothes make more than a fashion statement: They are chief indicators of what is going on inside a person at the deepest levels of the soul. If a kid's taste begins to turn toward "Goth" (gothic) attire, then it's reasonable to believe that his interest levels may include a heavy preoccupation with the occult and that his favorite books may be by authors like Anne Rice, who writes bloody tales about vampires among us.

But in this post-Columbine age we live in, we *should* watch our children for signals as to where their interests lie. Sometimes, though, the signals aren't as clear. . .especially when witchcraft is "repackaged" as a best-selling book that every kid on the planet is clamoring to read.

THE TROUBLE WITH HARRY

So what's not to like about Harry Potter? He's a cute kid—right? His story is one of pathos—dead parents, raised an orphan by hateful relatives who make him live in a cupboard under the stairs, much like the pitiful characters we grew to love in the pages of a Charles Dickens novel. But then. . .something happens to Harry. He learns he is not just an ordinary child, after all, but the child of parents who were witches, and once he is shipped off to Hogwarts School of Witchcraft and Wizardry, he learns that he, too, is a witch—and that's where he really comes into his own.

Children around the globe are devouring the Harry Potter books—written by J.K. Rowling, who claims since she didn't use real "spells" in her books, their magic will be of no particular use to her young readers. With millions of copies in print, translated into forty different languages, Harry Potter has become as close to a household word as you're ever going to get. And this worries a lot of contemporary theologians, not to mention Christian parents who are concerned that their children are being directed down dark corridors of fantasy that may eventually lead all the way into the occult.

What child wouldn't want to read of Harry's amazing adventures? He goes from nerdy unwanted boy to the most popular kid in class, winning the broomstick-riding tournament hands-down and running for his life from the death-curse placed upon him by the evil Voldemort, the malevolent wizard responsible for killing his beloved parents. He casts spells and curses, talks to snakes, and somehow manages to come off as perhaps the first contemporary "cool" good kid.

But that's what worries Christians most—that Harry's cool-but-somehow-good behavior is not based upon biblical foundations, or adhering to an intrinsic knowledge of the difference between right and wrong, but upon advancing in children the idea of the "possibility of the impossible." And this has nothing at all to do with faith, but with the concept that through the use of witchcraft, kids can use spells to get what they want in life—and quick. Some children have reportedly been trying this method to pass tests and attract boyfriends and girlfriends.

All this exploration into the strange world of the occult is now possible and made easy due to the internet, where there are hundreds of sites covering a range of occult interests and telling kids how to do everything from joining Wicca to worshipping Satan and conjuring up a quick-and-easy spell to pass that nasty school exam.

Lindy Beam, a youth-culture analyst from *Plugged In*, a Focus on the Family newsletter, states, "Children who read about Harry will probably discover little to nothing about the true world of the occult. We know God hates the practice of witchcraft. But we have committed a fault of logic in saying that reading about witches and wizards necessarily translates into these occult practices. I would propose instead that reading *Harry Potter* produces *curiosity* and that it is what we do with that curiosity that makes all the difference."[7]

However, her colleague at Focus on the Family, John Andrew Murray, had harsher things to say about Harry: "By dissociating magic and supernatural evil, it becomes possible to portray occult practices as 'good' and 'healthy,' contrary to the scriptural declaration that such practices are 'detestable to the Lord.' This, in turn, opens the door for kids to become fascinated with the supernatural while tragically failing to seek or recognize the one true source of supernatural good—namely God. What comes across is a kind of dualism, the idea that there are two equal, uncreated, antagonistic forces, one good and one evil, and that choosing between the two is purely a matter of personal opinion. Rowling's readers are ultimately left in a morally confused world."[8]

To be sure, the Harry Potter books are filled with boyish adventures that virtually thrill their young readers, many claiming to enjoy reading for the first time in their young lives since signing on to read about Harry and his thrilling alternate lifestyle. But while some Christians have their feet planted firmly in the "anti-Harry" camp, there are those—including Charles Colson and Fuller Seminary president Richard Mouw—who do not take exception to a Christian child being exposed to the adventures of Harry in wizard-school.[9] Instead, they cite the wonderful virtues that are modeled in the pages of Rowling's 700-page books and merely caution parents to discuss them with their children as they read them, in the light of biblical truth.

NOT EXACTLY LIKE 'HANSEL AND GRETEL'

Some argue that there is really not much difference in the tales of Harry Potter and, say, the tales of the Brothers Grimm. After all, the tale of Hansel and Gretel contained some of the same themes—an evil witch who wanted to cook them and eat them, for instance. It was the children who had to decide how to best outsmart the witch while overcoming the temptation to eat her "candy house."

It all boils down to the place of fantasy in encouraging a child to develop his imagination. But what kind of fantasy? Will any sort do?

In a fascinating article appearing in *Christian Research Journal*, Gene Edward Veith explores the difference between "Good Fantasy and Bad Fantasy."[9] "The Harry Potter books may be the biggest success story in children's literature. The series by a British woman named J.K. Rowling, who started writing them as a divorced single mother on welfare, has sold over 12 million copies, dominating the best seller lists for over two years. At one point, Harry Potter books ranked nos. 1, 2, and 3, the first time one author had ever taken the top three spots," writes Veith. "The fourth Harry Potter book was a best seller based on advance orders alone—before it was ever published—and when it finally arrived, the whole publishing industry could hardly meet the demand.

"Amazingly, most of these book buys, who have taken over the adult best seller charts, are children. Many of them, reportedly, are enjoying a book for the first time in their lives. Parents and teachers are saying that the Harry Potter series is turning on thousands and thousands of young people to the pleasures of reading. Boys, in particular, who have usually been more resistant to books than girls, are turning off the TV and the video games to spend time with a 'good' book…. Surely, this is good news. Yet, something about the Harry Potter series makes Christian parents squirm: The novels are about a school for witches."

Veith continues, "In a time when real witchcraft is in vogue, with Wicca chapters being recognized on university campuses as another legitimate campus ministry, these entertaining novels make witchcraft sound appealing. True, these broom-riding witches and wizards are a 'good' version of fairytale characters—not the neopagan goddess and nature worshippers of Wicca. Nevertheless, Christian parents still worry that it could be a small leap from fascination with Harry Potter to overt involvement with the occult."[10]

In the film, "Harry Potter: Witchcraft Repackaged. . .Making Evil Look Innocent," Robert S. McGee makes some of the same observations. McGee, author of *The Search for Significance*, states, "If you believe there is no real power in witchcraft, then you should have no problem with the Harry Potter books. But then you are denying the experience of hundreds of thousands of individuals who have practiced witchcraft."[11] Witchcraft, the author explains, due to its nature of putting one into bondage and becoming subject to its control, opens the door to many forms of obsessive behavior—including drugs, alcohol, and promiscuous sexual activity. After a young person has been captivated by witchcraft, he says, they often do not choose to come out of it until after they have spent many years living in misery.

But while the Harry Potter books do not seem at all harmless, McGee and others worry that they set the stage for an absorption in material with stronger occult themes—and that may, in fact, lead to a young person getting into the occult all the way to the hilt.

"Harry Potter is only one example of how today's young people are awash in fantasy," writes Veith. "Video games may be high-tech, but they often portray archaic realms of swords and sorcery. From Pokemon card games, they graduate to Magic the Gathering and other role-playing games, ranging from Dungeons and Dragons to Vampires. On TV they watch Xena Warrior Princess, Buffy the Vampire Slayer, and Sabrina the Teenage Witch. Movies popular with children and teenagers are often science fiction-tinged fantasies, such as the *Star Wars* series, or contemporary redactions of old fantasy motifs, from genies in a bottle to talking animals.

"In fact, fantasy has always been a staple of children's entertainment, including the most wholesome. Fairy tales also have witches in them but are currently under attack by feminists and others for conveying values that are 'too traditional.' Some of the best Christian writers, from John Bunyan to C.S. Lewis, have used and defended the genre of fantasy. Lewis's *Chronicles of Narnia* have helped thousands of children and their parents understand the gospel. The problem is not with fantasy, which is simply an exercise of the imagination. A work of fantasy can shape the imagination of its audience in either harmful *or* helpful ways. The challenge is to discern the difference between good fantasy and bad fantasy, recognizing not only its content but also its effects on the reader."[12]

IS HE A GOOD WITCH...OR A BAD WITCH?

The idea, in and of itself, that there can be a difference between a "good" witch and a "bad" witch is contrary to Scripture, which condemns *all* witchcraft as an abomination to God. So then, the main problem Christians have with Harry is that books about him put a positive top-spin on "witchcraft." No one, it seems, has as much a problem with the fantasy elements of the Harry Potter series as with the fact that, at its core, the Harry Potter series glosses over witchcraft and makes it seem at once inviting while implanting in children the idea that maybe...just maybe...it would work if a spell were tried in order to pass that test, confront that challenge, meet that trial.

Veith suggests that the best antidote to Harry Potter—as well as the negative effects of other non-Christian fantasy—is to ground their children in positive literature and, above all, in the wonders contained in the Word of God. "Children who have a strong sense of fictionality and who know that there is a difference between the story and the actual world are inoculated against most of the bad effects of fantasy," writes Veith. "It is when the child takes the fantasy world as the real world—that is, when it ceases to be fantasy—that problems can arise. When the child understands the difference between fiction and reality, however, stories of all kinds can both teach and delight."[13]

So is Harry Potter harmless fiction? Or a dangerous "mind game?" Is it just a story, or yet another example of "witchcraft repackaged" to fit our modern world?

You decide.

CHAPTER SIXTEEN

A Demon in Every Bush?

Satan uses mind games to ensnare men and women into a psychic trap, in which they are always searching for a deeper knowledge or a greater power but never quite attaining it. The enticements put before mankind have created a tremendous interest among Christians regarding the power of Satan. That's why we have seen a number of books being sold in Christian bookstores over the past several years attempting to describe the devil and his wiles.

Unfortunately, many of these books are based mostly upon the perceptions of the author's *experience* rather than upon *sound biblical theology*. There is a tendency within the Christian community to accept someone's experience as solid evidence without asking hard questions. In fact, those who question the validity of another person's testimony are castigated for not "walking in unity." For example, when André and others rejected Mike Warnke's wild tales of demon worship, they were criticized for not supporting a fellow believer—until a series of investigative articles proved that Warnke was not the "former Satanic high priest" he had claimed to be. Sometimes a healthy skepticism is good for the body of Christ.

Perhaps all the interest in Satan and the alleged psychic powers he is using has begun to create an unhealthy fascination with demonic activities—one in which some people have begun to see a demon in every bush. A recent Christian television show offered a preacher warning that "demons" were keeping people poor. Another blamed "the demons of illness" for giving somebody the flu. And a popular book suggests that demonic forces can place a "curse" on a family, so that the members are fated to fall into the same pattern of sin as their forebears. It is in this forum that we encourage Christians to remember the advice of C.S. Lewis:

> *There are two equal and opposite extremes into which our race can fall about the devils. One is to disbelieve in their existence. The other is to believe, and to feel an excessive and unhealthy interest in them. They themselves are equally pleased by both errors and hail a materialist or a magician with the same delight.*[1]

It is imperative that the modern church, which is under attack by the powers of hell, maintain a balanced perspective between recognizing Satan's existence but not becoming engrossed in his work. For though the devil is a powerful foe, he has already been defeated by the shed blood of our Lord Jesus Christ.

Our purpose in writing this chapter is not to prove the existence of Satan, though out of necessity we will touch on our reasons for believing in him, but to come to a biblical conclusion as to exactly what he can do. We firmly believe that some of the recent teachings in the Christian community are based on faulty theology and usurp the majesty and sovereignty of God.

THE ONE BEHIND IT ALL

Let's be clear as to *what Satan can do* in this world. The Bible is clear that Satan exists[2] and that he was originally perfect in wisdom and beauty, but that his heart became full of pride and false ambition so that he was deposed and cast out of heaven.[3] Satan's problem was that he wanted to *be like God*—the very sin he now tries to draw people into! He is crafty and deceptive, and he has the power to create *false* signs and wonders.[4] The devil likes to appear as an "angel of light," pretending to lead people to greater knowledge and freedom but actually dragging them into greater confusion and bondage.

We know from the Scriptures that Satan has access to God's presence,[5] that he inhabits the spiritual realm,[6] and that he is active upon the earth.[7] The apostle Paul referred to Satan as "the god of this age"—an apt description for the one behind all our culture's interest in psychic phenomena.[8] His work on earth includes causing suffering,[9] luring mankind into evil,[10] and ensnaring men and women in sin.[11] He does this through blinding our minds,[12] dissipating the truth,[13] and promoting evil acts through his followers.[14] Satan takes special delight in making life hard for Christians by resisting them, accusing them, and testing them regularly.[15]

He has an army of helpers, called demons, who are spirit beings with personal intelligence.[16] They are vile and degenerate disembodied spirits[17] who produce moral impurity,[18] bring affliction upon people,[19] and occasionally take possession of the bodies of human beings.[20] However, the Bible tells us that Satan and his minions are a conquered enemy,[21] perpetually cursed and destined for the lake of fire.[22]

Satan *wants* people to believe in the lie of psychic power. He uses mind games to attract men and women seeking spiritual knowledge, promising them supernatural power but never delivering it. And the deeper people get involved with psychic activity, the more entangled they get with the devil and his army of demons. They become blinded to the truth and resistant to the things of God. The more an individual gets involved in the search for psychic miracles, the more deceived he or she becomes.

THE LIMITS OF SATAN

Though it is apparent that Satan has tremendous powers, there are definite limitations to his power. *Nowhere in the Bible are we told that Satan can perform genuine miracles.* To suggest he can do so is to go beyond Scripture. He is not God—he cannot create life, foresee the future, transform matter, or perform miracles. We must be very careful about accepting stories of those who claim to have heard of Satan's power when their claims are not consistent with Scripture. Consider the Biblical record:

- There is no evidence that Satan can cause people or things to levitate, though stories about levitation abound.
- There is no evidence that a demon can transform matter from one object into another. Jesus proved He could when He changed water into wine, but Satan cannot.[23]
- There is no evidence that Satan can predict the future. Billions of dollars are spent each year on astrologists, palm readers, channelers, and psychic friends, but the money has so far produced not one example of genuine prophecy.
- There is no evidence that Satan can create life nor that he can take life, though God may sometimes use him for such a purpose.[24]
- There is no evidence that the devil can make a person wealthy, though he clearly promises to do so.
- There is no recorded instance of a demon manifesting itself as a man, though there are examples of angels doing so.
- There is no evidence that Satan can manipulate the weather, calming a storm or stopping the sun the way God can.
- There is no evidence that the devil can perform miracles, though he can produce "counterfeit miracles, signs and wonders," according to 2 Thessalonians 2:9. A counterfeit miracle is a lie—something posing as the genuine article.

It is unfortunate that the term "supernatural" is used when describing the abilities or powers of Satan and demons since most people equate the word "supernatural" with the miraculous. Only God can perform the miraculous. The supernatural is only a higher degree of the natural, it is the SUPERnatural, but not miraculous. No degree of the natural can ever be equated with the miraculous. A miracle is an act of God—only He can perform one. On the contrary, Satan is the ultimate master of deception; he tries to imitate or simulate the miraculous, but he can never perform a genuine miracle, only "counterfeit miracles" or "lying wonders."

In the words of Francis Anderson, "Satan may be the chief mischief maker of the universe, but he is a mere creature compared with the Lord. He can only do what God permits him to do."[25] In other words, the devil does not have miraculous power but, as we stated earlier, a *supernormal* power. He is able to utilize natural laws in an advanced way. Dr. Norm Geisler has articulated it well:

> *In spite of Satan's super power, he cannot do truly supernatural things as God can do. For example, he cannot create life or raise the dead. Although it isa debated point, Satan probably cannot suspend natural laws, but he can certainly utilize them in unusual ways for his own purposes. We know that he can cause a "fire...from the sky" and even cause "a mighty wind"—of course, modern science can do things like this too. In this sense, Satan is the Super Scientist. As such he can perform advanced wonders of science that seem to be supernatural but are not.*[26]

Satan's strength is found primarily in the mental and circumstantial arenas of life. As the author of confusion, his "mind games" can delude, depress, misguide, and set the most harmonious ideas and people at cross purposes. Although individuals do not have physical contact with Satan, there are times when they suffer physical consequences resulting from his mental and emotional harassment. Satan's limited knowledge and abilities are based on his limited experience. He is not omniscient, omnipotent, or omnipresent as God alone is.

MIND GAMES

Because of God's desire for the welfare of His people, He frequently admonishes them to bring their thoughts under His control through the power of the Holy Spirit and His commandments for right living. Ephesians 6 warns us to put on the armor of His strength in order to withstand the schemes, strategies, and tricks of Satan; and Philippians 4 emphasizes the importance of keeping God's Word and truth pre-eminent in the minds of His people. Throughout both the Old and New Testaments, God spoke to those who revere Him about guarding their hearts and minds, knowing that the real struggle is not against people made of flesh and blood, but against the powers of darkness and spiritual forces of the unseen world.

Each of us needs to put into proper perspective the contrast between God and Satan. God spoke and more than a hundred billion galaxies were created. Satan can speak nothing into existence. He is no more than a reprobate angel, a created being who couldn't even create a piece of bubble gum on his own. How ridiculous to compare Satan's limited abilities to God's unlimited power!

No individual can therefore be given miraculous power by the devil. A man can exercise and develop his athletic abilities in order to lift several hundred pounds. And some would argue the Scriptures indicate a demon possessed man would have the *super*natural ability to lift even more. But if this were true, the "more" would just be a little more of the natural; it would be another thing for someone to miraculously levitate several tons without any physical effort extended—*that* would qualify as miraculous.

It is critical to recognize the difference between what Satan can do and what God can do. The essence and heart of the issue is realized in that the difference is not a *comparison of degree* but a *contrast in kind*.

If we were to take a rock and compare it to a plant, we would find one has life and one does not. No matter how much we polish that rock, it would *never* have life; yet the plant would have life from the very beginning. In the same way, no degree of the supernatural can *ever* produce the miraculous. What God possesses in the miraculous, Satan does not have. Being able to perform the miraculous is part of God's

262

inherent being. This is one of the qualities that sets Him apart from anything or anyone in the universe.

Why is all this important? Because recently we have observed many believers granting Satan far too much power, and thereby falling victim to his mind games.

POSSESSED BY DEMONS

On April 5, 1993, the national television show *20/20* stirred up much interest in the subject of demonic power when it offered viewers the opportunity to watch an exorcism performed upon a young woman named Gina. The ceremony, performed by Father James LeBar and an anonymous "Father A," was done because members of Gina's family claimed she had incredible strength, could speak in unknown languages, was clairvoyant, and levitated over her bed. We watched the program with interest.

Unfortunately, none of those four things occurred. They kept Gina strapped to her bed (unfortunate, since nothing would have been more convincing then watching her float around the room like a balloon), she didn't burst from her bonds, and the exorcism was planned in secret—though if she were really clairvoyant, that shouldn't have mattered. What did happen was that Gina ranted in strange voices, sometimes clearly and sometimes inarticulately. Despite the touted exorcism, Gina was back on antipsychotic medicine soon afterward in order to keep her personality stabilized.

Was Gina "possessed" by a devil? Perhaps, but what good the Roman Catholic priests did by waving crosses and making her drink holy water is a point of dispute. Possession is a biblical fact, but the attaining of supernatural power by doing so is not, regardless of what appears in movies like *The Exorcist*. The demon-possessed man in Mark 5 and Matthew 8 was able to break his shackles, but that does not immediately prove he had supernatural strength. As a matter of fact, members of a Christian performance group, "The Power Team," do so on stage each night.

Our concern is that many Christians have come to believe that Satan holds some sort of incredible power, and that he can wield it to control us or keep us in bondage. Clearly a Christian *cannot* be possessed by a demon, for we belong to Christ, and He claimed that "no one" could take His people out of His hand.[27] If we have been made alive in Christ, filled with the Spirit, and adopted as sons of God, then it makes no sense that Satan would be able to "own" us or possess us in some way. As Thomas Ice puts it:

> We do not believe that the Bible teaches a Christian can be possessed or indwelt by a demon. We *do* believe, however, that Christians can be severely influenced or oppressed by Satan and the demonic. The key issues on this matter revolve around the differences between *internal* control/inhabitation and *external* influence.[28]

This is not to say that Satan cannot *oppress* us. The devil is working overtime to accuse, ensnare, and confuse believers. But he cannot possess us. It is this belief in Christian possession which has caused an overreaction on the part of many believers to live in fear of their conquered foe.

It is a grave mistake to attribute a power to the devil that he does not have, for it only sensationalizes Satan. A study done by *Campus Life* magazine revealed that the reason people get involved with Satan in the first place is to acquire more power.[29] So when someone claims the devil was able to give a person power to levitate or predict the future, watch out! It only increases his attraction. To attribute more power to Satan than he deserves is to sensationalize him—perhaps even to glorify him. When we lift him up to be like God, we rob the Lord of the glory due only to Him.

GRANTING SATAN TOO MUCH POWER

Some of Christianity's recognized authorities on spiritual warfare have perhaps granted too much power to the devil. They have suggested he can foretell the future, reveal secret information, and perform miracles—none of which can be supported biblically. In recent years we have seen dozens of books and conferences created to help believers prepare for spiritual warfare, but we must make sure the proposed solutions are both practical and biblical.

For example, Dr. Neil Anderson is probably the world's best-known authority on spiritual warfare. We have great respect for Neil and the influence he has had in the lives of many people. Neil has helped thousands through his books about breaking the bonds of Satan, but believers have to be careful that his prescription for spiritual warfare not be taken as some type of magic formula for fending off every demonic attack. What Dr. Anderson describes are good guidelines and a fine tool to be used in spiritual warfare, but they have been misunderstood by some as being a type of magic words.

While there may be great benefit in praying through his "steps to freedom in Christ," they should not be considered as a solution that will work for everyone, at every time, in every situation. Similarly, the popular concept of "binding" Satan should not be considered a blueprint for every spiritual battle. The Bible says we are to *resist* Satan, but there are no references to our prayers "binding" him. What exactly does it mean to "bind" Satan? For how long is he bound? Who unlooses him? And why not "bind" whoever is doing the unloosing? While becoming involved in spiritual warfare is a necessary task for any believer intending to mature in Christ, we've got to be careful that our theology lines up with the Bible.

Some writers have proposed the notion that we ought to "confront" Satan verbally, but we can't find that teaching in Scripture. The single greatest chapter on spiritual warfare, Ephesians 6, never mentions it. Neither do James, John, Luke, or Paul. The very concept of verbally rebuking the devil is on shaky ground, since even Michael the archangel did not do it and said instead, "The Lord rebuke you!"[30] If we begin to grant too much power to our words, we start sliding toward the mind game of creating reality with our mouths.

Satan is a powerful enemy, and he can ensnare people into spiritual bondage, but we dare not grant him too much power. For instance, recent writings have proposed the concept of "claiming your children" from Satan. This raises a number of questions: What exactly happens when a child is "claimed"? Does it offer some sort of extra protection, and if not, why doesn't the parent simply share the gospel with the child? Furthermore, the idea that a newborn must be immediately "claimed" to negate demonic influences, or that an adopted child might have already been "claimed" by Satan, would appear to have no biblical support. However, we are called to *pray* for our children, that the Lord would protect and nurture them. We believe in a mighty God, who offers truth and freedom to all who follow Him.

When we begin to give the devil too much credit, it causes us to live in fear of him. So while we appreciate the good work many "warfare" ministries have had in the world, we struggle with the claim that "5 percent of the Christian community" has fallen victim to demonic "control"[31], and that a controlled person can free himself by saying certain words. These ministries provide some excellent prayers for those facing spiritual oppression, but we question both the math and the proposed solution, wondering how these apparently possessed Christians are supposed to free themselves simply by saying words that are "nothing more than a fierce moral inventory and a rock-solid commitment to truth."[32] To suggest that a believer can lose control to Satan, then turn right around and regain control by saying some stock phrases, is dangerously close to magic.

CURSES AND HEXES

Another concern we have is the emphasis which some ministries have placed on "generational curses." While alcoholism and abuse may pass through a family, there isn't any biblical support that Satan can place a spiritual curse on a family that will continue to impact the lives of people generations later. For one thing, a belief in the power of curses seems rather cultic. We've all heard missionaries tell stories about tribal people being scared of curses, but the story usually ends with the missionary leading the individual to saving faith in Christ. To think that a *believer*, who has been set free by the Lord, would fear anything as silly as a "generational curse" is antibiblical and accords Satan too much power.

"The last step to freedom is to renounce the sins of your ancestors and any curses which may have been placed on you," one author writes. "The fact that demonic strongholds can be passed on from one generation to the next is well-attested by those who counsel the afflicted."[33] But we can find no Bible verse that admits pagan curses have any power, and the fact that something is attested to by counselors is a far cry from it being attested to by Scripture. Again, we want to make sure *the Bible* is our source of authority, not someone's experience.

Christians used to scoff at the idea that a witch doctor could place a "hex" on someone. Now we are seeing people in the evangelical camp promoting the notion that spells and curses are real and we should defend ourselves against them. We have in the office a recent issue of *Charisma* magazine that contains an advertisement for the book *Curses: What They Are and How to Break Them*. The ad copy claims this to be a "much-needed exposé" which "explores generational curses, hexes, spells, territorial curses, neo-pagan curses, together with an effective strategy in Christ to dismantle and destroy their impact, power, and effect."[34] In other words, we have now apparently ceded power to Satan and are in subjection to him.

Frances McNutt, writing in *Ministries Today*, penned these words to pastors, revealing not only her belief in curses but her advice that they should in turn curse others:

> *I want to encourage all pastors and their spouses to begin each day by praying for protection.... Then in the name of Jesus and by the sword of the Spirit, we break ourselves free from any curses, hexes, or spells that may have been directed against us, commanding them to return to those who sent them to harm us.*[35]

The writers who are promoting curses always seem to rely on their own and others' experiences rather than on biblical support. For example, an esteemed missionary says in *The Handbook for Spiritual Warfare* that curses "release spiritual authority."[36] But in searching the Scriptures we can only find two types of curses: those that come from

God and those that are claimed by pagans. We believe completely in the reality of the former, but we reject the reality of the latter, and we notice that in Scripture these pagan "curses" didn't amount to much. Goliath cursed David, but was defeated. Shimei cursed the king, and it cost him his life. This is what we need to fear?

The futility of renouncing curses after one has become a Christian would seem to negate the clear teaching of the Bible: "For he has rescued us from the dominion of darkness and brought us into the kingdom of the Son he loves, in whom we have redemption, the forgiveness of sin."[37] We have not been delivered from "preconversion occultic sin," but from *all* sin—and from the authority of Satan! *Nowhere in Scripture can we find a prayer or confession offered "in order to walk free from past influences."*[38] In fact, we are not aware of *any* passage in the Bible that shows a saved individual under a demonic curse and requiring a confession, renunciation, or exorcism to be delivered from it.

There is a wave of mystical and superstitious thinking that has permeated the church over the past several years. It seems to accept the mind games of Satan, granting credence to the idea that he has power over believers. But if we look to Scripture as our authority, and not human experience, we will find solid truth that rejects superstition.

WHAT CAN WE DO?

Spiritual warfare is serious business. The apostle John tells us that "the whole world is under the control of the evil one."[39] Paul encourages us, in Ephesians chapter 6, to battle Satan by putting on the armor of God—the belt of truth, the breastplate of righteousness, the helmet of salvation, the shield of faith, and the sword of the Spirit. With those elements in place, we won't be as susceptible to the lies and attacks of the enemy.

Paul reminds us that "our struggle is not against flesh and blood, but...against the spiritual forces of evil in the heavenly realms."[40] If we are to understand what that battle is about, we cannot afford to confuse fact with fiction. The stories propagated by Christian ministries about levitations, curses, demons being sent out at midnight, and the like all contribute to the church taking its eyes off the real battle.

DIVINE POWER

This isn't the first time our culture has faced a serious crisis over the role of Satan. In the late 1500s believers were much concerned with the possibility of witches. As a devout Christian scholar, Sir Reginald Scot was bothered by the tendency of people to attribute their troubles to evil powers. Scot, who had a keen interest in magic as an entertainment, recognized the difference between the mighty power of God and the measley power of magicians. In 1581, he wrote *The Discoverie of Witchcraft*, explaining,

> *The fables of witchcraft have taken so fast hold and deep root in the heart of man that few or none can (nowadays) with patience endure the hand and correction of God. For if any adversity, grief, sickness, loss of children, corn, cattle, or liberty happen upon them, by and by they exclaim upon "witches." As though there were no God in Israel that ordereth all things according to His will, punishing both just and unjust with griefs, plagues, and afflictions in manner and form as he thinketh good, but that certain old women here on earth, called witches, must needs be the contrivers of all men's calamities, and as though they themselves were innocents, and had deserved no such punishments.*
>
> *Such faithless people (say I) are also persuaded that neither hail nor snow, thunder nor lightning, rain nor tempestuous winds come from the heavens at the commandment of God, but are raised by the cunning and power of witches and conjurers....*

But certainly it is neither a witch nor devil but a glorious God that maketh the thunder.... But let me see any of them all rebuke and still the sea in time of tempest, as Christ did, or raise the stormy wind, as God did with His word, and I will believe them.

Little think our witchmongers that the Lord commandeth the clouds above or openeth the doors of heaven, or that the Lord goeth forth in the tempests and storms, but rather that witches and conjurers are then about their business. . . .

But these make the devil a whole god, to create things of nothing, to know men's cogitations, and to do that which God never did, as to transubstantiate men into beasts, etc. Which thing if devils could do, yet followeth it not that witches have such power. But if all the devils in hell were dead, and all the witches in England burned or hanged, I warrant you we should not fail to have rain, hail, and tempests, as we now have; according to the appointment and will of God, and according to the con-stitution of the elements and the course of the planets, wherein God hath set a perfect and perpetual order....

Finally, if witches could accomplish these things, what needed it seem so strange to the people when Christ by miracle commanded both seas and winds, etc. For it is written: "Who is this? For both wind and sea obey him."

...He that attributeth to a witch such divine power as duly and only appertaineth unto GOD...is in his heart a blasphemer, an idolater, and full of gross impiety, although he neither go nor send to her for assistance.[41]

After much noise and a bit too much action, they determined that the worries had exceeded the actual problem. There was too much fancy and too little fact. Historian Nigel Wright has observed:

> *The great witch craze gathered momentum because people were too willing to believe in what the devil could do. In this mood they ascribed all manner of things to the devil. The power and presence of the devil thus became exaggerated because people were too willing to believe. Such an attitude is not altogether lacking in the contemporary church.... When this happens it is scarcely indistinguishable from superstition. So a demon consciousness arises which bears no relation to the actual situation and which distorts and degrades the individual.*[42]

Should Christians know about Satan and the tricks he pulls to ensnare or defeat us? Absolutely. Should we worry about the devil gaining power over us and resort to magic formulas to keep him away? Absolutely not.

The apostle Peter warns that the devil is like "a roaring lion looking for someone to devour," and he encourages believers to resist Satan by "standing firm in the faith." This means we ought to be strong in the Lord, know our Bible, and be ready to use it when confronting spiritual attacks. If we stick to those principles, we won't fall for the popular psychic frauds our culture has embraced.

Some believers have begun speaking out strongly against the mind games of Satan. For example, Roger McNichols, Neil Anderson's right-hand man at *Freedom in Christ Ministries*, was bothered by the popularity of psychic hotlines so he created his very own hotline—one that explains how the psychic hotlines work and introduces callers to the saving knowledge of Jesus Christ! Some ministries like *Jews for Jesus* and *Campus Crusade for Christ* have specifically reached out to people involved in these mind games, offering the truth of God to counteract the deceit of Satan. Jerry MacGregor offers a lecture in which he demonstrates how fake mind-readers trick people into believing they have psychic powers—even offering to duplicate any psychic trick performed by someone claiming supernatural ability. And André Kole, while performing his world-class magic show around the globe, gives a clear presentation of the gospel and offers a $25,000 check to anyone who can demonstrate genuine psychic ability.

In the sixteenth century, Reginald Scot worried that "the fables of witchcraft" had led men away from God, and toward Satan. Those same fables are still with us.

The problem we have in our culture today is the problem people have always faced: *They need God.* People want peace with God, and to find it they are willing to explore every crazy idea that comes around, in hopes of discovering the one idea that will work. When an unscrupulous person is willing to fake psychic ability in order to meet that desire, there is the possibility of grave danger. When a Christian begins to believe in psychic ability, "The possibilities of credulity are enormous. It becomes difficult to disentangle fact from fantasy.... It is possible to lose a proper sense of judgment and by a credulous attitude give to the power of darkness more power than it actually possesses."[43]

Rather than attributing psychic power to Satan, recognize that supernatural power resides in God alone. Instead of trying to tap into psychic power to discover deeper truth, open up your Bible and delve into the truth of the Word. Don't believe in the mind games of the devil, but rejoice in the fact that, as a believer, you have full assurance that God lives within you. Remember: Greater is He who is in you than he who is in the world!

NOTES

A World of Illusion

1. Reginald Scot, *The Discoverie of Witchcraft*, first published in 1581.

Chapter 1—They Told Me All About Myself!

1. Kendrick Frazier, "Articles on the Paranormal: Where are the Editors?" in *The Skeptical Inquirer*, Winter 1980–81, p. 2.

2. Ibid, p. 4.

3. Author's interview with Dr. Ray Hyman, professor of psychology at the University of Oregon and well-known skeptic and debunker of alleged paranormal events.

4. For more information see Elizabeth Loftus, *Eyewitness Testimony* (Harvard University Press, 1980) and *Eyewitness Testimony: Psychological Profiles* (Cambridge University Press, 1984).

5. See Norman E. Spear and David C. Riccio, *Memory: Phenomena & Principles* (Allyn Press, 1993) or *Memory Distortion: How Minds, Brains, and Societies Reconstruct the Past*, ed. Daniel Schacter et al (Harvard University Press, 1995).

6. For a thorough investigation of this incident, see Larry Kusche, *The Disappearance of Flight 19* (Harper and Row, 1980).

7. "The Amityville Hokum: The Hoax and the Hype," in *The Skeptical Inquirer*, Spring 1986, p. 3.

8. For more information, see "The Project Alpha Experiment" in *The Skeptical Inquirer*, Summer 1983.

9. See *Memory: Remembering and Forgetting in Everyday Life*, ed. Jane Nevins and Merry Clark (Mastermedia Ltd., 1995).

10. Dr. Jerry MacGregor has done this in public settings, asking people what they saw and duplicating it on stage. Magician James Randi has done the same thing on *The Tonight Show* and many other venues.

11. The authors wish to thank magician, researcher, and psychologist Dr. Ray Hyman for sharing his wisdom with us in regard to information and belief systems.

12. Carl Sagan, "Night Walkers and Mystery Mongers: Sense and Nonsense at the Edge of Science," in *The Skeptical Inquirer*, Spring 1986, pp. 23–24.

13. James Randi, "Paranormal Powers Are So Much Hocus-Pocus," in *Science*, January 25, 1980, p. 389.

Chapter 2—Your New Psychic Friends

1. Figures are taken from a *USA Today* story, n.d.
2. G.B. Sullivan, "Stop, Look, Choose . . ." *San Francisco Examiner*, July 26, 1976.
3. *Merriam-Webster's New Collegiate Dictionary*, Tenth Edition, 1996.
4. The definitions of psychic abilities are all generally drawn from Arthur S. Berger and Joyce Berger, *The Encyclopedia of Parapsychology and Psychical Research* (Paragon House, 1991). The definition of telepathy is found on p. 430.
5. Ibid, p. 330.
6. For further information on divination, see "How Pagans Divine the Will of God," in Bruce Waltke and Jerry MacGregor, *Finding the Will of God* (Vision House, 1995).
7. Gallup Poll, *Los Angeles Times*, August 8, 1993, p. E3; and "Current Research: Recent Findings on Religious Attitudes and Behavior," *Religion Watch*, February 1993, p. 3. The quotation on horoscopes is taken from Richard Morin, "A Revival of Faith in Religion," in the *Sacramento Bee*, July 4, 1993, p. 1.
8. Richard S. Broughton, *Parapsychology: The Controversial Science* (Ballantine, 1991).
9. The SPR still exists today, publishing the *Journal of the Society for Psychical Research* in London. The *American Society for Psychical Research*, started in 1885, publishes the *Journal of the ASPR* in New York.
10. Ray Hyman, *The Elusive Quarry: A Scientific Appraisal of Psychical Research* (Prometheus Books, 1989), pp. 99–106.
11. J.B. Rhine, *The Reach of the Mind* (Wm. Sloan Associates, 1947), pp. 33–96.
12. James Randi, *An Encyclopedia of Claims, Frauds, and Hoaxes of the Occult and Supernatural* (St. Martin's Press, 1995), pp. 49, 142.
13. D. Scott Rogo, "J. B. Rhine and the Levy Scandal," in *A Skeptic's Handbook of Parapsychology*, ed. Paul Kurtz (Prometheus Books, 1985), pp. 313–26.
14. Betty Marwick, "The Establishment of Data Manipulation in the Soal-Shaddeton Experiments," in *A Skeptic's Handbook of Parapsychology* (Prometheus Books, 1985), p. 287.
15. See Hyman, *Quarry*, pp. 20–75.
16. Committee on Techniques for the Enhancement of Human Performance, Commission on Behavioral and Social Sciences and Education, National Research Council, *Enhancing Human Performance: Issues, Theories, and Techniques*, ed. Daniel Dnickman and John A. Swets (National Academy Press, 1987).
17. See "Spiritualism Exposed: Margaret Fox Cane Confesses to Fraud," as quoted in *A Skeptic's Handbook of Parapsychology*, ed. Paul Kurtz (Prometheus Books, 1985), pp. 225–33.
18. Melvin Harris, *Investigating the Unexplained* (Prometheus Books, 1986), p. 176.
19. Cited by Harris, ibid., p. 182.
20. M. LaMar Keene, *The Psychic Mafia* (St. Martin's Press, 1976), p. 149.

MIND GAMES

21. Jeane Dixon, *Jeane Dixon: My Life and Prophecies, Her Own Story As Told to Rene Noorbergen* (William Morrow, 1969), p. 63.

22. See Jan H. Boer, "Opening the Reformed World to the Powers," in *Perspectives* (Reformed Church Press, February 1994), pp. 16–18.

23. See for example Watchman Nee, *The Latent Power of the Soul* (Christian Fellowship Publishers, 1972), pp. 18–36; John Ankerberg and John Weldon, *The Coming Darkness* (Harvest House Publishers, 1993), p. 263.

24. Terry O'Neill and Stacey L. Tipp, *Paranormal Phenomena: Opposing Viewpoints* (Greenhaven Press, 1991), p. 14.

25. Ibid., p. 23, citing David Marks, "The Case Against the Paranormal," in *Fate*, January 1989.

26. James Randi, quoted by Henry Gordon, *ExtraSensory Deception* (Prometheus Books, 1987), pp. 27–28.

27. Dan Korem, *Powers: Testing the Psychic and Supernatural* (InterVarsity Press, 1988).

28. The most fascinating account of Uri Geller can be found in Martin Gardner, writing under the pseudonym Uriah Fuller, *Confessions of a Psychic* (Karl Fulves, 1975).

29. "News and Comment," in *The Skeptical Inquirer*, Fall 1981, pp. 4–7.

30. The letter from the Atlanta police was read on Fox Broadcasting's "Ron Reagan Show" on September 19, 1991. When confronted with the truth, Ms. Allison claimed she had a tape of herself giving the name of the murderer to the police. Investigator Michael R. Dennet asked her for a copy of the tape, but to date Allison has yet to produce it. More details are in Michael R. Dennet's chapter "America's Most Famous Psychic Sleuth: Dorothy Allison," in *Psychic Sleuths: ESP and Sensational Cases*, ed. Joe Nickell (Prometheus Books, 1994), pp. 42–59.

31. Piet Hein Hoebens, "Gerard Croiset: Investigation of the Mozart of 'Psychic Sleuths'—Part 1," in *The Skeptical Inquirer*, Fall 1981, pp. 18–28.

32. Dave Hoy, *The Bold and Subtle Miracles of Dr. Faust* (Magic Inc., 1963), p. 31.

Chapter 3—The Limits of the Mind

1. Russel Targ and Harold Puthoff, "Information Transmission Under Conditions of Sensory Shielding," in *Nature*, vol. 251, October 18, 1974, pp. 602–07.

2. Ibid.

3. Ibid.

4. "Investigating the Paranormal," in *Nature*, vol. 251, October 18, 1974, p. 559.

5. Martin Gardner, "How Not to Test a Psychic: The Great SRI Die Mystery," in *The Skeptical Inquirer*, Summer 1983, p. 31.

6. Ibid., pp. 38–39.

7. All of these quotations are from the authors' personal encounters with Ray Hyman. To verify, readers can write to Dr. Ray Hyman, care of the Psychology Department, University of Oregon, Eugene, Oregon.

8. James Randi, "The Project Alpha Experiment: Part 1. The First Two Years," in *The Skeptical Inquirer*, Summer 1983, p. 31.

9. Persi Diaconis, "Statistical Problems in ESP Research," in *Science*, vol. 201, July 14, 1978, pp. 131–36.

10. Ibid.

11. Jim Parker, "Firewalking," in *Arizona*, July 8, 1984, p. 7.

12. Peter Garrison, "Kindling Courage," in *Omni*, 1985, pp. 84–5.

13. Ibid., p. 84.

14. Ibid., p. 84.

15. Luis W. Alvarez, "A Pseudo Experienced in Parapsychology," in *The Skeptical Inquirer*, Summer 1982, pp. 72–73.

Chapter 4—Magic and Mindreading

1. Dave Hunt, *Peace, Prosperity, and the Coming Holocaust* (Harvest House Publishers, 1982), p. 67.

2. Hal Lindsey, from his foreword to Johanna Michaelsen's book *The Beautiful Side of Evil* (Harvest House Publishers, 1982).

3. For more details (and an interesting read), see Lulu Hearst, *Lulu Hearst (The Georgia Wonder) Writes Her Autobiography and for the First Time Explains and Demonstrates the Great Secret of Her Marvelous Power* (Lulu Hearts Book Company, 1897).

4. Robert A. Baker and Joe Nickell, *Missing Pieces: How to Investigate Ghosts, UFO's, Psychics, and Other Mysteries* (Prometheus Books, 1992), p. 217.

5. Kurt Koch, *Occult ABC* (Kregel, 1982), p. 252.

6. Bob Passantino, "Fantasies, Legends, Heroes," in *Cornerstone*, vol. 18, issue 91, p. 23.

7. James Randi, "The Role of Conjurers in Psi Research," in *Skeptic's Handbook of Parapsychology*, ed. Paul Kurtz (Prometheus Books, 1985), p. 339.

8. For more thoughts on the attitude of performing mentalists, see Martin Gardner's *Confessions of a Psychic*.

9. David Marks, "The Case Against the Paranormal," in *Fate*, January 1989, p. 33.

10. For a great expose of Geller's magic, see James Randi, *The Truth About Uri Geller* (Prometheus Books, 1982).

11. North, *Unholy Spirits*, p. 182.

12. Brooke, *Lord of the Air. Tales of a Modern Antichrist* (Harvest House Publishers, 1990), back cover.

13. See Dale Beyerstein, *Sai Baba's Miracles: An Overview* (self-published, 1992).

14. *Illustrated Weekly of India*, December 12–18, 1992, p. 3.

15. "Interview with Dave Hunt," in *SCP Journal*, vol. 4/2, Winter 1980–81, p. 4.

16. Acts 2:22, emphasis added. See also Luke 5:17; John 10:32; Acts 19:11; Hebrews 2:4.

17. See 1 Kings 18:39,40; Acts 5:12–14.

18. See Exodus 4:1–5; John 14:11; Hebrews 2:3,4.

19. R.C.H. Lenski, *The Interpretation of St. Paul's Epistles to the Colossians, to the Thessalonians, to Titus, and to Philemon* (Augsburg, 1961), pp. 426–27.

20. John Walvoord, *The Revelation of Jesus Christ* (Moody, 1966), p. 208.

21. Anderson, *Bondage Breaker*, p. 118.

22. Jermiah 14:14, emphasis added. See also Isaiah 44:25; Jeremiah 27:9; Ezekiel 13:1–10.

23. See F.C. Cook, "Exodus," in *The Bible Commentary* (Baker, reprinted 1981), vol.1, p. 236.

24. See Acts 8:9–25.

25. David Marks, "The Case Against the Paranormal," in *Fate*, January 1989, p. 33.

26. For a great expose of Geller's magic, see James Randi, *The Truth About Uri Geller* (Prometheus Books, 1982).

27. North, *Unholy Spirits*, p. 182

28. Brooke, *Lord of the Air. Tales of a Modern Antichrist* (Harvest House Publishers, 1990), back cover.

29. See Dale Beyerstein, *Sai Baba's Miracles: An Overview* (self-published, 1992).

30. *Illustrated Weekly of India*, December 12–18, 1992, p. 3.

31. "Interview with Dave Hunt," in *SCP Journal*, vol. 4/2, Winter 1980–81, p. 4.

32. Genesis 3:5.

Chapter 5—Make Big Money: Become a Psychic!

1. C. Eugene Emery, "Telephone Psychics: Friends or Frauds?" in *The Skeptical Inquirer*, September/October 1995, p. 14.

2. Ibid., p. 17.

3. Rosemary Ellen Guiley, *Harper's Encyclopedia of Mystical and Paranormal Experience* (Harper Collins, 1991), p. 286.

4. Frances Vaughn, *Awakening Intuition* (Anchor/Doubleday, 1979), pp. 3, 4, 46.

5. Guiley, *Harper's Encyclopedia of Mystical and Paranormal Experiences*, p. 286.

6. Ibid., p. 259.

7. John Ankerberg and John Weldon, *Encyclopedia of New Age Beliefs* (Harvest House Publishers, 1996), p. 473.

8. Danny Korem, *Powers: Testing the Psychic & Supernatural* (IVP, 1988), p. 18.

Chapter 6—Can We Know the Future?

1. *Doctrine & Covenants* (Church of Jesus Christ of the Latter Day Saints, 1949), section 84:114 (written September 22–23, 1832).

2. Ibid., section 87:1–8 (written December 25, 1832).

3. Oliver H. Huntington Journal, Book 14, 1837 (original in Huntington Library, San Marino, California).

4. Joseph Smith, *History of the Church*, January 4, 1833, vol. 1, pp. 315–16.

5. James Randi, *An Encyclopedia of Claims, Frauds, and Hoaxes of the Occult and Supernatural* (St. Martin's Press, 1995), p. 64.

6. Ray Hyman, "Cold Reading: How to Convince Strangers That You Know All About Them," in *The Zetetic*, Spring/Summer 1977, p. 21.

7. *Parade*, May 13, 1956, p. 5.

8. A. Voldben, *After Nostradamus* (Citadel Press, 1974), p 54.

9. F.K. Donnelly, "People's Almanac Predictions: Retrospective Check of Accuracy," in *The Skeptical Inquirer*, Spring 1983, p. 49.

10. Ibid., p. 50.

11. *Doctrine & Covenants*, section 62:1, 6, 7.

12. Ibid., section 84:4.

13. Daniel St. Albin Greene, "The Real Story of Jeane Dixon," reprinted in *The Christian Reader*, April–May 1974, p. 70.

14. Ibid., p. 71.

15. Ibid., p. 74.

16. Fawn M. Brodie, *No Man Knows My History: The Life of Joseph Smith, the Mormon Prophet*, (Knopf, 1975), p. 405.

17. Ibid., pp. 457–88.

18. Joseph Smith, *History of the Church* (Deseret Book Company, 1957), vol. 4, p. 461.

19. Josh McDowell and Don Stewart, *Understanding the Cults* (Here's Life Publishers, 1982), p. 96.

Chapter 7—Talking with the Dead?

1. Quoted in Randi, *Encyclopedia*, p. 101.

2. *New York Herald*, September 24, 1888.

3. Randi, *Encyclopedia*, p. 102.

4. Harry Houdini, *A Magician Among the Spirits* (Harper and Brothers, 1924; reprinted by Time-Life Books, 1991), pp. xix, 270.

5. Raymond Fitzsimons, "Death and the Magician: The Mystery of Houdini," reprinted in *Reader's Digest*, July 1981, p. 205.

6. Allen Spraggett and William V. Rauscher, *Arthur Ford: The Man Who Talked with the Dead* (New American Library, 1973), pp. 245–46.

7. James Randi, *Flim Flam!* (Prometheus Books, 1982), p. 246.

8. Ben Alexander, *Out from Darkness* (Exposing Satan's Power Ministries, 1988), pp. 33–34.

9. Keene, *Psychic Mafia*, p. 101.

10. Raphael Gasson, *The Challenging Counterfeit* (Logos, 1966), p. 74.

11. Tony Corinda, *Thirteen Steps to Mentalism* (Tannens, 1968), p. 294.

12. Randi, *Encyclopedia*, p. 58.

13. Deuteronomy 18:9–12 TLB.

14. Keene, *Psychic Mafia*, pp. 147–148.

Chapter 8—Look into My Eyes

1. Randi, *Encyclopedia*, p. 126.

2. Peter Blythe, *Hypnotism: Its Power and Practice* (Talinger, 1971), pp. 6–7.

3. Ibid., p. 11.

4. Larry Bodine and Douglas Lavine, "Hypnosis in Courts: Still on Trial," in *American Way*, April 1981, p. 24.

5. Phillip J. Klass, "Hypnosis and UFO Abductions," in *The Skeptical Inquirer,* Spring 1981, p. 21.

6. Ernest R. Hilgard, "Hypnosis Gives Rise to Fantasy and Is Not a Truth Serum," in *The Skeptical Inquirer,* Spring 1981, p. 25.

7. Randi, *Encyclopedia,* p. 126.

Chapter 9—The Latest from the X-Files

1. In recent years, New Agers have pointed to the "Bimini road" as further evidence of Atlantis. This "road" is the submerged former coastline of Bimini Island, which breaks off in straight lines so as to appear almost man-made. Alas, the same formations occur in such disparate locations as Australia, Venezuela, and Tasmania, so there is no way to link this naturally occurring formation to Atlantis.

2. Peter Tompkins and Christopher Bird, *The Secret Life of Plants* (Harper and Row, 1989, rev. ed.).

3. Randi, *Encyclopedia,* p. 60.

4. Ibid., p. 2.

5. Charles Berlitz, *The Bermuda Triangle* (Doubleday, 1974) p. 11.

6. Ibid., p. 12.

7. Michael R. Dennett, "Bermuda Triangle, 1981 Model," in *The Skeptical Inquirer,* Fall 1981, p. 48.

8. Lawrence Kusche, *The Bermuda Triangle Mystery—Solved* (Harper and Row, 1975), p. 275.

9. This entire story is true, though we have changed some of the circumstances to protect the reputation of the institution.

10. Proverbs 18:17.

11. Though levitation stories abound, an experienced magician will tell you that there has yet to be an unexplained levitation, though any good magic book will reveal the secret of the old party gag of having several people "levitate" a man into the air using only two fingers.

12. Paul Bauer, *Horoskop und Talisman* (Klower, 1963), p. 13, other information pp. 11–12.

13. Elsie Wright, cited in Randi, *Encyclopedia,* p. 57.

Chapter 10—Beam Me Up, Scotty!

1. Hans Van Kempen, "Case #17 Revised: What did Kenneth Arnold Really See?" in *UFO Brigantia,* November/December 1987, pp. 28–31.

2. Ronald D. Story, ed., *The Encyclopedia of UFO's* (Doubleday, 1980), p. 220.

3. Sachs, *The UFO Encyclopedia* (Putnam, 1980), p. 203.

4. Ibid., p. 99.

5. For a resource, see P.J. O'Rourke, *Parliament of Whores* (Atlantic Monthly Press, 1991), pp. 86–87.

6. Philip J. Klass, "That's Entertainment! TV's UFO Coverup," in *The Skeptical Inquirer,* November/December, 1996, p. 30.

7. Alan Hale, "An Astronomer's Personal Statement on UFO's," in *The Skeptical Inquirer*, March/April, 1997, p. 29.

8. Cited in John Ankerberg and John Weldon, *The Facts on UFO's* (Harvest House Publishers, 1992), p. 5.

9. Gallup Poll done August 6, 1990, cited in *Time*, November 11, 1991.

10. Charles Bowen, "Behind the Times," in *Flying Saucer Review*, vol. 20, no. 2, p. 2.

11. Mjr. Donald Keyhoe, *Aliens from Space* (Signet, 1974), p. 242.

12. Hale, "Statement," p. 29.

13. See, for example, Jerome Clark, "The Strange Case of Carlos de los Santos," *UFO Report*, December 1980, p. 26.

14. See quotation from the Director of the British Astronomical Association in *The London Times*, June 27, 1987.

15. Janet and Colin Bord, *Unexplained Mysteries of the 20th Century*, (Contemporary Books, 1989), p. 55.

16. Story, *Encyclopedia*, pp. 366–69.

17. The authors wish to thank Bill Pitts for his insights into UFOs.

18. Gerald Jones, "UFO's," in *The Dial*, October 1982, p. 10.

19. Klass, *UFO's Explained* (Random House, 1974), p. 14, 22, 30, 89, 174, 233.

20. Particularly Wells' *Crash at Corona* (Marlowe & Company, 1994).

21. For details on this and other Roswell incidents, the best and most well-documented book is undoubtedly Kal Korff's *The Roswell UFO Crash* (Prometheus Books, 1997).

22. Ibid.

23. Jeff Wells, "Profitable Nightmare of a Very Unreal Kind," in *The Skeptical Inquirer*, Summer 1981, p. 51.

24. Ibid.

25. See Joseph A. Bauer, M.D., "A Surgeon's View: Alien Autopsy's Overwhelming Lack of Credibility," in *The Skeptical Inquirer*, January/February 1996, pp. 23–24.

26. See Trey Stokes, "How to Make an Alien Autopsy," in *The Skeptical Inquirer*, January/February 1996, pp. 19–23; and John English, "Anachronistic Danger Sign in Alien Autopsy," in *The Skeptical Inquirer*, July/August 1997, p. 5.

27. Timothy Spencer Carr, "Son of Originator of Alien Autopsy Story Casts Doubt on Father's Credibility," in *The Skeptical Inquirer*, July/August 1997, pp. 31–32.

28. Jacques Vallee, *Messengers of Deception: UFO Contacts and Cults* (And Or Press, 1979), pp. 19–21.

29. David Swift, "A Psychologist's Reaction," in Vallee's *Messengers of Deception*, p. 229.

30. Ankerberg and Weldon, *The Facts on UFO's*, p. 30. The authors would like to thank Ankerberg and Weldon for allowing us to access their thorough research on this topic.

31. Citation written by Lynn Catoe, *UFO's and Related Subjects. An Annotated Bibliography*, (U.S. Government Printing Office, 1969), preface.

32. John A. Keel, *UFO's. Operation Trojan Horse* (Putnam, 1970), p. 215.

33. Trevor James, "The Case for Contact—Part 2," in *Flying Saucer Review*, vol. 8, no. 1, p. 10.
34. Vallee, *Messengers*, p. 19.
35. Ibid., pp. 146, 159.
36. Whitley Streiber, *Communion* (Morrow, 1987).
37. Robert Sheaffer, *The UFO Verdict. Examining the Evidence* (Prometheus Books, 1981), pp. 212–13.
38. Larry Kusche, *The Disappearance of Flight 19* (Harper and Row, 1980), p. 172.

Chapter 11—Stargazing

1. Lawrence Jerome, *Astrology Disproved* (Prometheus Books, 1977), p. 172.
2. Derek and Julia Parker, *The Compleat Astrology* (Bantam, 1978), p. 178.
3. Gallup Poll taken October 19, 1975.
4. Gallup Poll taken May 1988.
5. Reported by Kurt Goedelman, "Seeking Guidance from the Stars of Heaven," in *Personal Freedom Outreach*, July/September 1988, p. 5.
6. John Anthony West and Jan Gerhard Tooner, *The Case for Astrology* (Penguin Books, 1973), p. 1.
7. Donald Regan, *For the Record* (Harcourt Brace Jovanovich, 1988), p. 3.
8. Jerome, *Astrology*, p. 31. See also Frederick H. Cramer, *Astrology in Roman Politics* (American Philosophical Society, 1954).
9. Randi, *Encyclopedia*, p. 18.
10. Michel Gauquelin, "Zodiac and Personality: An Empirical Study," in *The Skeptical Inquirer*, Spring 1982, pp. 57–65.
11. Paul Kurtz, "French Committee Announces Results of Test of the Mars Effect," in *The Skeptical Inquirer*, January/February 1995, p. 4.
12. John McGervey, "A Statistical Test of Sun-sign Astrology," in *The Zetetic*, vol. 1, no. 2, p. 53.
13. Kurz and Fraknoi, "Tests of Astrology Do Not Support Its Claims" in *The Skeptical Inquirer*, vol. 9, no. 3, p. 211.
14. Kelly, et. al, "The Moon Was Full and Nothing Happened," in *The Skeptical Inquirer*, vol. 10, no. 2, p. 139.
15. Cited in *The Skeptical Inquirer*, Spring 1986, p. 196.
16. Sir John Maddox, editorial in *Nature*, February 1986.
17. Linda Hill, cited by Frederick G. Levine in *The Psychic Sourcebook: How to Choose and Use a Psychic* (Warner Books, 1988), p. 196.
18. Dean et. al, "The Guardian Astrology Study: A Critique and Reanalysis," in *The Skeptical Inquirer*, vol. 9, no. 4, p. 178.
19. John Ankerberg and John Weldon, *The Facts on Astrology* (Harvest House Publishers, 1988), p. 10.
20. Jerome, *Astrology*, p. 22.
21. Edward Moody, "Magical Therapy: An Anthropological Investigation of Contemporary Satanism," in Irving Zaretsky and Mark Leone, *Religious*

Movements in Contemporary America (Princeton University Press, 1974), pp. 362–63.

22. Interview in *Los Angeles Times*, January 15, 1975.

23. Charles E. O. Carter, *The Principles of Astrology* (Theosophical Publishing House, 1977), p. 14.

24. Sepharial, *A Manual of Occultism* (Samuel Weismer, 1978), p. 3.

25. Deuteronomy 4:19.

26. Marcus Allen, *Astrology for the New Age: An Intuitive Approach* (CRCS Publications, 1979), p. 117.

27. Jeane Dixon, *Yesterday, Today, and Forever: How Astrology Can Help You Find Your Place in God's Plan* (Bantam, 1977), pp. 7, 9.

28. Ibid., p. 502.

Chapter 12—Amazing Operations

1. André Cole, *Miracles or Magic?* (Harvest House, 1984), p. 42.

2. Dr. Eric Chico, quoted in Richard Mayhue, *The Healing Promise* (Harvest House Publishers, 1994), pp. 52-53.

3. Ibid., p. 53.

4. William A. Nolen, M.D., *Healing: A Doctor in Search of a Miracle* (Random House, 1974), p. 265.

5. Ibid., p. 272.

6. Ibid., p. 274.

7. Ibid., pp. 292–93.

8. Randi, *Encyclopedia*, p. 14.

Chapter 13—Deception in the Name of God

1. It should be noted that two of the cases André personally investigated involved extensive medical treatment and surgery prior to the "healing." The health of the two people improved, but it could not be proven that it was Mr. Hinn's healing ability, and not medical science, that helped them.

2. Supplied to the authors by James Randi. Used by permission.

3. Ibid.

4. James Randi, "Be Healed in the Name of God!" in *Free Inquiry*, Spring 1986, pp. 12–13.

5. It should be noted that both authors have known people who have been miraculously healed by God of organic diseases. But Dr. Jerry MacGregor did follow-up research after three different faith-healing seances in Portland, Oregon, and could find no case of healing an organic disease that had been performed by any of the three preachers. Our problem is not with *God's power* to heal, but with the alleged power of the *faith healers*.

6. Randi, *Be Healed*, p. 11.

7. Ibid., p. 17.

8. Nolen, *Healing*, pp. 286–87.

9. Ibid., pp. 305–06.

MIND GAMES

Chapter 14—The Vision of the Anointed

1. John Ankerberg and John Weldon, *The Facts on the Mind Sciences* (Harvest House Publishers, 1993), p. 5.
2. Ibid.
3. 1 John 1:1, emphasis added.
4. 1 John 1:6,8.
5. From John Ankerberg and John Weldon, *The Facts on Spirit Guides* (Harvest House Publishers, 1988), p. 16., citing information from Jon Klimo, *Channeling: Investigations on Receiving Information from Paranormal Sources* (Jeremy P. Tarcher, Inc., 1987), p. 1.
6. Helen Schucman, *A Course in Miracles* (Foundation for Inner Peace, 1977). In order the citations are from vol. 2, p. 334; vol. 2, pp. 353–54; vol. 3, p. 81; and vol. 1, pp. 88, 53, 87, 47.
7. Jane Roberts, *Seth Speaks* (Prentice Hall, 1972), pp. 389, 7, and 405.
8. The first citation is from Ruth Montgomery, *A World Beyond* (Fawcett Crest, 1972), p. 66. The second is from Ruth Montgomery, *A Search for Truth* (Bantam, 1968), p. 160.
9. Nina Easton, "Shirley MacLaine's Mysticism for the Masses," in the *Los Angeles Times Magazine*, September 6, 1987, p. 33.
10. Ankerberg and Weldon, *Spirit Guides*, p. 8.
11. One disenchanted follower, Pamela McNeeley, reported that Knight once "impersonated" Ramtha at a party. "She did a better job of doing Ramtha than Ramtha," she reported. "In fact, we couldn't tell the difference." Quotation occurred in *Newsweek*, December 15, 1986, p. 62.
12. These quotations are from J.Z. Knight, *Voyage to the New World* (Ballantine, 1987), pp. 219, 61, 139, 60, 252, 130, and 251 respectively. The authors wish to acknowledge John Weldon for his research, used in Ankerberg and Weldon, *Spirit Guides*, pp. 21–22.
13. F. LaGard Smith, *Out on a Broken Limb* (Harvest House Publishers, 1986), p. 103.
14. Emanuel Swedenborg, *The True Christian Religion* (E.P. Dutton, 1936), pp. 667–69).
15. Malachi Martin, *Hostage to the Devil* (Bantam, 1977), p. 485.
16. Dave Hunt and T.A. McMahon, *The Seduction of Christianity*, (Harvest House Publishers, 1985), p. 186.
17. Carol Tavris, "The Freedom to Change," in *Prime Time*, October 1980, p. 28.
18. Romans 3:23.
19. Romans 6:23.
20. Ibid.
21. See 2 Corinthians 4:7-18.
22. John G. Lake, *Spiritual Hunger, The God-Men and Other Sermons by Dr. John G. Lake* (Christ for the Nations Inc., 1976), p. 96.
23. Norman Vincent Peale, *Positive Imaging* (Fawcett Crest, 1982), p. 77.
24. Quoted in Mack R. Douglas, *Success Can Be Yours* (Zondervan, 1997), p. 37.

283

25. 2 Corinthians 11:23–29.

26. John 15:20,21.

27. Cited in Laurie Warner, "New Age Energies," in *New Age Source*, September 1982, p. 13.

28. Psychosynthesis Institute, *Synthesis Two: The Realization of the Self*, n.d., pp. 119–20.

29. Yonggi Cho, *The Fourth Dimension* (Logos, 1979), p. 40.

30. Hunt, *Seduction*, p. 148.

31. Quotation taken from an audiotape by Amway Crown Direct Distributor Bunny Marks.

32. David Stoop, *Self Talk: Key to Personal Growth* (Revell, 1982), p. 135.

33. See, for example, C.S. Lovett, *Longing to Be Loved* (Personal Christianity, 1982), particularly pp. 13–16, 87–90.

34. Calvin Miller, *The Table of Inwardness* (InterVarsity Press, 1984), p. 93.

35. C.S. Lewis, *The Screwtape Letters* (Revell, 1978 edition), p. 34.

Chapter 15—Witchcraft Repackaged

1. Michael Shermer, in an article titled "Deconstructing the Dead: Crossing Over One Last Time to Expose Medium John Edward," *Skeptic*, February 27, 2001.

2. Ibid.

3. Ibid.

4. Ibid.

5. BreakPoint with Charles Colson, Commentary #010822 titled, "Is That You, Uncle Bob?: Flirting with Mediums," August 23, 2001.

6. Greg Barrett, newspaper article titled "Can the Living Talk to the Dead? Psychics say they connect with the spirit world, but skeptics respond: 'Prove It'," n.d., Gannett News Service.

7. Michael G. Maudlin, "Virtue on a Broomstick: The Harry Potter Books, and the Controversy Surrounding Them, Bode Well for the Culture," *Christianity Today*, September 4, 2000.

8. Ibid.

9. Gene Edward Veith, "Good Fantasy and Bad Fantasy," *The Christian Research Journal*, n.d.).

10. Ibid.

11. Jeremiah Films, *Harry Potter: Witchcraft Repackaged. Making Evil Look Innocent*, 2001.

12. Veith, "Good Fantasy and Bad Fantasy."

13. Ibid.

Chapter 16—A Demon in Every Bush?

1. C.S. Lewis, *The Screwtape Letters*, p. 9.

2. See Job 1:6; Zechariah 3:1,2; Matthew 13:19; John 13:2; Acts 5:3; Ephesians 6:11,12; 1 Peter 5:8.

3. See Ezekiel 28:1–19, generally believed to be a description of both Satan and the Prince of Tyre.

4. See 2 Corinthians 2:11; 11:14; Ephesians 6:11,12; 2 Thessalonians 2:9,10; Matthew 24:24; Revelation 13:11,14.

5. See Job 1:6; Revelation 12:10.

6. See Ephesians 6:11, 12.

7. See Job 1:7; 1 Peter 5:8.

8. 2 Corinthians 4:4.

9. See Acts 10:38; Luke 13:16; Hebrews 2:14.

10. See 1 Thessalonians 3:5; 1 Corinthians 7:5.

11. See 2 Timothy 2:26; 1 Timothy 3:7.

12. See 2 Corinthians 4:4.

13. See Mark 4:15; Matthew 13:19; Luke 8:12.

14. See Matthew 13:25–39; 2 Corinthians 11:13–15; Ephesians 2:2,3; Revelation 3:9.

15. See Zechariah 3:1; Thessalonians 2:18; Revelation 12:9,10; Job 1:6–12; 2 Corinthians 12:7-9; Luke 22:31.

16. See Matthew 8:29–32; Luke 9:38–42; Mark 5:2–15; Acts 19:13–16; James 2:19.

17. See Matthew 8:28; 12:43, 44; 15:22; Luke 4:33; 9:39; Mark 5:10–13.

18. See Mark 5:2; Matthew 10:1; Ephesians 2:2; 2 Peter 2:10–12.

19. See Matthew 12:22; Mark 5:4, 5; Luke 9:37–42.

20. See Mark 5:2–13; 9:17–27; Matthew 4:24; 8:16, 28, 33; John 13:27; Acts 8:7.

21. See Colossians 2:15; John 12:31; 16:8–11; 1 John 3:8; 5:18; Hebrews 2:14.

22. See Genesis 3:14,15; Revelation 12:9; 20:10.

23. The claim that Satan can transform matter is usually based on the story of Pharaoh's magicians turning a rod into a snake in Exodus 7, but the text clearly says they used their "secret arts" or "magic arts" to do so. In other words, they gave the *appearance* of creating a snake, but did not actually create life. Only God can create life.

24. The Scriptures are clear that God retains command over the power of life and death: Hebrews 2:10; Genesis 2:17; Deuteronomy 32:39; 1 Kings 2:6; Job 2:6; Matthew 10:28; Luke 12:5; 1 Corinthians 15:25ff.; Revelation 1:18.

25. Francis I. Anderson, *Tyndale Old Testament Commentary on Job* (InterVarsity Press, 1976), p. 83.

26. Norman Geisler, *Signs and Wonders* (Tyndale House, 1988), p. 104.

27. John 10:28.

28. Thomas Ice and Robert Dean, Jr., *A Holy Rebellion* (Harvest House Publishers, 1990), p. 119.

29. Diane Eble, "Satanism," in *Campus Life*, April 1990, p. 53.

30. Jude 9.

31. Neil Anderson, *The Bondage Breaker* (Harvest House Publishers, 1993), p. 108.

32. Ibid., p. 187.

33. Ibid., p. 201.

34. *Charisma*, July 1992.
35. *Ministries Today*, November/December 1993, p. 15.
36. Ed Murphy, *The Handbook for Spiritual Warfare* (Thomas Nelson, 1992), p. 442.
37. Colossians 1:13,14.
38. Anderson, *Bondage Breaker*, p. 203.
39. 1 John 5:19.
40. Ephesians 6:12.
41. Reginald Scot, *The Discoverie of Witchcraft*, p. 1.
42. Nigel Wright, *The Satan Syndrome* (Zondervan Publishing House, 1990), p. 26.
43. Wright, *Syndrome*, p. 14.

Mind Games
Order Form

Postal orders: Andre Kole
325 West Southern
Tempe, AZ 85282

Telephone orders: (800) 234-9549

E-mail orders: orders@andrekole.org

Please send *Mind Games* to:

Name: _____

Address: _____

City: _____ State: _____

Zip: _____

Telephone: (_____) _____

Book Price: $14.99

Shipping: $3.00 for the first book and $1.00 for each additional book to cover shipping and handling within US, Canada, and Mexico. International orders add $6.00 for the first book and $2.00 for each additional book.

Or order from:
ACW Press
5501 N. 7th. Ave. #502
Phoenix, AZ 85013

(800) 931-BOOK

or contact your local bookstore